CW01334597

WHAT WILL THE NEIGHBOURS SAY!

RICHARD LEE

ISBN:
9781983326608

Life isn't about surviving the storm, but learning to dance in the rain.

Anon

CONTENTS

Prologue – The Funeral

I've always hated funerals. Nothing very strange about that, I suppose, except that some people like them, enjoy them even. Me, I hate them, and I hate cremations most of all. The thought of it makes me shudder, I mean suppose you're not dead, just in a deep sleep, and along comes some plonker and says you're dead! Well, it will be a bit bloody late if you come to just as the flames burn your box, won't it? At least if you're buried, you can bang on the coffin lid – though knowing my luck, the gravedigger will be stone deaf! Still, at least I'll get a lie in.

Of course, the one good thing about funerals is the chance to meet people you haven't seen for years, unless you're the one in the coffin, of course. Still, even that has its compensations – you don't have to talk to them, you can just lie there and ignore the buggers.

I wish I could ignore my sister Jill, not that we are speaking to each other, apart from, "Hello," that is. She is my twin, and today we are burying our uncle, our late mother's only brother. I'm standing in my aunt's house in Romford, in East London. The house is much smaller than I remember it from my childhood and quite shabby. My aunt, bless her, will not be saying goodbye to the man she had spent most of her 82 years with, she is in a nearby hospital. She has dementia, poor love, and has no idea that her Billy-boy is dead. Apart from my cousin Caroline, my uncle's daughter, my sister and I are his last surviving relatives.

We would come to this house as kids with my mother (and sometimes my father, if they were on speaking terms) from our home in Enfield, North London. It was always a great treat, we regarded my aunt and uncle as our 'rich relatives' – well, they had a car! After our small terraced house – two up and two down, with outside lav – their 1930s three-bedroomed semi, with a bathroom and a garage for the old Ford Popular, was the bee's knees. There was the added bonus of my uncle always giving my sister and me five bob each, and a ride in the car to the bus stop in Gants Hill after our visit.

Since my mother's death, my uncle and I have had a strained relationship. I had not been at my mother's funeral, or that of my father some years later. The fact that I had no idea that they had died did not help my uncle understand my absence. I was the black sheep of the family. It was my beloved aunt who told me of my parents' passing. I had had a nightmare some years earlier that my mother was asking for me – we hadn't spoken for years because they were unable to come to terms with my homosexuality. After that nightmare, I telephoned my aunt only to be told that my mother was dead. When I asked my Aunt to tell my father that I would come and see him that afternoon, she then told me that he too had died, a few years after my mother. I was devastated. I blamed myself for being homosexual, and for the hurt I must have caused my parents, who despite everything I had still loved. I also blamed my sister for not trying to find me to tell me, firstly that my mother had cancer, and of my father's heart trouble. It wouldn't have been too hard to find me. After the break-up of my own doomed marriage, my sister knew that I was earning a living in the London pubs and clubs as a female impersonator, or a drag queen as we were later called. I would have had more chance with her had I been a mass murderer or even a rapist. At least if I had been a rapist, to her that would have shown some signs of 'normality'. I would have a chance to show I could be 'straight'. But nothing has changed – she still resents me being queer, even all these years later.

My uncle did speak to me in the last few years of his life. My aunt and my cousin did their best to try and make him understand that I didn't have a choice, I was what I was, and that being homosexual didn't make me less of a human being. l know that some people reading this will disagree. In fact, when I stopped doing drag and started working as a stand-up comic, in my uncle's eyes I became a bit more respectable. When I began writing for television, for such people as Michael Barrymore, and Bobby Davro, and my name would appear on the screen, then he started to tell his cronies about his nephew in show business.

My sister never changed. I used to think that my uncle's death would be the thing that would bring us back together. I had tried in the past after the loss of my parents. I got in touch with her, I even sent some friends in a Rolls Royce to take her to the London Hilton Hotel for a showbiz dinner, so that she could meet my friends. She came, of course, and had a great time chatting to the stars. It wasn't until the next day when the girlfriend of mine and her husband, who had taken my sister to the ball, phoned me and said what a rude woman she was. They had found her house, she kept them waiting outside, then got in the car and didn't speak to either of them there or back! When I phoned her, she simply said that as far as she was concerned they were her transport and nothing else, and anyway she had nothing in common with them!

I stand looking at my sister.as she chats to long-lost aunts and uncles. A big, smartly dressed woman, beginning to look her age, it is hard to believe that we were together in the same womb. She is strong-willed, a former Sunday School teacher. and has had anything but a successful private life. She has been married twice and has three sons from her first marriage to a barrow boy, of whom neither of our parents approved. She is narrow-minded and quick to judge, but also quick to forget her own misdemeanours. I once caught her with a married man, a leading light in one of the local youth organisations, that both he and his wife belonged to. Jill would have been about fifteen when I found her in a local park in the dark, in a compromising position with this guy. She has always denied it, but I have to admit it makes me smile sometimes when I listen to her preaching. She is one hard lady – even her sons didn't know that I existed until our half-brother Don came over from his home in Canada, and asked the eldest of her sons, Martin, if he ever saw me. The boy hadn't a clue what he was talking about, so Martin asked my cousin Caroline's husband Mick if he knew. When he had heard the story, he said he wanted to meet me. Caroline said it wasn't a matter of what he wanted, but rather what I wanted. She phoned me, and I said no, I didn't want to go through any more rejections, which I thought might be the outcome. I remembered him of course, I used to bounce him on my knee when he was a child. Mick then phoned me to say that Martin was a very nice guy, married, with his head firmly on his shoulders, and he too was now remembering the uncle who made him laugh as a baby, and he truly wanted to find me.

We arranged to all meet in a large country pub in Abridge, Essex. Caroline and Mick, Martin and his wife Kyla, myself and my partner of ten years, Ray. I made myself look as camp as possible, what with my long, hennaed hair. I wore a bright green and black check jacket, black trousers, a black polo-necked jumper and black suede winkle-picker boots, and of course my fly's-eyes white-framed glasses, just the sort of everyday chap you see in your average village pub. We arrived late, we could hear the strains of a jazz band playing. As we approached, I nearly chickened out, but Ray said that I had met all his family, and I was a firm member of that family – now he wanted to meet mine. I held my breath, pushed the door open and in we went. I swear that everybody turned and looked at me – the band stopped playing for a few seconds. I saw Caroline sitting with Mick, facing the door. Martin and his wife had their backs to us. Mick nodded to Martin, who turned around, saw me, got up and raced to meet me, throwing his arms around my neck. We have been mates ever since and I'm proud of him. But I digress.

As more guests arrive, my cousin puts another glass of lukewarm gin and tonic in my hand, kisses me and tells me not to let her (my sister) get to me. I smile at Caroline, take a swig of the tepid gin and promise her I won't. The car arrives and the funeral director is asking who should go in what car. As two of my uncle's last remaining relatives, my sister and I are told to go in the leading car with Caroline and Mick. My sister swishes out of the house and into the limousine, as though she was going to a film premiere. Caroline gets in next, then me and Mick, and their two children sit in front of me, on the fold-up seats that limos have. "Maybe now," I think, "now she might realise that we are about to say goodbye to the last of our past, maybe now we can be reconciled." I don't have to wait long for the answer to that little thought, she (dressed all in black) leans forward in her seat to look at me, dressed mainly in black but with a black and white polka dot shirt opened at the neck.

"I would have thought you could have made the effort, today of all days, to wear proper mourning!"

You can feel the atmosphere in the car. The kids turn round to look at me, willing me to answer back, I look down at my black suede winkle-pickers (I like black suede winkle-pickers), then without thinking it is out:

"Had I known how strongly you felt about it," I hear myself saying, "then I would have worn the little black dress I was wearing last night!" The other four can hardly stop themselves from laughing out loud, my sister sinks back into her seat, and we haven't spoken since.

It is a long drive to the crematorium, and as we drive through the streets of East London, my mind goes back to where it all began.

1 – THE BREAK

My sister and I were born in the East End of London, at the Salvation Army Hospital, in Hackney, in 1940, with just five minutes between our arrivals, my sister being first – a fact that she would remind me of with monotonous regularity. I was christened Richard Greene, and as a boy and young man I was always known as Ricky – Lee came later. I have no idea where or how my parents met. My father was originally from South London, having been born in the famous Lambeth Walk. My mother hailed from East London, and lived her young life in Silvertown, moving to Walthamstow after the destruction of the Brunner Mond factory, which once produced soda crystals and caustic soda. Opened in 1894, the plant lay idle for the initial period of World War I, but reopened in 1915 to process TNT for the Ministry of Munitions, and continued with its work until the explosion on 19 January 1917. It is believed that a fire broke out in the melting-pot room. The explosion occurred at 6.52 p.m., destroying buildings up to 400 yards away. Among the buildings destroyed were flour mills and the local fire station. A ship on the Thames, the SS Italia, was also destroyed. Molten metal, stones and bricks rained down, about seventy people were killed, and over a thousand injured, many seriously. My grandmother had been upstairs putting my uncle, then only a baby, to bed. As the house shook with the blast, she jumped down the full flight of stairs, with her baby in her arms as the roof and ceilings came crashing down. She undoubtedly saved his life, but was herself badly injured, and died some weeks later.

Later my grandfather re-married and my mother and uncle were brought up by their new stepmother, not at all the wicked stepmother that we read about in books, but a lovely woman, who died when I was fourteen, and who I still miss to this day.

Before she met my father, my mother was married briefly to another man, and she had a son by that union, my half-brother Don. After her marriage to my father, and our subsequent birth, we all moved to Enfield in North London and went to live with my father's mother. Unlike my other grandmother, she was a formidable lady, who stood no nonsense, and she never forgave my father for marrying a divorcée. We moved house a couple of times, then my father fell ill with a kidney complaint. He had to stop work, and we moved to a small two-up two-down terraced cottage, with no bathroom and the lav in the back yard. It meant that Don had to go back and live with my grandmother. He was now about fourteen, my sister and I about four. We lived in that house for the next eleven years, bathing in front of the fire in a big tin bath once a week, and playing in the long, long garden. My father got better after nearly a year off work, my mother also had to go to work, but in the main we were happy. Our parents' rows started to get worse but I think we pushed them to the backs of our minds. I did, at least, unless they were really bad and they started throwing things at each other – then I would hide in our bedroom.

At school my sister was top of the class, she also played for the school netball team, and was generally popular. As for me, well I hated school and couldn't stand sports – academically I was so-so. We had both failed our eleven-plus exam, much to my mother's disappointment, and we went to- a secondary modern school that was about forty-five minutes' walk away – and we had to walk, hail, blow or snow. As a boy, I was always shy and timid. The first couple of years at secondary school were hell, I would dread getting up in the mornings the walk to school was full of foreboding. My mother had forbidden me to play football, and although I didn't like sports I used to think that if I did play, then I wouldn't be such an outcast. After an accident at primary school, in which I sustained a fracture of my left leg– in fact, it fractured in three places – I was taken to hospital. My mother came straight from work, she held my hand and told me I would be home soon, but it was to be over a year before I would be able to go to school again or even to play in the street with my friends. I contracted osteomyelitis (a disease of the bone marrow); after spending months in hospital I was sent to a convalescent home on Hayling Island. I was put on a train in London by my Mum and Dad, as the train pulled out I wanted to get off, but I just sat there being "brave", as my Mum had told me. I was met at the other end by a little plump woman of about sixty. She wore a blue dress uniform with a dark blue cloak and a blue felt hat. She was the Matron of the convalescent home. She bundled me into a small Austin Ruby, and away we went. In my mind's eye, I had pictured this convalescent home as being like a hospital. It proved to be nothing more than a large Nissen hut at the side of the matron's cottage and occupied most of her garden. I was to spend nearly two months there. My parents couldn't afford to come and visit, so they would write to me every week, and send me a few sweets and my favourite comics. Radio Fun was one of my favourites, I used to love reading about "Cardew the Cad from St Fanny's", never dreaming that years later Cardew Robinson would be one of my closest friends, but the Matron would never give us our parcels. She would hand us any letters, then put any comics or toys in with all the others that were jammed into an old cupboard in our hut. I used to pull out the whole cupboard looking for the new comics. Tears would stream down my face. I could picture Mum and Dad buying those things they thought I would like, and I knew that they had little money to spare, and that's why I cried, not for me but for the sacrifices I knew they were making – and it was a sacrifice, times were hard, and money was scarce. When I came back from Hayling Island, my left leg was still very weak, and I walked with a limp. My mother in some unconscious way would limp with me, as though she were trying to take the pain for me. She became very protective towards me, fearing a reoccurrence of the osteomyelitis, which might result in my losing my leg altogether, so I wasn't allowed to play games. The bond between my mother and I was very strong. Little did I realise that the bond I held dear would one day turn to loathing, or that my mother would refuse to acknowledge me as her son.

When I was about fourteen my mates and I started to go to dance lessons. "That's where we'll pick up some girls," I was told by Eddie, one of my friends. The lessons were for ballroom dancing (rock and roll had yet to start) – much to my surprise, I liked it. Not only did I like it, I was also quite good at it, good enough to win a bronze medal anyway, and Eddie was right – we did pick up girls. We would tell each other how far we got with our particular girls. In truth, not very far at all, a kiss on the lips, maybe even a French kiss, very risqué in 1954, or maybe a hand up her jumper or even her skirt, but that was about it. Thinking back, it didn't mean a thing to me, but my mates did it, and it was expected. I left school at fifteen and went to work in Gamage's, a large department store, in Holborn, London. I worked in the menswear department, the head of the department put me in charge of selling hundreds of ex-Army demob suits, at 39'11" each). I quite enjoyed it, most of my friends had found work in local factories, and here was me working in London, and I was earning good money – £3 10' per week. My mother had wanted me to work in the Post Office like my uncle, but thankfully there were no vacancies. Still, as soon as one came along I was told it would be for me, I hoped it would never happen – I didn't fancy wearing a uniform and delivering telegrams, which is what the job entailed.

"You start there and work your way up, like your Uncle Bill, and you could end up like him with a good job and a pension when you retire," that was my mother's advice, what she wanted me to be like – her adored brother. "A pension!" I thought, "I'm only fifteen, the last thing I want to think about is a pension," but life has a way of not always letting you do what you want. After a couple of months at the store, I was to go into the stockroom and help another assistant to tidy it up. This other person was a small balding man about fifty, he scurried about the department like Mole from The Wind in the Willows. We had been in the stockroom for about an hour, when he told me to get up the ladder and tidy the top shelf, as I was getting up, he put his hand up between my legs and squeezed and rubbed my balls. I froze, I couldn't move. he kept on. Now I could hear him saying "I knew you'd like it," and he tried to undo my fly buttons – no zips then. I came to my senses and kicked him with the back of my heel. I caught him in the chest, he let go of my balls and yelled in pain, as soon as he released me I jumped from the ladder and ran from the stockroom back to my department, where I collapsed onto a pile of the cheap suits.

I was near to tears, shaking and trembling, I couldn't control myself. I fumbled for a cigarette, I lit it and took a long gasp. Right next to me I saw a telephone, I picked it up, and when the operator asked what department I wanted I said the police. A few minutes later the department manager came racing over me. "What's the matter, boy? Did somebody try to steal something?" I shook my head." The operator said you had asked for the police, is that true?" I could only nod. He pointed to the phone. "That's for internal use only, now tell me what your reason was for asking for the police."

I went with him to his office and told him what had happened, he sent for the man in question. When the accusation was put to him, he denied it, said I had imagined it, and that he was a respectable married man with boys of my age. All he had done was to help me up the ladder. He was sent out of the office and the manager told me I should be more careful before I make such rash statements, and that I was lucky he didn't sack me. Then he sent me back to work. I was still shaking inside when I got home that night and I begged my Mum to ask my uncle again about a job. I started with the Post Office two weeks later, I never did tell her why I wanted to leave Gamage's.

I thought about the incident a lot over the next weeks and months and each time I did I got excited sexually. I kept thinking about another guy who worked in the menswear department, a dark-haired Jewish man with olive skin, dark smouldering eyes. He was about twenty-five, his name was Max." Why couldn't it have been Max?" I kept thinking to myself, "if it had been Max, I would have let him carry on." I started to fantasize about him, wishing it had been him, imagining what it would have been like, then I would break out into cold sweats. I thought I was going mad. I found myself scanning the Sunday papers looking for stories about queers, putting myself in their position. I started to hate myself, I bought books like Health and Efficiency so that I could look at naked women and try to turn myself on, but it was only the naked men who turned me on. I was a freak. I was to feel like that for a long time.

My career in the Post Office didn't last long, I was sent to my birthplace, Hackney, as a telegram boy, and spent my days cycling around the streets, bringing good and bad news, and sometimes getting quite good tips. The talk among us, while we were waiting to be sent out on delivery, was of course sex. As a new boy, and not yet accepted by the rest, I would just sit and listen as they recalled their exploits of the previous evening. Gradually they brought me more and more into their conversation, and when they asked me about my girlfriends, or 'tarts' as they always called them, I would make up stories and swear they were true. The eldest boy, Mark, a dark-skinned good-looking Latin type, told by far the best stories, and the rest of us "Mergos", as they called telegram boys (I never did find out why, or what it meant) would sit enthralled by his tales, punctuating his words with the occasional, "You didn't?" "You lucky sod," or "Did she let you do it?" It made me feel even worse. "Why can't I be like them?" was the one question that kept going around in my mind as I pedalled my bike through the streets. I would try and put myself in Mark's position, I'd imagine him doing things to some 'tart', then I would find that I was thinking more about Mark than the girl. We kept our bikes in a shed at the rear of the Post Office. On one particular day, I went out to the shed to get my bike, as I went in I heard a noise from the back of the shed, behind some old junk. It startled me and I jumped. "Who's that?" I called out trying to sound unconcerned.

"Only me, is that you Rick?" I recognized Mark's voice.

"Yeah – what are you doing back there?"

"Not so loud," he hissed, "come back here." I picked my way through the junk, and when I reached the back, Mark grabbed me and pulled me into where he was hiding. It was pitch black.

"What's up? I asked.

"Nothing, and keep your voice down, I just felt like a bit of fun, all right?" I could feel him getting closer, then he pulled my hand down between his legs. I realised that his trousers were around his ankles. I tried to pull away.

"What are you doing?" I nearly screamed, he put his hand over my mouth.

"Sssh! The whole fucking office will be out here, you yelling like that." He let go of my mouth, then pushed himself closer to me. He took my hand and said, "Just hold it for me, I've seen the way you look at me so I know you want to." He guided my hand to his dick, I could feel it throbbing, it was hard and stiff and very big. "Go on take it, hold it." I did as I was told. I was shaking, as I touched it he sighed. "Harder," he breathed. I let my fingers tighten around it, it felt warm and welcoming, then he was fumbling with my fly buttons. I found myself helping him, his hand went into my underpants and closed around my now very hard dick. I felt dizzy, I wanted to run, but at the same time, I also knew that I wanted to stay. He moved his hand faster inside my underwear, his head was nearly on my shoulder by this time, then I felt his body go rigid. He gasped, then pulled himself away, at the same time pulling his hand from my trousers. "Have you come?" he asked me.

"Come where?" was my innocent reply. I didn't have a clue what he was talking about, I heard him laugh, and pull his trousers back up, then he was gone. I stood there for what seemed an age. I did my flies up. I couldn't believe what had happened, but I did know that unlike the last time, this time I wasn't about to tell anybody – not because I didn't want another telling off, but because I had enjoyed it! Mark never ever mentioned the incident, it was as if it had never taken place, and it certainly didn't happen again. He still spoke to me but only when he had to, he would smile now and then, but I could feel a chill in the air if we were ever alone together. The job was getting me down, I began to feel depressed. I found myself thinking about what had happened and wanting it to happen again, then I would hate myself for having those thoughts. I was telling my sister that I didn't like my job, and she told me that there was a vacancy at the place she worked, an insurance brokers' in the City. My mother threw a fit when I told her I was leaving the GPO: "I don't know what your uncle Bill will say when he hears, after all he's done for you, put his own neck on the line for you," and so it went on. I started at King William Street House a couple of weeks later, the job I had taken was that of a claims broker. It was my job to try and get American aviation and non-marine claims settled with the underwriters concerned. Six or seven of us brokers, mainly young guys like myself, would be given files of claims in the morning. These we would read through, then we would all troop down to the Lloyds Building in Leadenhall Street, a great Victorian pile, inside of which was The Room, a vast open room on two floors, in which sat hundreds of underwriters and their clerks. They were all split into syndicates, and each syndicate sat in Boxes. The boxes consisted of a couple of high-backed wooden settles, facing each other with a large wooden desk in between, the sort of thing you would have expected to find in one of the London coffee shops in Victorian London and before – and it was in one such coffee-house where Lloyds of London was born. All the major insurance companies sent their claims brokers to the Room – some were very nice and polite, others very snooty. We would usually have to queue at a Box in order to see an underwriter, and as everybody was called "Sir," you would approach the Box you had on your list and say to the chap at the end of the queue, "Good morning Sir, are you last?" and he would reply "Good morning to you, yes I am," – or not, if that was the case. It was all terribly polite, and it took me some time to get used to people, even underwriters, calling me Sir. About the only people who had called me Sir at that time were the salesman at Burtons" the tailors, where I bought the charcoal grey suit that I wore in the Room. I was as green as grass in the ways of the upper classes. Most of the people who worked in the Room were from (or as I was to find out later, WISHED they were from) the smart areas in and around London, so it came as quite a surprise to me when one Friday, as I was standing at a Box talking to another broker about God knows what, when a very dapper young man in a very well-fitting tweed suit approached me and asked the usual question – was I last in the queue? He had soft brown hair quite long, he was also very good-looking and about my age, maybe a year or two older. His voice was very cultured – in those days I would have called it posh. I told him that I was indeed last, at which he looked me up and down and then said quite loudly, "I see you're not going to the country this weekend."

I looked at him, I was speechless, then I said, "I beg your pardon?" He then repeated the question, but this time he had a smirk on his face and I knew he was trying to take the piss. "Oh," I said in my most cultured tones, "as a matter of fact I live in the country, Manor Farm Enfield, do you know it?" He looked a bit surprised.

"No, I don't think I do, how many acres has it?"

I looked him straight in the eye, and said "600, or thereabouts." By this time all the people around us including the underwriter were listening.

"Is that arable, or livestock?"

"Bit of each," I said quite nonchalantly, "you must come down and stay."

His face broke out into a smile." Thanks, old boy," he gushed at me, "is it easy to find?"

"Yes," I assured him, "just drive down the A10 into Enfield, keep going until you see the crematorium on your right-hand side, and just past there on your left-hand side is Manor Farm, you can't miss it, it's a fucking great council estate! Just ask for Ricky, they all know me." His face turned to fury as everybody laughed, he flushed bright red and left very quickly.

"It's about time someone put that little prat in his place," it was the underwriter talking, and he was not a man known for his humour, in fact the reverse. I smiled." Well done," he said, then hurried his nose back into a file.

The other young broker, a guy about my own age, smart in his dark blue suit, blue striped shirt with a stiff white collar and dark tie, with fair hair and vivid blue eyes that sparkled as he laughed, said, "That was brilliant." He held out his hand. "I'm Alf, you're new here, aren't you?" I told him I was and he asked who I worked for, it turned out we both worked for the same company, but he dealt with marine claims, so was on a different floor back at Head Office. "What are you doing lunchtime?"

I shrugged my shoulders." Nothing much."

"In that case let me buy you a drink, and I'll introduce you to some of the other guys," he shook my hand again, "is it a deal?"

"Deal," I said as we both shook hands.

That was to be the start of a friendship that was to endure for many years. It was also one that was to cost me a lot of heartache, none of which was Alf's fault. We met for lunch, then went for a drink in one of the market pubs – Leadenhall fruit market was still thriving in those days, I'm not sure if it still is. Alf introduced me to some of the other fellows as he had promised, and he told them all about my run-in with the guy at the Box. It turned out that everybody knew the bloke, his name was Norris. What I didn't know was that, for all his airs and graces, Norris came from Petts Wood, itself a large council estate just outside Orpington, south of London, – but since working in the Room, poor Norris had all but elevated himself to the peerage! Working in that environment could and did affect and change some people, some for the good and some for the worst, like Norris. I and the other guys from working-class homes were, after all, rubbing shoulders and getting on first-name terms with lords, earls, and lots of Hons. The vast majority of them were utterly charming and helpful, the people who were difficult as a rule were those like Norris who had forgotten their roots. I still see that today, only now it's so-called stars of showbusiness who smile at their fans from a stage but hold them in contempt in private.

Alf and I became almost inseparable, meeting at Liverpool

Street Station in the mornings and walking to work from there, meeting for lunch and then walking back to the station after work, calling in a pub on the way. He played football for the company, so at weekends you could usually find me standing on the touchline cheering on the team, but in truth the only one I was really cheering was Alf. I had fallen in love with him, but I dared not show it, and this was the difficult bit. I knew he wasn't like me, in fact I didn't think anybody was like me. I felt completely alone. Some of the lads would make comments like, "Are you two Siamese twins?" or "What's going on between you two?" Alf would laugh, then say, "We're having it off! Ain't that right Rick?" then it would be my turn to laugh and agree, and all the time I would be thinking, "If only it were true."

To help me cope with the strain of all this I started to write Alf letters.

I never posted the letters, of course, I would tear them up after a few days, then write another. I would write with passion all the things I wanted to say to him but couldn't. I would even write about things I would like to do in bed. I found it helped, I was having a secret love affair, and writing to Alf about it made it all seem so real. When I read the Sunday papers and saw articles about queers and the twilight world in which they lived, I wondered if I were part of that world, and I wondered also what would happen to me if I were found out, would they send me to prison?

The evenings were the worst. When I came home from work, my Mum always asked how my day had gone, or my sister would tell me of a girl in the office who fancied me. "Why don't you ask her out?" she would say, then Mum would say, "Bring her home for the weekend." I would go cold. I'd tell my sister that I didn't fancy the girl, she would then ask why, and so it would go on. "You have to get married sometime, and they're a better class of girl, those who work in offices." If only she knew some of the girls I worked with, most of them – including my sister– wore their drawers permanently round their ankles! They were man-mad, but having said that so was I! Well, mad about one man at least. While we were walking to work one day, Alf asked me what I was doing the coming Bank Holiday. "Nothing that I know of, why?

"How would you fancy a trip to North Wales? I've got a great-aunt living there, we could stay with her."

"Would she mind?" I asked

"No course not, that's why I'm suggesting we go, what do you say?" Well, of course I said yes, the thought of my spending a whole weekend alone with him made my heart jump.

"How much is the train fare? I haven't got that much saved."

"Don't worry about that," he said airily, "we'll hitch!"

"Hitch!" I stopped walking, "hitchhike to North Wales?"

"Yes, why not, where's your spirit of adventure?"

I didn't know but I was going to find out.

We started our trek at five in the morning, by about seven we had travelled about eight miles. We were about to get disheartened when a large lorry came into view, we both thumbed and to our delight it stopped. Alf told the driver where we were heading, and he said he could take us part of the way, but we would have to ride in the back. Well, the fact that it was an open-backed lorry didn't deter us as we scrambled aboard – it was only when we fell into the open back that we had second thoughts. It was carrying sand, not just sand but wet sand, but by this time it was too late. The lorry had moved off, we were now travelling at about sixty miles an hour and the noise was deafening, so even if we had wanted to get out, the driver would never have heard our calls.

The temperature that morning had seemed quite mild, but in that open-backed truck, the wind was freezing. When eventually it did stop and the driver yelled, that was as far as he could take us, we literally fell from the open back onto a grass verge. The lorry pulled away and we lay where we had fallen frozen stiff. It was to be another nine hours before we arrived at our destination, tired and hungry but happy to have arrived. We set about finding Great-Aunt Rose.

We were in Haverfordwest, we might as well have been in China as we tried to follow directions that would lead us to our destination. After what seemed an age we found the little row of terraced houses where Great-Aunt Rose lived. Grinning as we walked up the little garden path, Alf knocked at the door – nothing. He knocked again – still nothing.

"I bet she's gone down to see your Mum," I said to Alf, half-joking, and half-thinking that I could be right.

"That," said Alf, "is not remotely funny," and he banged on the door even harder. Then we heard a noise coming from inside the cottage. The door opened and a scruffy man in a flat cap asked what the bloody hell we wanted, at least that's what we took it to mean.

Alf tried to explain who he was, but the old boy just told us to sod off and come back later.

We walked dejectedly out of the street, and into a nearby field. Neither of us spoke, I sensed that he was feeling bad about the situation. We fell onto the grass. "Look on the bright side," I told Alf. He looked at me.

"What bloody bright side?"

"Well, now I can tell Norris that we spent the weekend in the country!"

We both laughed and then fell asleep.

It was about eight o'clock when Alf woke me.

"Come on, let's go try again."

This time the door opened almost as soon as he had put the knocker down, a woman of about sixty with greying carrot-coloured hair tied up in a bright turban.

"Now who have we here? And what do you mean by banging on me door, as though you meant to break it down?" We may have been in Wales but this lady was most certainly Irish.

"Are you Aunt Rose?" Alf said weakly.

"And suppose I am, what's that to you?"

"Well," said Alf, a little brighter, "I'm your great nephew, Alf, and this is my mate Ricky, we've come to see you."

"Oh, you come to see me so you have, and why should I want to see you, sure I haven't seen your mother in twenty years."

"She sends her love."

"So it's her love that's she's sending is it, and you two are part of the package, is that it?"

We looked at each other, and Alf just shrugged. "Suppose so," he whispered.

"Well don't be standing on my step, sure the neighbours will think I've been invaded by beatniks, give your old Aunt a kiss."

With that, she grabbed Alf and smothered him in sloppy wet kisses. I was so glad she wasn't my aunt, that is until she grabbed me and gave me the same treatment. After the trial by saliva, she ushered us down a narrow hallway, into the back room. It was tiny and crammed full of furniture, pictures, and bric-a-brac. As it was nearly dusk, it was also quite dark in the room, the only window being covered by a pair of heavy dark-green curtains. Suddenly there was a grunt from a pile of clothes on an armchair that was at the far side of an old kitchen range.

"Are you not even going to say hello to me long lost great-nephew, who's come all the way from London with his friend just to see me so he has?"

Another grunt from the armchair. Alf and I both said our hellos.

"Take no notice of him, lazy old sod, sure he wouldn't even go to the front, door if he thought I could bring it in. Now sit yourselves down, you must be famished" We sat down and she gave us a huge meal of ham, eggs and chips with platefuls of fresh bread and butter and endless cups of tea.

After the meal she asked us if we would like to go to the local club for a drink, we said we would.

"Right then, me man there," pointing to the pile of clothes that hadn't moved since our arrival, "will take you both, he always goes about this time."

More grunts from the corner, then the pile of clothes started to move and made for the door.

"And don't you be bringing them back here drunk, sure isn't one drunk enough for me to cope with," then she turned to us, "off you go and enjoy yourselves, and don't spend too much on that old bugger, and I'll have your room ready by the time you get back so I will." We thanked her and followed the old man out. We walked behind him all the way to the club, he never spoke once, we tried, but soon gave up. When we reached the club, he muttered something to the bloke on the door. He, in turn, looked at us, nodded and we were in.

It was the local working men's club, a long low room, with a bar running down one side. The room was packed, mainly with men of all ages – there were a few women, but only a few and those were middle-aged and over. The noise was deafening, a duo was bashing out some old standards from a small stage at the far end, and the air was thick almost yellow with pipe and cigarette smoke. The old guy pushed his way to the bar, nodding to various cronies as he went. We followed, and the eyes of a hundred or more followed us. The old man ordered a drink, and I told the barmaid to make it three. I put the money on the counter, the old man picked up his drink, then without a thank you went and joined his friends.

"Cheeky old sod," said Alf.

I laughed. "Who cares – let's get pissed," and we did.

When it was time to go, the old man just pointed to his watch and then the door. We finished our drinks and followed the old guy out. Still he didn't say a word. He walked on in front, and we took the piss out of him behind his back, then we broke into song, singing songs like "Apple Blossom Time" and "Georgia". The old boy kept turning round and yelling at us to shut up, but we were drunk, so we kept singing.

By the time we reached the house, the old man was nowhere to be seen, he had hurried on leaving us to our sing-song. Aunt Rose was on the step.

"Do you want to wake the whole town?" We both shut up when we saw her. "I'll have the devil's own job with the neighbours in the morning so I will."

"Sorry, 'said Alf, "did your husband tell you?"

"Sure he had no need to tell me at all, sure couldn't I hear you three streets away? and don't you be taking any notice of your man" she laughed as she closed the door behind us," if you had been singing, "We'll Keep a Welcome in the Hillside", the old bugger would have joined in."

We doubted that.

She gave us a supper of cheese and pickle, washed down with mugs of cocoa.

"Now I expect you're both ready for your bed, you must be ready to drop. Follow me and I'll show you your bedroom." She led the way up a narrow dark staircase, up yet again to an attic bedroom, with one bed, a washstand and a small wardrobe. The room smelt of mothballs, it reminded me of my gran's in Walthamstow.

"Now I know it's not what you're used to, living in your fancy London houses like you do, so there you are – take it or leave it."

I just stared at the double bed. "Christ," I thought, "I am going to sleep in the same bed as Alf!" I was sure they must be able to hear my heart beating with excitement.

"That's great, Aunt Rose, just like home." Alf lied, I hadn't seen his bedroom at home but he was always moaning about the way one of his younger brothers, with who he shared, was forever making a mess, and this little room with the patchwork quilt on the bed was spotless.

Aunt Rose bid us goodnight and left.

"I could sleep for a week, couldn't you," Alf said through a yawn.

"Yes, not half," I said, trying to pretend that I too was yawning – in fact, I was wide awake.

"Well I hope you don't snore," he yawned again as he took his trousers off. He was naked except for his underpants, which were pale blue, quite novel in those days, when men's underwear was purely practical, not the fashion accessory they are today. So tight fitting pale blue Y-fronts were very trendy, and against his slightly tanned, sinewy body, almost too much for me.

I lay in the dark, scared to move. I could feel the warmth from his body, he turned his back to me, and I felt his buttocks gently pressing on my leg, now my head – amongst other things – was throbbing with excitement.

Some guys who are, for want of a better word, 'straight', will experience, or want to experience a relationship with another man, but some most definitely do not. At that time in my life I knew nothing of homosexual society, in fact, I didn't even know that I was what was called homosexual. What I did know was that I was drawn sexually to other men. I hadn't even met, nor did I know anybody with the same feelings, apart from my two brief experiences at Gamage's and at the GPO. I was completely ignorant, but I did know that by making a move towards Alf, or indeed anybody else I would be running a grave risk. At school, and with my limited experience in the world outside of school, I had become aware of the hatred and ridicule that was shown towards 'queers' and 'poofs' in the playground and workplace. Jokes about them were an everyday thing, and I have to say some were very funny – well, anyway, I used to laugh at them, along with the rest. Not always because I thought they were funny, but because if I hadn't have laughed, it might have made people point the finger at me, and in the 1950s that would not have been funny.

As I lay there, I prayed that he would make some advances towards me, but of course, he didn't. I so wanted to put my arms around him, to tell him how I felt, the frustration was almost unbearable, then a sort of panic set in." Was this to be my life? What will happen if anybody finds out? Maybe I'm ill, perhaps I should see the doctor!" Then I thought of our family doctor, a jolly red-faced Scot, Dr Stevens – but he was the family doctor, and I thought he would tell my parents, so I decided there and then that I would tell no one, that I would find a girlfriend, and try and be like my mates. That night seemed to go on forever. I didn't dare sleep, in case I did something without realising. I couldn't take that risk.

Next morning, Aunt Rose was banging at the door telling us breakfast was on the table, Alf moaned and groaned, and got up after Rose, calling for the umpteenth time, threatened to come upstairs and drag us out!

We spent that day looking at the local landmarks and visiting any pub we came across. By late afternoon, we decided that we would go back to London that night. I was pleased because it meant I wouldn't have to spend another night lying awake and wishing.

Aunt Rose said she was sorry we were going, and how much she had enjoyed seeing us both, which I thought was nice of her. Even the old man managed to smile as he grunted his goodbyes. Mind you I could be wrong – it could have been wind!

The evening was warm and balmy as we left Haverfordwest and headed back to London. Traffic was light, but it didn't bother us for the first few miles. We walked along country roads, enjoying the scent from the fields and laughing at this and that. Aunt Rose had given us an old Army sleeping bag. "You never know," she said, "and your man will never miss it."

It started to get a bit chilly, the miles wore on and we were still only about fifty miles from Haverfordwest. Darkness seemed to fall suddenly. Just as it did a middle-aged woman stopped in a battered Ford. It was, I thought, very brave (or silly) of her to stop for two youths she didn't know – now, of course, she could be risking life and limb, or worse. She took us about forty miles, she chattered away quite unconcerned about us. When she dropped us off she warned us to be careful about who we accepted a lift from. We climbed out from the back seat, and I was just about to close the door after saying thanks when she suddenly reached for a paper carrier bag next to her on the front seat. "Be a love, put this in a waste bin, there's a dear," she handed me the bag, "don't want my husband knowing all my little secrets, do we!" Then she slammed the door and drove off. We watched as the little car went off weaving from side to side.

"She's pissed," Alf said in amazement.

I looked into the carrier bag. "I'm not surprised, look." I showed Alf the contents of the bag. "Two empty vodka bottles!

No wonder she told us to be careful!" We both fell about laughing.

We were not laughing half an hour later, it was by now bitterly cold, and pitch black, we hadn't seen or heard a thing since the battered Ford had gone off at speed.

"This is madness," groaned Alf, "we better find somewhere to kip, and get warm, before we freeze to death."

This did not prove to be an easy task. Because it was so dark, we could not actually see very far, so any shelter more than a few feet away went completely unnoticed.

Then, "Oh shit! that hurt," it was Alf. He had walked into a broken-down fence. The road had turned sharply, but we, of course, couldn't see it.

"You all right?" I said as I edged towards Alf's cursing and swearing.

"Yes, who wouldn't be, lost in the middle of Welsh Wales, in the pitch bleeding dark, freezing cold with half a rotten fence stuck in me, oh yes I'm fine."

When I caught up with him and saw him sitting on the ground, picking splinters of wood from his hands, God knows why, but I laughed.

Alf was not amused." Don't just stand there laughing, help me up!"

And that's when I saw it.

"Quick," I said, as though what I had seen would vanish if he didn't see it at once. Ignoring his outstretched hand, waiting to be pulled up, I stepped past him. "Look!" I was getting excited by my find now, "our hotel for the night!"

Alf was now up and at my side, and we were both staring at the wreck of an old car.

"Don't know about a hotel," Alf said, as we both went nearer our find, "looks more like a very cheap boarding house."

As we got right up to the wreck, our hopes of a warm bed faded. The car was indeed a wreck, and much too much of a wreck to be of any use to us. The doors were missing, and the seats had been ripped out.

"Well so much for me and my hotel, now what?"

There was no reply, I looked round and Alf had vanished,

"Alf, where are you? Alfie, for Christ's sake stop sodding about."

"Over here."

His voice came from out of the blackness that was all around me.

"Where the hell's here?"

"This way, follow my voice, but be careful, we're in a breaker's yard."

I followed his voice, picking my way over and around piles of old tyres, and heaps of old cars, that loomed out of the dark, like great metal monsters, I didn't so much find Alf, as walk into him, I had put my hand out to grab at what I thought was a post, in order too steady myself, and I grabbed Alf by the neck, the scream of fear that came from him that night still makes me fall about laughing to this day.

"You stupid bastard – oh fuck, me heart's stopped! Stop laughing, you could have killed me."

I was almost rolling on the ground. When I touched him, I swear he must have jumped ten feet in the air, what with that and the scream – well, I just couldn't contain myself.

"Will you get up and shut up."

I was trying to tell him, through my laughter, what he had looked like, but the more I tried to tell him the more I laughed. The tears were running down my face, now he too was laughing. We hung on to one another while we nearly split our sides with laughing. When at last we did calm down, Alf pointed to the ghostly shape of an old ambulance, its white paintwork standing out in the dark night.

"Now that's what I call a hotel," he said as he led me closer, "and look all the doors are on." We went to the back of the ambulance, and Alf tried the handle. "Let's hope the stretchers are still inside," he said as he pulled the doors open. We both peered inside but could see nothing, so we climbed in. Alas, it was empty, everything had been removed.

"Still at least we'll be out of the cold, and we'll be dry," I said as I fell to the floor. I hadn't realised just how tired I was, Alf was now at my side.

"I'm shagged out," he said, as he spread out the sleeping bag." Come on we'll share Aunt Rose's present."

We both lay on the hard floor, on the sleeping bag, in case the floor was dirty, but soon it was so cold that we pulled the bag over ourselves and huddled together in a vain attempt to keep warm. I could feel the warmth from Alf's body, his face touching mine, and his breath on my cheek. Any other time and I would have been in my seventh heaven, but then and there I just wanted to be warm. Nothing else mattered as we lay there shivering in the dark.

We both slept fitfully. I woke early the next morning – I was freezing. For a moment I lay there not knowing where I was or what I was doing there. My arm was around Alf's waist, he with his back to me was still snoring. I looked around me trying not to wake him, what I saw made me yell out, "Oh for fuck's sake!"

Alf was awake in an instant. "What is it? what's the matter?" he said as he struggled to get out of the sleeping bag.

"That's the matter," I was laughing now." That's the bleeding matter!" I pointed to the windows.

"You mean we have been trying to get warm all bloody night and the windows have been wide open!"

"Well, it was so dark last night I didn't think to check if they were closed or not."

"And I thought it was the black glass. What a pair of prats, don't for Christ sake tell anybody they will think we are mad for not checking."

"They probably will," I thought, "but at least I got to sleep close to you."

"Oi! did you hear me?"

"Yes of course I did." I was still laughing but also thinking about being so close to him and how good it felt." Come on, let's get out of here before somebody comes and tries to charge us for our 'hotel room'." We picked up our things and made our way back to the road.

It took us another five hours before we got anywhere near London and by this time we were tired and hungry and out of cigarettes. We pooled the last of our money and bought five "Weights" (you could buy the cheap brands of cigarettes in packets of five then). Then we went into a café and bought two steaming hot mugs of tea and two slices of toast. Now we really were skint, but as we sat there taking deep drags on the cigs and clutching our mugs of tea, we hadn't a care in the world. If I could have been frozen in time then I would have been perfectly happy, but as I was about to find out life just ain't like that.

When I got home, Mum asked if I had enjoyed my weekend. I said I had and told her some of the highlights, she then told me that she had a row with my Dad and they were not speaking yet again. This situation could last for weeks or even months, I didn't bother to ask what had caused it this time, it was always the same answer anyway: "Gambling". My father was addicted and that was that. My mother was telling me the ins and outs of the argument, but I wasn't listening. Both my sister and I had become expert in saying yes and no in the right places whenever either my Mum or Dad was giving us their side of things. It was a very unhappy marriage in the main, sometimes they would seem truly happy but it never lasted. Now when I look back on it I can never remember ever seeing them kiss or give each other a hug or hold hands. Come to that, my sister and I never got hugs, but that's the way they were – they loved us, and they loved each other but other things got in the way. Lack of money for one, the fact that they both worked so hard all their lives and had little to show for it, and of course my Dad's gambling. He was so sure that one day he would be rich, one day he would be able to give us and my Mum all that money could buy. Neither of them could see that all either of us wanted was to know that we were loved.

I love them still and I have spent a lifetime of regret that I didn't tell them so. at the end. I have never even been able to visit their last resting place. I went to the crematorium and was given a map of where they were at rest, but I could never find the spot, I went twice searching for them, but to no avail, and my sister never offered to show me so I guess I'll never know.

After that holiday I changed. I knew I couldn't go on the way I was. I kept writing my letters to Alf, and that helped me cope, but inside I was breaking up with both fear and self-loathing. Suppose someone finds out the truth about me, how will people react towards me, what will Mum and Dad say? I didn't have long to find out, and it was to set me on a path that would lead me almost to self-destruction-.

Arriving home from my job, my mother was in the kitchen. "Hello, Mum. Oh! What a day!"

"Don't 'hello mum' me." She spat the words at me. I looked at her and saw that she'd been crying. I went to put my arms around her.

"What's up Mum?" She pushed me away.

"Don't you dare touch me."

I couldn't understand what was wrong. My Mum did have a temper but she was normally a loving mother. But now she was very angry and upset.

"Just tell me what's wrong Mum, for Christ's sake!"

"This is what's wrong," she pulled a letter from her pocket. I felt myself go red, then I broke out into a cold sweat. She pushed the letter into my face. I recognised it. "Well, do you know what's in it? Do you?" I nodded." You need to hang your head down in shame, you pervert. Tell me it's not true, tell me, please tell me." She was crying and sobbing now. Once more I tried to put my arm around her but she pushed me away again.

The letter was one of a number I had written to Alfie but had never sent. They were love letters.

"Please Mum, let me try and explain." I didn't know how to explain because I didn't understand it myself.

"Oh, so you want to explain, do you? Well go on – try, try and tell me why I've got a queer for a son. Go on – tell me that!"

"I'm not a queer, really I'm not."

"You're not, aren't you? Then what's this, this filth? Let me read a bit to you."

"No, please Mum, I don't want to hear it." I put my hands over my ears as my mother, the Mum that I loved, read or rather screamed lines to me that I had written to Alf, who had no idea of how I felt. The tears were now streaming down my cheeks, they were tears for my Mum and tears of humiliation. I was sixteen and I wanted to die right there and then.

"Well, do you deny you wrote this filth?" I shook my head then I felt like my head had left my shoulders as my mother slapped me around the face. I felt it burn and I could almost feel her handprint on my cheek.

"Get upstairs and pack your bag and get out of this house before your father comes in and kills you."

"Where can I go?"

"That's your problem. Go to your boyfriend's."

"But he doesn't even know, Mum. I can't tell him. What will he say?"

"What will he say? I don't care what he says. What's the family going to say? What are the neighbours going to say? Tell me that." Her tears had stopped now. "She's not worried about me," I thought, "it's the neighbours she's really worried about."

"It's not me you care about, is it?" I said, "It's her next door or my sister or the rest of them, but what about me? Don't I count?

Don't I matter? I'm your son."

She hit me again even harder, it knocked me off balance, I felt my cheek and I could feel it burn again. I don't think she realised that I would feel that slap for the rest of my life. I pleaded with my mother to let me stay one more night. She agreed so long as I stayed in my room and didn't speak to any other member of the family.

The next morning I left home.

At six o'clock on a frosty morning, I made my way by bus to Walthamstow, East London. Shocked, scared and fearful of the future. I got on a trolley-bus to Bruce Grove, the trolley glided through North London like a huge, silent monster. Everything seemed so unreal. I rubbed the condensation from the window and stared out at the Saturday morning crowds, all hurrying around to do the weekly shop. I wondered if any of them felt as lonely as I did.

"Come on mate. I said where to?" I looked up at the bus conductor.

"Sorry!" I said.

"Cor blimey, if it ain't young Ricky, whatcher up to then?" I recognised him as being one of my Dad's mates, Dad was also a bus conductor.

"Hello Mr Shaw, I'm going to see my Gran." I lied.

"'Ow far you going, young 'un?"

"Oh, Bruce Grove please."

"Righto cocker, if a jumper (a ticket inspector) gets on, you're my grandson!"

He patted me on the head with his money-blackened hand.

"Thanks Mr Shaw," I murmured, "thanks a lot."

I sank back into my seat. I began to feel strangely excited. I wondered what Mum had told Dad and what he had said. I really did love them both. I put my hand to my face and could still feel the smart in my cheek. I changed buses at Bruce Grove and said goodbye to Mr Shaw. The next bus would take me to Walthamstow in East London. It was my mother's birthplace and the home of my favourite Gran until she had died two years before.

It was also the place where my best friend lived, the boy who I had written all those letters to. It was only a short ride to my stop at Blackhorse Road, but I put my case under the stairs and went to the upper deck. I wanted a good look at my new home town. I remembered when I was a child and my mother used to take my twin sister and me to visit Gran, I always loved the top deck of the bus. As we approached Walthamstow I could smell the place, it was a magic smell that to me as a child meant seeing my Gran and eating stewed eels and mash covered with a bright green gravy called liquor. At my stop in Blackhorse Road stood the Ever-Ready battery factory. It was from here that the magic smell came. At the side of the factory was a 'graveyard' for old London buses. I used to love looking at those old buses and trams.

I left the bus and started to walk towards the High Street where I hoped to find a room. I found a newsagent's with a large board outside that was full of ads offering anything from rooms to wheelchairs to ladies with large chests for sale! I scribbled down some addresses, this was easy I thought. Now it had started to rain, not heavily, but a fine penetrating rain. The first address was Coppermill Lane, which had been the road my Gran lived in. Coppermill Lane stood at the bottom of the High Street. It was a long, straight road lined on both sides with plane trees. Behind the trees stood the houses, large, Victorian houses that were once the pride and joy of local businesspeople. Now they were a motley assortment of bedsitters and run-down guesthouses. Most had peeling paintwork, the front doors that had once sported stained glass windows now had a mish-mash of frosted glass or were simply boarded up. A once elegant street of houses now stood shabby and forlorn.

I found number 73. I could hardly see the front downstairs windows through the thick privet hedge that all but filled the small front garden. I knocked on the door, its paint all grimy apart from a bright patch near the lock which was now shiny with wear.

At the sound of footsteps, I pulled my coat straight. The door opened and a thin, tired-looking woman appeared, her head wrapped in a bright scarf tied in a turban. She wore a flowered overall tied tightly around her waist. A cigarette hung from the corner of her mouth, she took the cigarette from her mouth with long, bony, nicotine-stained fingers.

"Well, what do you want? I ain't buying nothing."

"Er, I've just come about the room that's for rent." I almost whispered.

"What?" She snapped.

"The room you have for rent, I'd like to see it please."

"Oh you would, would you? Well hard luck mate, cos it's gorn, went weeks ago."

"But I've just seen the ad in the news—" She cut me short.

"I know where you saw it, but like I said, it's gorn, you deaf or something? Try 'er at 87." She pointed down the street, then turned and slammed the door shut.

I didn't try 'er at No.87. Instead, I went to the local newsagents with a Wanted Ads board outside. I found an address for a room to rent in Eastfield Road, I found the address, it was a smart 1930s semi. I walked up the short path and pressed the bell on the bright blue door. After a moment the door opened and I was looking at a small very plump boy about 12 years old, "What do you want?" he almost sneered at me.

"I'd like to speak to your Mum or Dad please," I said, in my most sarcastic voice.

"Who's there, Jacob?" came a shrill voice from inside.

"Don't know, said he wants you or Papa," said the brat. A woman twice as large as her offspring pulled the door further open, she was about 40 and well-dressed.

"What can I do for you?" she said sharply.

"Oh, good afternoon, I've come about your room you have to rent," I replied.

"Oh, do you work?"

"Yes," said I, "I'm a broker at Lloyds of London." Her face showed a faint look of delight. She looked me up and down, then invited me in.

"Follow me," she said as she climbed the stairs, still talking." This is a nice clean Jewish house, we don't supply food and it's two pounds a week in advance." She reached the top of the stairs and opened the door of the box room, standing to one side she ushered me in. It was a box room, about the size of a box! Inside was a small bed, small chest and a narrow wardrobe, plus a small table at the foot of the bed with a small portable electric stove on top, but it was very clean." Well?" she said.

"Oh, very nice I'd like to take it please Mrs err—"

"Gold!" she snapped. "All right. No loud music and no beer or spirits allowed, bed changed once a fortnight, use your own towels and soap, and one bath a week."

Christ, I thought, this will be fun. I paid the rent and moved straight in. There were no pots and pans for the tiny oven so I went to Woolworths and bought some cheap aluminium pans and a kettle.

I loved listening to the radio on Sunday mornings, there were repeats of all the week's comedy shows, Round the Horne, The Clitheroe Kid, Take It From Here and many more, I would be laughing out loud, but not too loud or I'd have someone banging on the door yelling "Keep the noise down, this is a nice Jewish house!" I wanted to call back, "My mother is Jewish and she keeps a nice house!" but I didn't.

One Sunday I was trying to cook eggs and bacon – I know, I know! It was a Jewish house – but we had bacon at home. Those cheap pans were useless everything seemed to stick and burn, I was getting in a real state when Mr Gold banged on the door. "Someone to see you." I opened the door. If looks could kill, the look he gave me would have struck me down there and then. "That smell! Can't you smell that the smell of the cooking is all over the house? Don't you know that it is a good, clean Jewish house?"

"Yes," I said, I did know. He turned and stormed back down the stairs. I threw the remains of the eggs AND the frying pan into the waste bin, and followed him downstairs. When I reached the front door, Alfie my friend was standing there, with a look of amazement on his face.

"Who the bloody hell was that?" he said, as I showed him into my room.

"That was Mr Gold my landlord, and when I say Lord, I mean Lord."

"Christ, what an old bastard. How do you put up with that?"

"I've got to have somewhere to live."

"Well you can't stay here," he said, "come on, let's have a cuppa in the Black and White."

The Black and White was a milk bar, all the rage in the fifties. It had a black and white painted front, inside the walls were covered in black and white tiles, the tables were covered in black and white plastic cloths, and just in case you might think it was a red and green or a blue and pink milk bar, the words "Black and White Milk Bar", were picked out in (yes, you've guessed) black and white tiles on the wall behind the counter.

As we crossed the High Street towards the café – sorry, the milk bar – I was glumly listening to Alf telling me that my digs were no good, I must be mad not to move and that he was going to help me find somewhere else.

"I wish I could live with you," I thought, as we entered the milk bar, "then everything would be OK." I just knew it.

"Sit down," Alf said, "I'll get the teas, do you want a Banbury?" A Banbury was a flat cake stuffed with currants.

Since my breakfast was in the bin I said I would. I sat down at the table in the window. Outside the market was getting in full swing even though it was only nine o'clock. The windows were steamed up, so I rubbed them with damp nylon curtains. I peered out into the street.

"What the hell have I done? I'm sixteen and I'm in love with my best friend, had a row with my family and now I have to change digs." I hadn't even written to Mum and Dad to say sorry or that I was OK, I should really, but I just didn't know how to say what I felt. I glanced across the room to where Alfie was standing, talking to Anne the manageress, a brassy blonde about forty, with a coarse laugh and huge tits. She always wore green nail varnish, it looked awful when she was serving cakes, picking them up with those evil-looking talons – they looked like poison tip darts to me. I looked at Alfie, I wondered if he had any idea about my feelings for him. I didn't think so, he was a man's man and I knew it, he loved the girls. I feared if he ever found out I would surely lose him completely. Now both Alf and Anne were looking at me. Anne waved, I waved back. We knew her quite well, we were always in the Black and White, especially at weekends. I looked at them laughing and thought that Anne fancied him. For a moment I hated her, then I thought, "Well, let her, she won't ever get him." I thought about the girls at work, always chasing after him, flirting with him, I didn't really care, as long as no other bloke fancied him! I looked through the misty window again and imagined the two of us, just me and Alf, living in a bright green valley, with nobody to spoil it.

"Wakey, wakey, I've got some news for you." It was Alf. He put a tray down on the table. "Anne was saying you look fed up, so I told her about old man Gold, and she said she has a spare room at her house, so we're going to see it tonight, great eh?"

"Oh yes, great! Imagine living with those green fingernails!" I thought to myself. "Yes, great!" I said, aloud. "Great!"

Saturday night was the big night out of the week, and we really looked forward to it. I met Alf early at the Black and White so that we could go and see Anne. He was already there when I arrived, he was sitting on his own by the window. He waved to me as I came in and his clear blue eyes seemed to shine. My heart leapt. He was wearing a dark blue suit and blue checked shirt, with a blue tie. My suit was the same colour, but I had put on putty-coloured shoes, a white shirt with a knitted tie to match my shoes and – to finish it off – a handkerchief in my top pocket of the same putty colour.

"You look great," he said." Do you want a coffee or shall we see Anne?"

"Better get it over and done with," I said, "apart from anything else, we won't get a seat in the pub."

Anne lived in Carlo Road, just around the corner from the Golds. It was a larger house, not so well cared for, but by no means a slum. Alf rang the doorbell, a dog barked, and kids yelled. The door was opened by a little girl, about nine years old, and behind her was another girl about seven.

"Are you Ricky?" she asked.

"Yes, that's me, in the flesh," I laughed, "how do you know my name?"

"We know his name as well," said the seven-year-old, and they both giggled.

"Oh yes," said Alf, "well, you better go and tell your Mum that there's two good-looking blokes at the door."

They both ran back down the hallway calling, "Mum, Mum, they're here Mum."

Anne appeared, "Oh shut your bleedin' noise up, they'll think it's a bleedin' madhouse. Come on in lads," she smiled, "don't take any notice of them, they're bleedin' man-mad! Well, let 'em get past Anne!" The elder girl moved back and in we went. Anne showed us into the front room. "Sit down, drink?" I always have one about this time."

We sat down and she crossed to the cocktail bar, a shiny cabinet with a walnut finish. She pulled down the flap and a light came on to expose a whole range of drinks. We both had a vodka and tonic, Anne had something called a "Green Goddess", I supposed to match her nails! The room was large and comfortable with an assortment of furniture. The wallpaper was a large leaf design, and on it hung various photos of the family, some living, some long since gone. At the windows hung heavy green striped curtains. We sat on an old real leather settee, it was deep and soft, and although it had seen better days, it was the only real nice piece in the whole room. In front of that stood a long coffee table topped with fake marble.

"Well now," said Anne sitting herself between us, "got yourself in a right old mess and no mistake."

"Well things could be better," I admitted.

Anne patted me on the leg. "Well you're lucky, I do let rooms, and I've got a spare bed in one of them, you don't mind sharing, do you?"

"Well not really, I suppose, but – er—" Here I started to fumble with words again.

Anne said, "Don't worry, it's with my son, Brian, he's about your age. I wouldn't put you in with any old fogey."

"Thanks," I said.

"I've got six bedrooms here, me and Dave, he's my husband. You won't see much of 'im, he works nights." She said that with what sounded like relief in her voice. "He's my third, I must have been mad." She laughed, so did we, a half-hearted laugh, smacking of embarrassment. She sipped her "Green Goddess" and smiled. "Then there's the two girls, you met them, they have a room. My young son has the box room, more like a cupboard really – still, he likes it. You and Brian are in the large back room, two busmen share the top attic."

"Christ," I thought, "not more busmen."

Anne was still going through her "paying guests" as she liked to call them. "Then in the top back attic, I have two retired gentlemen, Mr Hardman and Mr Silver." As she spoke their names she developed a pseudo-upper-class accent. As though she were speaking on hallowed ground. "Anyway," she continued, "I'll get Brian to show you the room. BRIAN! BRIAN! Come in here."

She yelled so loudly, so suddenly that I nearly jumped out of my new putty-coloured shoes. The door opened and Brian did indeed come in. He was a dark Italian-looking boy about my age – he may have been a year older. He was very good looking with black wavy hair, his teeth were like those you see in films, straight and pure white, but his fingernails matched his hair – they were disgusting, as were his clothes, all black with grime and grease-stained.

"Oh Christ Brian, you could have washed yourself, this is Ricky." I nodded and smiled, he smiled back.

"He's going to be sharing your room." He groaned. "Cut that

out! We need the money, he needs the bed. Well, don't just stand there – take him up to have a look at it."

I went upstairs with Brian, he asked me if I had a motorbike. I told him "No", then he told me that was all he really wanted and did I think that the Norton was better than the BSA. I hadn't a clue what he was talking about! So I got him to tell me what he thought, then I agreed with him!

We went into the bedroom. It was quite large, with a big double bed against the inner wall, and a single bed under the window. Two huge old-fashioned wardrobes stood along the third wall. At one side of the fireplace was a dressing table and on the other side a tallboy. On top of this were bits of motorbike. The walls were, in the main, covered with pictures of motorbikes and motorbike riders – there was here and there the odd picture of a naked girl. When I pointed to the bits of machine on the tallboy Brian merely said that he was trying to build his own bike. "Good job he's not into cars," I thought, "he'd never get it up the stairs!" We went back downstairs. Brian was still talking bikes, I was still nodding and yessing, in what I hoped were the right places.

Brian went straight to the kitchen, as I opened the door of the front room, Anne jumped up from beside Alf, and went over to the cocktail cabinet. Alf blushed. Anne snapped, "Blimey! You were quick."

"Sorry," I said.

"No need to be sorry love. I was just getting Alf a drink, want one? Well come on – did you like the room? It's got to be three quid a week, but you can have all the tea you like, and I'll do you sandwiches to take to work, how's that eh?"

"Oh, that's great," I said. "Can I move in next week, I paid the Golds a week in advance."

"Course you can – what's your favourite sandwich?"

"Er – cheese and pickle." It was the first thing that came to my head, but I was to regret it later, as I had cheese and pickle sandwiches for the duration of my stay at Anne's!

We left the house and were walking down the street to go to the pub when Alf turned to me and said,

"You'll be all right there, she let me grope her tits, I bet she's a real goer."

"Leave it out Alf, I don't fancy her, don't tell me you do?"

He laughed, "No, course I don't, but well, we are young and we do need all the practice we can get, don't we?"

I went numb, but he laughed, and I pretended to laugh with him, but inside I was beginning to have misgivings about Anne's place. I think I also knew then that Alf was meant to be my friend and nothing else. At last, we got to the Lord Palmerston, a big Victorian pub, in Forest Road, already we could hear Tommy and Billy, the pub 'band', belting out the latest hits. We walked into the pub like a couple of Jack the Lads. Most people in there knew us, because at about half past ten on a Saturday night we would get up on the stage and sing a couple of songs, never on our own, we didn't have the nerve to go solo, and in fact the only reason we sang at all was because it was a sure way of getting a free drink! Somebody always bought the singers a drink, some nights we would get three or four! Our three numbers were "Someday", "Cherry Blossom Lane", and "Woman from Liberia", always the same songs, but not always in the same order!

The pub was typical of the East End pubs, packed with people who worked hard all day on the docks and in the local factories. Mixed among them were, of course, a sprinkling of petty crooks (and some not so petty), good-time girls, costermongers and anybody else that wanted to let their hair down on a Saturday night, and in the East End of London they all wanted to do that!

Tommy and Billy were really great musicians, able to play any song that was thrown at them, and who could make good singers sound great and bad singers, like us, sound good. Or was everybody so drunk that it just sounded like that? We got really drunk that night, walking home holding each other up, and singing our lungs out. I loved it, I was with Alf, and I didn't care about a thing that night. I walked to his house, he said he would walk back to mine, at my digs I turned round and walked back to his place again, so we went on, still singing but so happy.

At last, we got back to my digs – it must have been nearly two in the morning. We were nearly sober, but I was in a silly mood. Alf said he would like a cup of tea, so I opened the front door as quietly as I could. As we crept up the staircase, Alf slipped and crashed down about six steps. I grabbed him and pulled him up and into my room. We fell on the bed, rolling around laughing. I had my head on his shoulder. Suddenly the door opened, and standing in my room, like something out of a Tom and Jerry cartoon, was Mr Gold. What he saw was Alf and I hugging one another, with laughter – what he thought he saw, I don't have to explain. He screamed he would call the police if Alf didn't get out, and that he had never realised he had a dirty queer living in his good clean house. Alf flew at him yelling we weren't fucking queers, and that he had a dirty fucking mind, and if he didn't shut his mouth, then Alf would!

Mrs Gold now put in an appearance, ranting and tearing her hair. I made Alf go – as he fled down the stairs, he threatened anyone who hurt me and that he would be back in the morning to make sure I was OK. I felt a lump come to my throat. Alf did care – he wasn't like me, but he did at least care what happened to me – and I had a feeling that he knew more than I gave him credit for. The Golds told me I had to go at the end of the week. I had great pleasure in telling them that I had already had new digs, and I was going anyway.

2 – IT NEVER RAINS

It was early spring in 1957. I jumped off the 7.53 train from Walthamstow to Liverpool Street in the heart of the city. Alf and I had spent the weekend as usual, getting drunk in the Palmerston and filing ourselves with pie, eels and mash in the market on Saturday. Monday never was a good day, but that morning the sun was shining, and there was that feeling of spring and a fresh start. Money was getting to be a problem for both of us. Alf came from a large family and he was the eldest son. There were five brothers in all and Alf's mother, a small wiry woman who worked long and hard for her family. Both she and her husband (a strong man, a man's man, who could be very distant) did all they could to make sure the family didn't go without, but they still relied on Alf to more than help out.

I was living at Anne's. It had been uneventful, Anne and Dave had bitter rows now and then, but that was about all. Christmas had been good except that I did miss my family. I did send a card but I didn't put my address on it. I had spent my Christmas bonus on Alf and Anne's family, but now it was spring and I needed some new shoes and a couple of shirts.

As we had time and it was such a nice day we walked from Liverpool Street to the office, which was at London Bridge. It also saved a couple of bob on the underground and meant that we could stop off at Gino's in Leadenhall Market and have coffee and toast. We walked along talking about this and that – and as usual with Alf, 'the other'. We weaved in and out of the other office workers, the men mostly wearing black pinstripe trousers and black jacket topped off with a black rolled umbrella and, of course, a black bowler hat – it was almost a uniform. The women, sensing spring, wore bright coloured dresses with full skirts but, being sensible, most had left their cardigans on!

I was telling Alf that the time had come for me to ask for a rise in my salary and he agreed. I had even stopped having Sunday lunch at Anne's because I had to pay three shillings and sixpence extra on my rent for it. Anne had asked me if I could cook. Well, I had watched my mother and didn't see any problem so I said "Yes".

"Right," said Anne. "In that case, you can cook Sunday lunch for all the family and guests and have yours free!!"

So I did. I got up early on Sunday morning, after a heavy night of drinking, and I cooked lunch for eleven people!! But I saved three and six!! I was nearly seventeen years old.

We reached Gino's in Leadenhall Market. It was, as always at that time of day, very busy. It was packed with market porters, city gents, office girls and boys, and cleaning staff on their way home. Gino was a small balding Italian, who was always smiling (probably because of the money he was making), as we walked in he called "Morning lads, had a good weekend, plenty of womans eh!" he laughed.

"Not as many as you, you dirty sod!" I called back. This time the whole café seemed to join in the laughter, spring was definitely on the way! We took our coffee and toast to a corner table where some of our workmates had gathered. We swapped stories about the weekend, each of us building a bigger picture than the truth. Alf and I were always in demand for these stories, ours being that much more over the top – and of course, we had each other to back the stories up.

"This dirty little git pulled a right little cracker on Saturday night," said Alf pointing at me, "he took her outside of the pub, he was gone at least an hour."

"Was she a goer?"

"What 'appened? Did you give 'er one?"

"He's only got one!" laughed Alf, "I told 'im it wouldn't take me a bloody hour!"

They all oohed and ahed. "Lucky sod, did she have big tits?" and on and on. In truth we had met a couple of girls, I got the ugly one and she felt faint (or so she said) so I took her outside for some fresh air and while she was trying to throw up I was at the shellfish stall outside the pub, eating a plate of cockles – and very nice they were!

When we got to the office I sat at my desk wondering how to ask for a rise. Bertie Smallwood, my office manager, came in and slapped me on the back as usual and gave me his Monday morning greeting. "Morning Lad, bowels all right!" It was the same every Monday, I told him I was OK and that everything was in order, then I asked him if I could have a word with him in his office.

Bert Smallwood was an ex-Navy man. He gave the impression as he recounted his war stories, that he had been an Admiral of the Fleet, a Commander or at the very least a Captain – he was, according to somebody who had served with him, a Petty Officer. He was brusque, brash but fair. I told him of my problems about money and my having to cook for eleven on Sundays and not eating much the rest of the week and he told me he would have a word with the director concerned.

Late that day I was summoned to the director's office, a Mr Greystone. He was so like his name. He was a small thin man with thin lips that never smiled. The other thing in common with his name was his eyes, they were cold and grey. He sat behind a huge desk and wore a red carnation in the buttonhole of his black jacket. Nothing in the office was out of place. Papers, pens and files were all placed in neat piles or rows. I stood in front of him, he never asked me to sit down.

"Now what's all this nonsense about you not being satisfied with your job or your salary?" He looked down at his blotter the whole time he spoke to me, looking up only when he had finished.

"But I—" I started to explain.

"Be quiet lad, I'm talking to you, I'll let you know when and if I want you to talk to me!" He banged his fist on the desk. My legs turned to jelly, I wanted to run or the ground to open up and swallow me, I could hear him going on about my not being grateful, about people of my age having no respect for money or anything else. "I asked you a question, are you deaf? Well, are you?"

"No Sir." I was visibly shaking now.

"Very well, I'll ask you again – and stand still boy, when I'm talking."

I wanted to scream "Shut up, you old bastard," but I just stood there rooted to the spot by fear.

"Now how much do we pay you? Do you understand the question?"

I nodded.

"Pardon?"

"I understand the question, Sir."

"Well answer it, stupid."

"£400 per year Sir." My voice was shaking now.

"£400 a year, and you have the nerve to tell me you can't manage. Well, I've got news for you laddie, you are going to have to manage and if as you say you are not getting enough to eat, then eat more potatoes and bread! Now get out of my sight and get back to work!"

I crawled out of that office, my tail between my legs, I was close to tears, that pig, that bastard. I went to the lavatory and locked myself in, then the tears came in a flood. I vowed that no one would talk to me like that again. I was going to be wrong but at that moment I meant it. I had no idea of what was to come. I washed the tears from my face and went back to work as ordered. Bert Smallwood came from his office and looked at me in a knowing way. He winked and I tried to smile. I picked up some papers and out of one that I was working on, I saw an envelope on my desk addressed to me. I opened it and inside were two crisp pound notes with a typewritten note attached. It read, "Have a meal on me" signed "a friend". I looked up in time to see Bert's office door close. The tears filled my eyes and although I knew he didn't want me to thank him, maybe because of his reputation, I've never forgotten that moment and I've never forgotten him.

I met Alf in the main entrance hall that night and told him what had happened. "The bastard," he said as he let fly a kick at the lift doors." But who would have thought that old Bert would have done that! Are you sure it was him that lent you the two quid?"

"Who else?" I replied. "Nobody else could afford to chuck two quid away."

"He didn't chuck two quid away, he gave it to you, at least he understands how bad things are."

"Oh, come on," I pulled his arm, "let's have a couple of pints on Bert."

"Are you sure? He gave the money to you for food."

"You're my friend Alf, always will be and we always share."

"Well," he looked at me, "if you're sure," he grinned, "but only one each."

"That'll be the day. Anyway, we're going to celebrate!"

"Celebrate what?" He had to wait for my answer because he was now in the swing doors trying to catch me up.

"Anything," I said as I stepped onto the pavement.

"You're a bloody nut case, do you know that?" Then he put his arm around my shoulder, "And you're right, we're mates."

I felt ten feet tall as we walked into the city pub packed with homeward bound office workers. As we pushed our way to the bar a voice said, "What'll it be, lads?" It was Bert Smallwood.

"It's OK Bert," I smiled, "I'll get these."

"You're chucking your money around, aren't you?" said Bert.

"Well, a – er – a friend of mine gave me a couple of quid."

"I wish I had a friend like that, "he squeezed my arm and pushed his way past. "Now let another friend buy you and young Romeo here a drink." Alf was always called "Romeo" by the male members of the staff. He was, as I said, always chasing and chatting up the girls. "And whoever your friend is that gives you gifts of money, look after yourself and don't let him down."

"I won't Bert, I promise. Could we have two light and bitters please?"

He bought the drinks, said "Cheers" and went over to a group of his cronies who were in the bar.

"Well bugger me," said Alf as he stared at Bert crossing the room." He's treating you well, you don't reckon he fancies you, do you? After all, he was in the Navy and you know what they say about sailors. I reckon old Bert fancies your arse!"

"He's got a hope," I said nearly choking on my beer, "he would have to be a lot younger than he is and a bloody sight richer!" Now we both laughed. I'm sure I must have gone bright red at Alf's remarks, but if I did Alf never said a word, thank God. We left the pub at closing time, the two pounds well and truly spent and the two of us well and truly pissed! In fact, as pissed as parrots as my dad would have said. We walked to the railway station and just caught a train back home. The train was nearly empty so nobody minded us singing the tops of our heads off – if they did they didn't tell us. I got out at Hoe Street and Alf went on to Wood Street. I danced a little jig on the platform as the train pulled out, with Alf hanging out of the window yelling obscenities at me. I gave my ticket to the collector.

He said, "I bet you ain't so bleeding 'appy tomorrer mate!" He laughed, I shrugged my shoulders.

"Sod tomorrow, it's now what counts."

When I got back to my digs everybody was in bed. I crept into my room. I heard Brian snoring as I opened the door, I closed it quietly and didn't put the light on. I undressed in the moonlight that was streaming through the window. I looked at myself in the dressing table mirror. I was tall, just over six foot in fact, and slim, my hair was dark and quite long. I rubbed my hands over my naked body. "Not bad, not bad at all," I thought to myself. I didn't hear Brian but I saw him in the mirror. He was standing behind me, like me he was naked. As I turned round to face him he put his hands between my legs. I tried to pull away but I couldn't. I looked down and saw that he had an erection and by now so had I! He put his other arm round my waist and pulled me towards him. I felt our bodies touch, my heart was beating like a drum. Neither of us had said a word, I looked into his dark eyes, they seemed to flash in the moonlight.

"I fancied you when I first saw you."

"But you couldn't have." It was a stupid thing to say, but I didn't know what to say!

"Well, I did!" I couldn't believe this was really happening. "And what's more," he said, "I knew you'd like it!"

Then he kissed me on the mouth. I pulled away, I was in a panic. "Well I don't," I lied, "leave me alone. I'm not like that."

"You've got a hard-on, so have I, that must mean something," he whispered. Then his hands started to caress me between my legs, I felt a thrill in my whole body. "Maybe you like this?" He sank to his knees and I could feel his soft warm mouth kissing me on my stomach. Still further down he went, his tongue now searching and probing until it found my erection. Then his mouth closed around it warm and soft. He used it with skill as he moved my penis in and out, slowly at first, then faster and faster until I climaxed. I felt the sperm leave me and he pulled me to him even tighter. He led me over to his bed and pulled the bedclothes back and told me to get in – I did.

Once in bed, he put my hand between his legs and rubbed himself against me until he too had climaxed. Then he kissed me and put his arm around me and went to sleep.

I lay there, my heart still pounding. This was my first real experience of sex. Oh, I had played with a few girls' tits and had 'snogging' seasons and I had thought that daring and great!! I used to jerk myself off after those sessions but it was never anything compared with what I had experienced tonight – tonight was bliss!!

When I woke up in the morning I was in bed on my own. It was late, Anne was yelling up the stairs. Why hadn't Brian called me, why had he just left me there? I felt empty and used. That day at work was hell. I spent the whole time looking at the clock. All I wanted to do was race home and see Brian but the day seemed endless, time seemed to stand still, almost as though it were mocking me. At last, of course, it did end. I raced down the stairs to meet Alf in the lobby, he was late and by the time he did arrive I had worked myself into a real frenzy. When at last he did arrive, the anger must have shown on my face but I bit my tongue and said nothing. As we walked to the station Alf was chatting away but I was hardly listening. I thought I was saying yes and no in the right places but I wasn't really bothered. Alf interrupted my thoughts.

"You OK? You don't seem your old self."

"No, no, I mean yes. I'm all right, nothing's wrong."

"Are you sure? I mean nobody's had a go at you, have they?"

"What do you mean – had a go at me?" I snapped.

"Hey!" Alf took my arm. We stopped walking and he looked into my eyes. "I'm your friend and I know when something is wrong with you, so tell me."

I wanted to. Oh, how I wanted to tell him. To say, I had sex with Brian last night and I think I'm in love with him. "After all, Alf," I thought, "I can't have you and I do need someone. You should be pleased, Alf – it lets you off the hook." All this I wanted to say but, of course, I couldn't. "I'm sorry Alf. I'm just tired. I didn't get much sleep last night." (Ain't that the truth, I said to myself.) "I'm sorry, really."

He slapped me on the back." I bet it was all that booze last night."

"Yes." I nodded." You're right, it must have been." I ran down the street, opened the front door and rushed straight into the front room. Anne and the kids, along with some of the other "guests" were watching TV. "Hello love." It was Anne speaking to me. "'ad a good day 'ave you?"

"Oh, so-so Anne," I said, 'so-so." Brian didn't even look up, not a smile, not a nod, nothing.

"Want a cuppa love? There's one in the pot and it's still 'ot. Oo 'ark at me, I made a funny!"

"Ow Mum shut up," said young Anne, "we can't hear the telly!"

"It's all right Anne, I don't want any tea. I've got a headache, I'll just go straight to bed."

Brian continued to stare at the television.

"Oh, all right love, but the way you came racing in here, shouldn't have thought you 'ad time for a headache. Still, if you want an aspirin there's some in the kitchen by the sink."

I thanked her and said goodnight. I heard a couple of grunts but nothing from Brian. I closed the door and went upstairs. I lay on my bed. My head was throbbing. What the hell was wrong with me? Why wouldn't Brian speak to me? I didn't expect him to say, "Hello love, you were great in bed last night!" or anything like that. Maybe I had imagined it all. I was very drunk last night. No, I couldn't have imagined him kissing me, caressing me, it had been real. So why hadn't he spoken to me? Didn't he like it? perhaps I was no good at it. Yes, that must be the answer. I was no good at it. But it seemed good, it was good – maybe he was just ashamed of himself or maybe he despised me for letting him do it. The questions kept racing round in my mind and my head still ached.

Then the question of why. Why did I have to be like this? Why didn't I fancy girls, like I fancied boys? After all, I was built the same as the other boys – in fact, when I was at school and we had to take a shower after a games period, I was built bigger than most boys. Girls seemed to like me – I even had a minor problem trying to fight them off. So why couldn't I feel about them as I did about Alf and now Brian?

I lay there on the bed for the rest of the evening trying, without success, to find the answers to those questions. My mind went back to my childhood searching for some clue, anything to unravel the puzzle. Home was ordinary enough – although my elder brother Don I hardly knew. He had been away from home for years and had only recently returned. As a kid I had been forbidden to mention his name. It was only later that I discovered the reason for this, he had spent quite a lot of his life in Borstal and prison, mainly for theft. My parents had disowned him and it was only the pleadings of my sister that brought him back into the fold. My mother and father used to argue, not about work but about gambling. We would hear these rows as we lay in bed, often we would hear the crash of china as my mother threw the crockery at my dad. I once heard my mother say to an aunt, "If only he would come home drunk, at least I could see where the money had gone."

But for all her pleadings my father would still gamble and the rows still went on often resulting in them not speaking to each other for weeks, even months. My mother still scrubbed and cleaned the house. The windows and curtains were still spotless, as was the rest of the house. She still cooked his meals but would leave them steaming on a saucepan with a lid over them. She would never serve them to him and if he didn't go and get it, it would be thrown in the pig-bin. In those days, all waste food was placed in a special bin, put in every street by the council. The scrap food was then fed to pigs. All this was to help feed the people after the war.

Mum would scrimp and save to take my sister and me on holiday, which used to be a week maybe two in a caravan and we loved it. Sometimes if Mum and Dad were speaking he would come as well and that was even better, but I had known them to row on holiday and my father would pack his case and leave us. It wasn't all fights though and although she threatened to leave him she never did. I really believe that they did love each other but the lack of money and the sheer hard work were the main reasons for their fights.

I had hated school. I had a bad stammer as a kid and was held to ridicule by some of my classmates. To get over this I became the class prankster. That way the kids would laugh when I put stink bombs on the fire or chewing gum on the teacher's chair and then I was one of them. The fact that I used to get a belt across the bum with a gym shoe or a whack round the head by some irate teacher only built me up in the eyes of the other kids. I hated P.T. and disliked sports of any kind, except running. I always found sports a waste of time but I went through the motions just to keep face.

But was all this enough to make me 'queer'? My mind raced. Was I really queer? Maybe I only thought I was because I hadn't yet 'made' it with a girl. I must try, I really must try.

About two weeks later I came home from work and walked into a row between Brian and Dave. The two of them were yelling and swearing at each other.

"I'm bloody well going," screamed Brian.

"No, you're sodding not," yelled back Dave, "I'm your father and you'll do as I tell you."

"You're not my father," Brian screamed back, "he was Italian. You're only my stepfather." He spat the last few words at Dave.

As I walked in Dave said to me "You talk some bloody sense into him will you, 'cos I can't."

"What the hell's wrong?" I replied, surprised at Dave's sudden trust in my ability.

"He wants to go to an all-night party. He's only seventeen for Christ's sake!"

"Oh, so that's it." I was quite disappointed. I thought it would be something really important. "Well it'll be all right, I'm sure. After all, he's not a yobbo, is he? He knows right from wrong." I stressed the words right from wrong. Brian looked at me and blushed. "You have to trust him, Dave. He's a man now. Anyway, I don't know why you're asking me I'm younger than he is."

"But you got more bloody sense, his mother will go mad when she finds out."

"Oi," said Brian, "I'm here you know. Will you stop talking about me like I was a bit of the bleeding furniture?"

I looked at Dave." He's right, Dave."

"All right, I can tell you're on his side." He looked at Brian, "Go to your bloody party but if the Old Bill come round here I'm not standing bail for you. Got it?"

"What bleeding bail," cried Brian, "I'm only going to a party I'm not going to do a bleeding bank raid."

Dave's face was white with rage." I don't care what you do, you ungrateful little shit, but if you get into trouble you're on your own. I mean it!"

With that, he stormed out of the room slamming the door so hard that a photo of some long-dead aunt fell from the wall and crashed to the floor. Brian picked it up and put the shattered pieces on the coffee table. He looked at me, hung his head and said, very quietly, "Thanks"." Then he too went. I went into the kitchen and put the kettle on. I made some tea and pinched a piece of cake from the larder.

Anne came home at about eight o'clock. She had been having a driving lesson. I was still in the kitchen reading the local rag. As she saw me she said with some surprise, "Hello luv, what are you doing sitting in the kitchen?"

"Oh, I like kitchens, always have."

"Gawd you're a funny one and no mistake."

If only you knew, I thought, if only you knew.

"That bleeding driving instructor's a bit of a lad, 'e kept missing the gear stick and putting his hand on my leg." She giggled like a schoolgirl." Saucy sod. Any tea in that pot?"

I nodded.

"Mind you," she continued as she poured the tea, "'e is a bit tasty. Where's Dave? Gone to bloody work early again, I suppose," answering her own question, "and where's Brian? He's late home from work."

"He's gone to an all-night party." As soon as I said it I wished I hadn't.

"An all-night party," she looked at her watch, "at half-past bleeding eight!"

"I-er-I think he's gone to meet some friends first. Dave said it would be all right." Another boob, I thought as I waited for the bang. I didn't have to wait long.

"Dave said it was all right?" I thought she was going to explode, "Bloody Dave said it would be all right! I'll kill him when I see him. No wonder 'e's gone to bleeding work early."

On and on she raved, "Who's he going with?", and "Where is he going?" I poured her another cup of tea and she quietened down. "Don't you get any of his fancy ideas, you're a good lad – stay that way." She patted my arm and I promised I would. Anyway, I didn't much like parties. I didn't add that I had never been to a real adult party, all-night or not! We had a little party at home at Christmas or on birthdays, but I hadn't been to a real booze and birds party.

"I think I'll nip down to the Palmerston and have a drink with Alf, fancy coming?" I didn't think she would so I was on a safe bet but I did have to get out.

"You and that Alf, always together. You should find a nice girl, you should. It's not natural you two always together. I was only saying the other night to the rest of them. 'It's not natural,' I said. Not that I'm prying mind."

I felt myself colour up. I was mortified. She kept on talking.

"But you 'ave to be careful, don't you? Anyway, Brian said you couldn't be," she hesitated, "well, you know, 'funny', cos 'e said you and 'im were always talking about girls." I knew well enough what "funny" meant and I had to put her off the scent.

"Do you mind! It's like Brian says, course I'm not!" I said it as though I had been accused of murder.

"Well, that's all right then. Anyway, I don't think I'll come for a drink, I'll see you later maybe. All right ducks?"

I left the house and walked towards the bus stop. I was thinking about what Anne had said about Brian. He had told her I was all right, I wasn't "funny". He had stuck up for me and in fact, I supposed, he had protected me. It was a surprising thought, but it was true.

I did see Alf in the pub. We had a couple of drinks but he had some girl or other with him so I didn't stay long. I had become used to Alf and his girls. I used to get upset about it but not any more – I knew that they didn't really matter to him.

I arrived home quite early, about ten-thirty, nobody was in the front room so I watched some TV, read the paper, tried to do the crossword and went to bed. I had only been in bed about an hour and I was still half awake when I heard a noise in the room. Now I was wide awake.

"Is that you Brian?" I called softly. "Brian, you're home early." Then I heard Anne's voice and I nearly had a heart attack.

"It's not Brian ducks, it's me!" I sat upright in the bed, I had to let my eyes get accustomed to the light. Then I saw her at the foot of the bed.

"What's wrong?" I called.

Then I really had a shock. I could see her more plainly now. She was dressed in a full-length see-through housecoat and a pair of brief panties. Her face was fully made up and her hair newly brushed. My head started to swim. It wasn't helped by the overpowering stench of cheap perfume that was now drifting over the bed towards me. That's not all that was drifting towards me, for now she was moving from the bottom of the bed up towards me.

"There's nothing wrong ducks," she cooed. As she got nearer her heavy breasts swung to and fro. Her stomach was full and flabby, hanging over her panties as though it was trying to escape. It too swayed as she moved. She was talking to me in soft tones. "I thought to myself, what that boy needs is a real woman. So here I am, ducks." She pulled back her housecoat." You just help yourself."

I tried to speak but my mouth dried up. I could hear the words in my head but no sound came from my throat. I kept trying to yell, "Go away you stupid cow, go away."

She pulled my bedclothes back and slipped out of the housecoat, her huge white thighs now almost on top of me. She bent over the bed, her lips pursed, I tried to turn my face but it was too late. Her hands had my head in a vice-like grip as she tried to force her tongue down my throat. I felt sick, I kept my mouth shut.

"Don't be scared luv, I'm only going to fuck you, not kill you, least I hope not!" She giggled.

I was, by this time almost paralysed with fear, unable to move, unable to speak. It was a nightmare, I felt her hands running all over my body. Then suddenly she turned herself around so that her head was between my legs. Then she put her leg over me and pushed her arse into my face. I screwed my eyes shut tight and tried to turn my face but I couldn't. I could smell her odour, I reflexed and as I almost threw up I could feel her mouth trying to swallow my manhood but I didn't have an erection and I knew, what's more, that I wouldn't get one. I thought "I must try, I must get a least a semi-erection. If I don't she really will start to put two and two together." I tried to think of her son Brian and how it had been with him but knowing this creature laying on top of me was his mother didn't help. Then I tried to imagine what it would be like with Alf. This I had known to work on numerous occasions, but it did no good on this night.

"Come on ducks, try to relax," Anne moaned as she fought a losing battle with a penis that, by now, would have made a new-born baby blush!

Then we both heard something that made us both react. It was the front door slamming. She cursed and almost fell on the floor in her haste to get off the bed. I just breathed a sigh of relief. Anne cursed under her breath and ran for the door, only to come back and frantically grab her housecoat and snarl at me. "One word from you, you bastard and you're OUT."

She had hardly left the room when the door opened and Brian came in. I had never been so pleased to see anybody in my whole life.

"You're early," I whispered.

"Christ, you still awake? Yes, the party was a bit of a flop. Still, I did get my end away with one of the birds."

"Oh, did you, I'm glad," I lied. I watched him undressing. His muscular body made what I had just seen look like something from a horror film. It had also felt as though I were in a horror film! He was naked now and standing where I had first seen his mother stand only twenty minutes before.

The erection that had failed to happen for his mother was now very much in evidence, throbbing between my legs. He gently caressed his own body, then said.

"Are you really glad I got my oats tonight?"

"Yes, of course I am. If it made you happy."

"Thanks for standing up for me tonight. Dave's such a pain."

"Oh, it's nothing."

He walked towards me. My heart jumped. He pulled back the bedclothes.

"Christ," I thought, "like mother like son, and both on the same bloody night." I moved over in the bed and he climbed in. He ran his fingers over my stomach and down between my legs. I moaned with pleasure. Then he straddled my chest so that I was looking up at him. He bent down to kiss me. I took his tongue deep into my mouth, his moist lips and his tongue were searching my face and neck.

"Take this for me," he whispered. He climbed further up my body until his rock-hard erection was pressing on my lips. I opened my mouth and devoured it. He moaned with pleasure and pushed himself further in. Then suddenly he withdrew, slid down on me again and kissed me. "Oh Ricky, I'll tell you what, you're better than that bird I had tonight."

I pulled him to me.

"I want to take you all the way tonight, do you mind?" I asked him what he meant. I hadn't a clue! "You know, fuck you, ride you, do you mind?"

"No," I said. I didn't mind.

He got out of the bed and went over to the dressing table. He came back with a small tin." Don't worry, its only cream. It'll help. I wouldn't hurt you." Then he went down on me, his mouth and tongue finding the most sensitive parts of my body. I arched my back and writhed around the bed in ecstasy. As he took my penis in his mouth I was about to climax. He sensed it and released his grip. He said, "Lie on your stomach." I turned over, he pushed my legs apart, then I felt his lips and his soft warm moist mouth on my bum, gently kissing and again, his tongue probing. Then I felt him reach for the tin. He smeared the cold cream on me then asked me to put some on his penis, I rubbed it on and lay back as I was.

Then he was on top of me again, his fingers now easing my buttocks apart. Then I felt him enter me. Slowly at first, then faster. It hurt but I didn't care. Then as he moved even faster I wanted him to stop, but I prayed he wouldn't. Now I was in rhythm with him further inside me. He pushed faster and faster. Then his body went rigid. He pushed his hands down on the bed and raised his body, his penis still inside me. I felt him climax, he put one hand under me and made sure that I too reached my climax. As soon as his hand touched me I let it flow. He lay on my back kissing my neck. We were both sweating, it made it all the more exciting.

"You're great," he said, "you're great." I told him he was also great and that I was no longer a virgin.

The next morning at breakfast Anne was not only cold towards me she was positively icy. I tried to sound natural as I said, "Good morning." The girls were bright and replied with gusto, chatting about God knows what! Brian gave me a wink and a really big smile. Old Mr Silver who was deaf and probably hadn't even heard me say "good morning" but had guessed, was nodding away like one of those model dogs you used to see in the rear windows of cars. Dave was his usual self, having just got home from the night shift. He sat at the table with his head buried in a copy of the Daily Mirror, but he did give me a grunt. Only Anne said nothing, except, "Tea's in the pot."

"Thanks," I replied.

"Don't thank me, it's cold. If you want fresh then make it!" And with that she stormed out, slamming the door behind her.

"Christ, what's got into her this morning?" asked Brian.

"More like what hasn't got into her!" I thought.

"Oh," mumbled Dave from behind the newspaper, "it's probably the wrong day of the month."

"What's wrong about today?" said young Jeanie, "how can it be the wrong day and if it is, when will it be the right day?"

"Shut up and eat your toast," snarled Dave still buried in the paper.

"But I—" continued Jeanie.

This time Dave lowered his paper and cut her short. Staring at her from across the table with a look that would kill he growled back, "I thought I told you to shut up, now do JUST that."

The child recognised the look and knew just what it meant. She lowered her head and began to play with a piece of toast that she had on her plate. Dave, satisfied now, pulled the paper back over his face. Then the elder girl, Anne, leant across to her sister and whispered, "I'll tell you later." If Dave heard this he chose to ignore it, probably grateful that at least he didn't have to explain, thereby saving himself a great deal of embarrassment. I grinned at Brian.

That morning Alf wasn't hanging out of the railway carriage window as usual. "Silly sod's overslept," I thought. I climbed into the already crowded train and tried to find myself a seat. "Sod Alf," I said under my breath – he always had a seat saved for me. I sat down in the middle of one of those bench-type seats in a third-class compartment. It was filthy already, with the floor littered with cigarette ends, sweet papers and orange peel. I sat squashed between a city gent, or at least somebody who thought he was a city gent and wanted his neighbours to believe it as well. He wore the 'uniform – black bowler hat, black jacket, pinstripe trousers and a stiff white collar that was so stiff I felt sure that if he had turned his head quickly he would have cut his throat. The stiff white collar was atop a dark red striped shirt and to finish off the whole outfit he had a dark red carnation in his buttonhole and, of course, a rolled umbrella plus a copy of the Financial Times. For all the world a city gent, except, of course, that he was in a third-class compartment! A real city gent wouldn't have been seen dead in such a place, a real city gent would rather stand in a first-class carriage than sit in a third-class compartment!

At the other side of me sat a large woman with a huge shopping bag on her lap, from which came a strand of wool. She had two of the largest knitting needles I had ever seen and there she sat, void of pattern book, her arms going sixteen to the dozen and the needles clicking away like demented chicks.

I was so squashed in my seat that I had little or no chance of reading my copy of the Daily Herald, it not being a tabloid meant that you needed quite a bit of space in order that the pages might be opened and turned. So I just sat there and let my thoughts wander back to last night's events. They seemed unreal. First Anne trying to seduce me and nearly crushing me to death with those huge thick white thighs. Then trying to smother me by shoving her equally fat and revolting arse in my face while at the same time trying to eat my manhood! I wondered if the woman knitting next to me had ever tried that! I glanced at her. Her hair was in neat little curls. The hands were thick and pudgy and well cared for. "Hm," I thought, "probably the type who would have to wear gloves to handle the beastly thing!" I grinned to myself. Then it was Brian's turn. God, what a surprise HE had turned out to be! What's more, he was good at it. I could still feel the sensation I had when he first entered me. I felt exhilarated, but of course it was also absolute madness. I knew I couldn't go on living at Anne's, she had ruined that. One day she would find out about my affair with her son if I went on living there. That would put the cat amongst the pigeons and, of course, Brian might find out about his mother and I couldn't bear that. I would have to leave and as soon as possible before the shit hit the fan. I wondered if Brian would come with me but I quickly put that thought out of my mind, I knew the answer already.

Now, of course, the problem was where to go? I wished Alf had been on the train that morning. At least he could have made a few suggestions. I would also have to give him a reason for my leaving. He mustn't find out about Brian. What a bloody mess, but what a bloody night!!!

When I reached work, there was a note on my desk asking me to see Bert Smallwood as soon as I came in. I tapped on his office door." Now what?" I thought. He called for me to go in. When I saw him, he wasn't his usual happy self.

"Sit down lad." He sounded glum.

I sat down and Bert fiddled with the papers on his desk. Then he asked me how my digs were. I was a bit surprised.

"Oh, they're fine." I lied. Then he asked me if I was eating well, was my health OK, more and more small talk – at last I could stand it no longer. "Bert, what's wrong for Christ's sake? Have I made a balls-up or what?"

He looked at me with sad eyes." No of course not. I wish you had lad, it would make it easier. I've had a memo from Mr Greystone, it appears we are over-staffed. I have to let you go, I'm sorry lad, I really am sorry." He was trying so hard to be matter-of-fact but it wasn't working.

"Go?" I was stunned." Go where?"

"You must leave," he said gently." I have to give you a month's notice." This had to be a joke. He was pulling my leg, he couldn't sack me.

"What have I done?" My head spun." Why, Bert? Why me?"

"They, rather Mr Greystone, informs me that the company is over-staffed and that it must reduce costs."

This wasn't happening." But how can my four hundred a year help? It's nothing to a firm this size, nothing. I mean they are turning over millions."

"To be fair laddie, they are giving a month's notice. It will give you a chance to look around." Then suddenly he slammed the file down on the desk. The noise made me jump." No, they are not being fair, laddie." He stormed, "Those bloody upper-class twits. They are not being bloody fair."

He walked round the side of the desk and put his hand on my arm." I'll help you all I can lad, I'll help you find another job."

I left the office in a daze. Sacked, what would I do? How would I live? Pay my rent? Buy food? I went to look for Alf only to be told he was out sick.

"Not as sick as I am, I bet."

"Pardon?" said the clerk in charge. "I thought you of all people would have known he was sick. After all, you are his best friend, aren't you?"

"Sarcastic sod," I said to myself. That night I didn't get off the train at my usual stop. I carried on and left the train at Wood Street which is where Alf lived. I wanted to see what was wrong with him and to tell him about my getting the sack.

As I went through the barrier I was surprised, to say the least, to see Alf standing there waiting for me. He even paid my excess fare.

"What the bleeding hell you doing here? I thought you were ill."

"Did you?" He laughed. "Where's my grapes then?"

"I'll give you bleeding grapes. I was worried."

"I know you were. I'm sorry. I did phone in sick but I've been with a girl all day and I knew you would come and see me tonight, so here I am!"

"Oh, I see. So, I meet you and if anybody sees us I'm your alibi, right?"

"Got it in one." said Alf, "Come on, I'll buy you a drink, you look as though you could do with one. Come on. Don't get pissed off, I did pay your excess fare didn't I?" He took my arm and led me across the road and into the Railway Arms. "Come on, cheer up or did you want me to be ill?"

"No, you silly sod, of course I didn't. Get me a Scotch, will you?"

I sat down while he went to the bar. When he had put down our drinks I told him my news.

"I don't believe it."

"It's true Alf. I only wish it wasn't."

"But why? Did you have a row with someone? Didn't you do your work? There must be more to it than that."

I drank my whisky." I think it was that bastard Greystone. The one I had to see about a rise? He didn't like me. Thing is, what do I do now?"

"Well, the first thing is another drink." I didn't argue. He got up and went to the bar. I looked at him and thanked my lucky stars I had him for a friend. He came back with the drinks. "First thing we must do," he said as he passed me my drink, "is to find you another job. Let's face it, there are a few about."

"Oh, I know that Alf, but I won't be working with you, will I?"

"Well we don't really work with each other now, do we? OK, we are in the same company, but I hardly see you all day – and anyway, we would still see each other, you nutcase. We're mates – so I'll see you after work and at the weekends. It's your round." He laughed." Come on, cheer up!" I bought another round of drinks. Then I told him about Anne. "Christ, you really have had a time of it. Did you give her one?"

"No!" I yelled at him." I didn't, I didn't fancy her, all right!"

He looked amazed. "What's fancying her got to do with it? If they put it on a plate, take it."

"I was tired," I lied.

"Blimey, I would have soon woken up." He laughed again.

"Anyway, I thought you might come with me on Saturday to see my mum. I don't want to stay at Anne's after that."

"You mean you want to go home?" He looked disappointed.

"I don't want to go back but if I don't get a job and I can't pay the rent, what choice do I have?"

"Go on the dole." He said." They pay your rent and give you money to live on. I know it's not much but it will see you through."

"No," I replied." Besides, I want to see my mum and dad."

That Saturday saw us both in Enfield. We had gone by train using our weekly tickets. It was the long way round but it did save money. As we walked through the town I began to have misgivings. I wasn't sure what sort of reception I would get. Alf told me not to worry. "After all, they are your parents," he pointed out." Not strangers." Then I saw my mother, she was walking towards us, I pointed her out to Alf.

"That's her, that's my mum."

She was wearing a green and white print dress. As she got almost level with us I wanted to run to her and put my arms around her. She looked towards us, at me, right through me, and finally right past me! I stood there looking at her walking away from me and I couldn't believe it. I felt the burn of her hand on my cheek and the sting of the tears in my eyes. Alf was talking to me.

"I thought you said that was your mother?"

"It was." I looked at him. "That was my mother."

"Oh come on, she didn't even stop and talk to you. Any mother would have done that, if only to tell you off. You're winding me up."

"No, no I'm not. I'll prove it later. Let's have a cup of tea or something."

We left Joe Lyons (as Lyons's tea shops were always called) about an hour later and caught a bus to my home. I had to see if my mum really meant to snub me. The estate hadn't changed much. Dogs still barked, kids still screamed as they played and neighbours still stood on doorsteps and gossiped. We reached our house and I stood at the front door, almost afraid to knock.

"Well don't just stand there," said Alf, "Knock!"

So I did. We waited a couple of minutes then the door opened and there was my mother wearing the same green and white print dress. Alf's mouth dropped.

"Hello Mum, this is Alf – can we come in?" The words came out in a whisper.

"If you must." Her voice was cold. We followed her into the kitchen." Well, what do you want? Have you come home for your birthday present?"

All the time she spoke she had her back turned while she stood at the sink filling the kettle.

My birthday! Shit, I had forgotten it was June, I would be seventeen in two days' time!

"No Mum – I'd forgotten about it."

"Hmm," was the reply as she banged the kettle onto the stove. As she turned round I could see her eyes were red and moist.

"Well, what have you come for? I hope it's not for money – your father and I only just manage."

"I didn't come for money." I could see that by this time Alf was getting embarrassed." It's just that I keep telling Alf here about you and he wanted to meet you." I held my breath. She looked at me, then at Alf, and a smile crossed her face.

"Would you like a piece of bread pudding? It's fresh made."

I breathed a sigh of relief.

We drank the tea and ate the bread pudding and we talked. We talked about everything from the weather to the world situation. I was a little nervous. It was all going well, too well in fact. Then it happened. My mother suddenly turned to Alf and said, "Did you know that friend of Ricky's at work? The one he writes letters to yet never posts?"

Alf looked at me. I wanted the floor to open up and swallow me. The kitchen was silent, nobody said a word for what seemed like hours. Suddenly I found some courage.

"Thanks Mum, the tea was very nice. We have to go."

Alf got up and thanked her and we made our way to the front door. As she opened it, she said how nice it was of us to drop in and that we must do it again sometime. It was as though we had all met on holiday or at a dance somewhere. Not as if I was her son. The son she hadn't seen for months. The son whose face she slapped. Then out of the blue came her parting shot.

"Don't forget to ask Ricky about his friend, Alf. You might have a lot in common." The sarcasm in her voice could have been detected even by somebody who was profoundly deaf. I felt my face burn.

"What was that all about?" Alf asked as we walked from my mother's house towards the bus stop. I didn't know how to answer him.

"What's all this about you writing letters to somebody at work?"

"Look Alf, I don't know what she's talking about. I think she might even be going a bit—" I hesitated for a moment, "I think she might be going a bit potty." I lied yet again, but I knew I had to keep the truth to myself.

"I think you could be right." was his reply.

The next month seemed to fly by. Bert Smallwood arranged some interviews for me. They all seemed to go well, but nobody offered me a job. I tried for jobs myself but again without success.

I couldn't understand why I wasn't being offered work until I phoned one company back and asked them why, only to be told that my references were not up to standard.

"That bastard Greystone must really hate me," I thought to myself as I slammed the phone down. My birthday came and went. In fact, if Alf hadn't sent me a card I wouldn't have known. Things at Anne's were now at a low ebb. I gave her two weeks' notice. Everything I did or said was wrong. To make things worse, Brian had gone on a work training course for two weeks, so I didn't have him to talk to or to sleep with! Dave was off work with a bad back and that cramped Anne's style even more and did nothing to improve her temper. I, on the other hand, thanked my lucky stars that Dave did hurt his back. Two weeks with Brian away and Dave on night work – leaving me alone with Anne – didn't bear thinking about. On my last day at the office, my friends gave me a Good Luck card and some of them had a whip round and bought me a pint tankard and a pair of cufflinks. I was quite moved. I hadn't really expected to be missed, but I would be, and it made the parting all the more sorrowful. But at the same time, I was pleased that I wouldn't be forgotten, at least not at once. I received four weeks' pay plus two weeks' holiday money less, of course, deductions for income tax and insurance. That left me with the grand total of something like forty pounds to last me the rest of my life, or until I found work. I was now just turned seventeen.

3 – BROTHERLY LOVE

I had decided to spend Saturday looking for new digs but when I awoke a thought struck me like a bolt out of the blue. Don! Of course, my brother Don! I would go and find my brother. I was sure he would help me. We were after all now both 'black sheep' of the family. Trouble was I didn't know his address – but I did know one of his favourite haunts. It was worth a try a least.

I dressed quickly and packed all I wanted to take. Then I wrote a note for Brian and hid it in one of his girlie books. I was sure he would find it sooner or later. I left the house at about seven-thirty in the morning, and being Saturday, nobody was up. I had left my key on the hallstand and as I closed the gate I also closed another chapter on what was going to be a very crowded life.

I made my way to the bus stop and got on a bus for Bruce Grove. There I changed buses and caught a 629 to Waltham Cross. I had a good idea where he would be. I had often heard my mother and father talk about Vi's café and my brother Don in the same breath. I knew exactly where the café was.

My father, as I said, was a busman, first a driver then a conductor. My sister and I had spent many a summer holiday just riding on the trollies with our Dad. My mother was at work so if my dad had a day shift we would have to spend the day on the bus so that he could keep an eye on us. If he was on a late turn we would go with my mother to one of the canteens she managed. I loved that, watching her and her staff cooking mounds of food for the factory workers. I loved also the back-chat between my mother and the workers as they queued and were served their lunch. When we were with my father, Waltham Cross was the end of the bus route, so my dad and his mates would have a break at one of the two cafés at the terminus. He always went to the café opposite the bus turn, a few others would go to the café behind the terminus, and that café was Vi's. When I once asked my father why we never went into Vi's he snapped and said simply "Because I say not," and I knew better than to ask why he said not.

I pushed open the door of Vi's and stepped into the shoddy interior. The place was little more than a large shed. Inside on the filthy concrete floor stood about eight tables piled with dirty crockery. There were two windows on opposite walls – both were filthy, as were the shreds of curtains that hung at them. Steel framed chairs, their paint chipped and dirty, stood round the tables. The whole place was lit by two fluorescent tubes from which two dirty, fly-covered sticky papers hung down over the tables. At the far end was the counter, behind which stood a man of about fifty – he could have been forty, but he looked older. A cigarette end hung from the corner of his mouth – the hand-rolled cigarette had long since gone out.

Seated at the tables were an assortment of men, one or two busmen, an old tramp huddled in one corner, some workmen. One or two spivs were playing on the pintables. As I walked in they all seemed to turn around at once and stare at me. I walked to the counter, trying to look as casual as possible and failing miserably.

"Yeah?" said the scruffy man behind the counter, his lips hardly moving and the cigarette staying put.

"Er – has my brother been in today?" As soon as I had said it I knew it was a stupid question.

"'Ow the bleedin' 'ell should I know?" said Fag End." "Oo's yer bruvver anyway?"

"Sorry," I replied." Don, Don Parsons."

"Oh yeah, and 'ow do I know that, I should like to know?"

"What's the matter, Andy?" A woman had appeared behind the counter. I guessed it was Vi. She was fat, about forty years old, her bleached hair was pulled up on top of her head in a bun with a gold band around it. Her fingers were covered in diamond and gold rings. From her ears hung two whole gold sovereigns, more full sovereigns and gold chains hung around her thick neck.

I had never seen so much jewellery on one woman and never at nine o'clock in the morning!

Fag End spoke to her. "This 'ere geezer is asking for Don." He pointed a nicotine-stained finger at me.

"What's your business with Don then, young feller?" She looked at me the whole time she was speaking, her eyes searching my face, almost daring me to lie. Her eyes were as hard as the diamonds on her fingers.

"He's my brother. I've come to see him, that's all." Even as I spoke I was beginning to wonder if I had done the right thing.

"Well you're too early – he don't come in until about eleven." Then she turned to Fag End." Give 'im a cuppa and some breakfast." She looked at me now. "I take it you're 'ungry?"

"Yes, starving," I confessed.

"Right – sit over there in the corner." She pointed a stubby but rich finger in the direction she meant. "Andy 'ere will bring it over when it's ready."

Then she turned on her heel and was gone.

I heard the back door slam shut and I wondered if she was going to find my brother. The breakfast was greasy and didn't look very appetising but I was very hungry. The cup of tea looked even greasier than the food but they both tasted good. I didn't dare use the condiments. The brown sauce bottle looked as though it hadn't been cleaned for weeks, the top being covered in thick brown goo.

I looked around the café. The other 'diners' had long since lost interest in me. A few more had come in since I arrived. Nobody spoke to me and for that I was grateful. Most of them looked like crooks or gangsters. (I was to find out later that most of them were!)

Just before eleven o'clock the door of the café opened and in walked a tall man, his black hair plastered straight back over his head, revealing a high forehead. He had a prominent nose and dark swarthy good looks. He was dressed in an expensive-looking dark blue suit, white shirt and blue tie. On his feet he wore light tan chukka boots. It was Don, my brother. I made as to wave to him but he hadn't noticed me in the corner. The rest of the customers had noticed him! From all sides people yelled at him, "Watcher Donny boy! 'Ow are yer Don mate?" He walked to the counter, acknowledging the inquiries as he went. I began to wonder if Vi had told him I was looking for him, or maybe he didn't want to know anyway. After all, I hadn't seen him for nine, maybe ten years. Vi was back now and behind the counter. They were both deep in conversation. She nodded in my direction. He looked over, smiled and waved. I waved back and breathed a sigh of relief. He made his way to my table, stopping every now and then to talk to his mates.

When he reached my table, he offered me a cigarette and said, "Hello bruv, wot brings you rand 'ere?" His voice was deep and gruff, but kind, his accent thick cockney.

"I've left home." I didn't look at him but twiddled with a teaspoon.

"Oh I see, left 'ome 'ave we, and when did all this take place?"

"Months ago," I told him, "I was doing all right but then I got the sack and I couldn't pay the rent. Now I don't know what to do!"

"Get a bleedin' job young 'un, that's wot you gotta do, got any dough?"

"Yes, I've got a few quid, but it won't last long."

"'Ang on to it. So you come to see yer old bruvver eh! Well you can't stay wiv me cos I'm living wiv Eileen, you know Eileen?"

I shook my head.

"Well you will, anyway as I said I'm living with 'er and it's a bit cramped, but I'll try and fix you up wiv somewhere, but it won't be till Wednesday or Fursday OK?"

Again I nodded, "Wednesday or Thursday, Christ!" I thought, "Christ."

"In the meantime—" Don was talking again, "'ere, you listening to me?"

"Yes, yes I am."

"Right," he continued, "in the meantime, you will have to kip down wiv a mate somewhere. You 'ave got a mate?"

"Yes of course I have. I'll stay with my friend Joe for a couple of days." Another lie, I didn't have a friend called Joe or any other friends in that area for that matter. I couldn't tell him, I didn't want him to think I was completely useless.

"That's all right then. Anyfink you want? Food, tea, fags. Ask Andy (Fag End) or Vi to put it on my tab OK?" Then he got up from the table, "I'll see you tomorrer. Be lucky bruv." He rubbed his hand through my hair and was gone.

He went to the counter, pointed to me and I saw Fag End and Vi nod. Then he waved to me and left.

I hung around the café until about three o'clock. I asked Vi to look after my suitcase.

"Course you can leave it 'ere ducks! Andy! Take 'is case and put it out the back." Andy did as he was told.

He grinned at me with blackened teeth, "Staying 'ere wiv us, are yer?"

I grinned back and told him I was. He introduced me to some of the other customers as Don's brother and they in their turn shook my hand, offered me cigarettes or a cup of tea. It was clearly obvious to me by now that my errant brother was a bit of a local big shot. It made me feel quite important and excited to think I was mixing with the local 'underworld.' The fact that most of them were only petty crooks didn't mar the feeling.

The Embassy was the better of the two cinemas in the Cross. It was showing A Town Called Alice. I went in and sat through the film three times. It was a good film I remember, but not that good, but as I had nowhere else to go it was at least somewhere to pass the time. I left there and went into the Castle, a small friendly pub. It was packed with couples laughing and petting. I bought a pint of lager and stood in a corner watching everybody enjoying themselves. Then, once again, the questions came flooding into my mind. Why me? Why didn't I have a girlfriend? Why didn't I feel the same way about girls as I did about some boys? My mind was confused. Maybe it was a phase I was going through. Maybe it would soon pass. But suppose somebody finds out? I could go to prison and I couldn't face that, Christ no, not prison. I'd die. I drank my drink and left the pub. But the thoughts didn't go away. As I walked my thoughts were of my brother. What if he found out? What would he say? I walked and walked. My legs ached but I kept walking, the questions crowding my mind. Was it possible that I was the only person like me? I knew that Brian had slept with me but he did have girlfriends. I was sure that he slept with me for the sake of sex and nothing else. If he had the choice of me or a girl I knew he would pick a girl. But with me, it was the other way round. I wanted a boy to love me and that was crazy, or maybe I was the one that was crazy. Yes, that had to be it, I was mad, I must be. I was also alone and lonely. Well if I was mad I might as well end it all now – I didn't want to go through life mad and on my own. My walk broke into a trot, then a run, I was running faster and faster, I ran and ran. Die won't you just die. My legs gave way, I had a bad stitch in my side. I collapsed on the grass verge near a factory estate. I lay there panting and crying, my chest heaving. As I fought to get my breath I crawled over into a factory car park, wishing I could die and praying that I would. But I lacked the courage to do anything about it. I found a wreck of a lorry, climbed in, drew my legs under me, lay down and cried myself to sleep. I slept in that lorry alone for nearly three weeks!

My brother did find a room for me, but I couldn't afford the rent. I didn't tell him that, I merely said that my "friend" had said I could stay on at his place, but of course there was no "friend". It was another lie.

During the next few weeks, I was to leave my lorry 'home' early in the morning at about six or six-thirty, before anybody discovered me. Then I would walk to Vi's. The walk took about half an hour, the café opened early for the workmen's trade and the all-night drunks. Once there, Vi or Fag End would let me wash and shave in the kitchen and get a change of clothes from my case. As the days grew longer my supply of clean clothes grew decidedly smaller so I had to get new shirts and underwear from the market. My money was fast running out, but because I was always clean and tidy my brother thought I was managing OK.

One day a tall good-looking bloke came into the café. He was about twenty-four or five. He wore a light grey suit with a white shirt and a blue paisley cravat at his throat. I recognized him as being my old school captain, Steve Shaw. When I had been in the first year he had been the star footballer and athlete of the school. I used to watch him on school sports day, not I think in any sexual way, I just admired his skills as a player and an athlete. He went to the counter and bought a cup of coffee. Then he looked around the crowded café, he saw me looking at him and I felt myself blush. I turned my head away. The next thing I knew he was sitting next to me.

"Mind if I sit here?" He sat down.

I shook my head. "No of course not, be my guest."

He thanked me. "I haven't seen you in here before. What brings you to Vi's?" he said, as he stirred the third spoonful of sugar into his coffee.

"Oh, nothing much," was my reply. "Actually, you have seen me before. Not in here though, at school. I was in the first year when you were the school captain at Albany Road."

"I thought I recognised you," he said still stirring the coffee. I felt flattered. "You still haven't told me what brings you to Vi's."

"Well, to tell the truth, I'm looking for a job and somewhere to live. I'm Don Parsons brother. I left home a few months ago, lost my job and – well I came here. Don's trying to help me."

"So – you're Don Parsons brother, eh? The big man around here."

"Yes, so it seems. It was quite a surprise for me, I can tell you."

He looked at me with blue-grey eyes that sent a thrill through me.

"Look," his voice was soft but sounded like gravel, "your brother's a good friend of mine. Tell you what, I've just split with my wife. So why don't you doss down at my place? It would be company for me and help you at the same time. What do you think?"

"Really? Do you mean it?" Me staying with Steve Shaw! I thought I felt my heart start to thump.

He put his hand on my arm. "Course I mean it. I wouldn't have said it, would I? Anyway, how can a former school captain see one of the juniors in a fix? It can't be done. So, you'll come then?"

We both laughed.

"OK, great. I'll tell Vi and she can tell my brother."

He cut me short, "No, no don't worry Vi. You can see she's busy. I'll make sure Don knows. Like I said, he's a mate."

I thanked him and he went to the counter and bought me another cup of greasy tea. We stayed in the café until about five, talking about a number of things, from school days to jobs. Then I got my case from behind the counter and followed him outside to where he had parked his small van. On the drive back to his flat he told me about his wife and kids and how he had come home early one night to find his wife in bed with another feller. There was a fight and he threw his wife and the kids out. I said that was a bit harsh on the kids but he said after what she had done, he wasn't even sure they were his kids. Then he told me he had met another girl and was getting a divorce. We arrived at the flat. It was the top floor of a semi-detached house in a nice part of Enfield. He led the way up the stairs.

"It's not very grand. He said as he threw my case on the double bed. Then he looked at me, grinned and said, "I hope you don't mind sharing?"

Mind! My heart was REALLY thumping now.

"No, it's great. It looks a nice place – and of course I don't mind sharing at all."

"That's great." He smiled. "Well if you have been sleeping rough you'll want a bath. Not that I think you're 'soapy'," he said quickly, in case he offended me. "But, well – you'll want to freshen up." He led me to the bathroom. "All the towels you'll need are here." He opened the bathroom cupboard, then pointed to the window ledge. "And there's all the talc and aftershave. Just help yourself." I thanked him. He smiled and left closing the door behind him. I turned on the bath taps and poured in loads of bubble bath, then I lay in the bath full of bubbles and scented soap. It was bliss.

When I got out of the bath I caught sight of myself in the mirror. I had an erection. "Oh god," I thought, "if only he fancies me." I dried myself and smothered myself in talc and aftershave. I decided not to get fully dressed, so I combed my hair and put on a clean pair of underpants that I found in the cupboard and I walked into the lounge.

Steve was lying on the couch watching TV. As I entered he looked up at me and smiled. "Feel better?"

I nodded. "Er – I'm sorry but I pinched a pair of your pants."

"Don't be sorry," he said, "they look good on you. Hungry?"

"Yes," I could feel myself blush, "I am a bit." He went into the kitchen and came back with a plate full of sandwiches.

"I made them while you were in the bath. I hope you like what's in them." I told him I was sure that I would and that it was good of him to go to so much trouble. All the time I was eating I was conscious of him looking at me.

At about ten o'clock he said he was going to bed early as he had to be up at six the next morning, he asked if I wanted to go as well because I looked tired. I told him I would as I hadn't seen a real bed for weeks.

I followed him into the bedroom. A thrill ran through my body. "He wants me," I kept telling myself. "He wants me, that talk about my being tired was just to get in bed." I was trying not to show my excitement but it was difficult.

The bedroom was fairly large and well furnished. The double bed was covered with a thick expensive candlewick bedspread. "Any side you like," he said and pulled the covers down. By this time I could hardly control myself. To go to bed with someone like

Steve Shaw was more than I thought possible. To think that only a few months ago I was lonely and felt unloved. Now I was going to bed with a real man! I could see him looking at me through the mirror. So I played it up. I took off my underpants and stretched myself before climbing into bed. By this time, he was about half-undressed. I lay there and watched him get ready. He knew I was watching. As he slowly pulled down the zip of his trousers I looked at his naked upper half, it was beautiful, strong and tanned. I hoped he couldn't hear my heart beating. He sat on the edge of the bed, took off his shoes and socks, then stood up again. Facing me he slowly let his trousers slip to the floor.

His body was beautiful. He arched his back and he too stretched himself. I could tell by the bulge in his underpants that he was well built all over! My heart beat even faster as he took his briefs off to reveal stark white buttocks.

"That's quite a tan you have." I heard myself saying.

"Like it?"

"Yes I do, very much."

"Good, I'm glad." Then he turned around and put the light out. He quickly got into bed.

I lay there hardly daring to breathe. Waiting for him to touch me." Oh for God's sake touch me." I was saying to myself. I could feel his body next to mine. I could also feel his arm rubbing up and down his own body.

Suddenly he said, "There's quite a lot of talk about you down the Cross."

"Really? Is there? What sort of talk?"

"Some say you're queer. Is that right? Are you a queer?" His tone sounded threatening. I began to sweat and my heart beat faster, but for different reasons. "Well, answer me. Are you a queer?" He was getting angry now. I felt numb, my throat was dry.

"No." I croaked." In fact, I hate queers. Really hate queers – I do."

"I think you're lying to me. I think you are a queer." His voice was quiet and menacing.

"I told you I'm NOT!" I tried to move away from him without being obvious. But I was too scared to move.

Suddenly he grabbed me round the throat and was half on top of me. I could hardly breathe. I thought he was going to strangle me. He put his face close to mine, so close I could feel his lips on my cheek – the same lips I had wanted to kiss only a few moments ago. He was trembling.

He squeezed my throat tighter, then whispered." You are a queer and I'm going to give you what all queers should get."

Now he was right on top of me. His lips now kissing me. He still had one hand round my throat. Then he brought his other hand, clenched into a fist crashing into the side of my head. I tried to scream but no sound came. He hissed at me. "That's just a sample of what you'll get if you don't do as you're told, got it! Let me know you understand, you bastard, or I'll give you another one and you don't want that, do you?"

I moved my head from side to side to let him know that I didn't want to be hit anymore.

"That's good." Then he kissed me full on the lips. He pressed so hard, I thought my lips would split.

Then he whispered again." Now I'm going to take my hand from your throat. If you yell I'll kill you, understand?"

I nodded. He took his hand from around my neck. I gasped for breath and he pulled himself up in the bed until his erect penis was on my face.

"Open your mouth," he ordered. I didn't and his fist came crashing down on the side of my face. I went to yell with pain and fear but he filled my mouth before a sound came out. He thrust himself deeper and deeper into my mouth. I thought that this time I really would choke to death. I tried to struggle but his legs were wrapped around me like a vice. He kept going faster and faster, deeper and deeper. I couldn't breathe. Now I was fighting for air, my arms flailing. He climbed down as if he knew that he would kill me if he didn't stop.

"Just stay calm," he told me, "stay calm, nearly there, nearly there."

A few seconds later he climaxed in my mouth. I felt the warm bitter sperm fill my throat. He took his penis from my mouth then put his hand across my mouth and told me to swallow his sperm. I did as I was told. When he had finished with oral sex he knelt over me.

"There, queer boy. Didn't you like that? Tell me you like that." Again, I did as I was told. "By the way queer boy," his hand came round my throat again, "If you're thinking of telling your big-shot brother about this, forget it. Firstly, he's my mate, so he wouldn't believe it anyway, and secondly, if it did get out that you really were queer, just think what a lemon he would look in front of his mates. He would be a laughing stock, so much so that he would probably kill you himself, get it?" He shook me. "I said, get it?"

I said, "Yes, I get it."

"You never said a truer word."

I saw him raise his right arm, I even saw it come towards me and I felt the pain as it crashed into my jaw. But I don't remember any more after that until I came round. Then I couldn't breathe. Something was crammed into my mouth. I was lying face down on the bed. I couldn't move my arms or legs. The light was on. I moved my head and saw that my arms were tied to the bed and my feet tied to the bottom of the bed. I struggled but the bedhead kept crashing against the wall. The more I struggled the louder the crash. I felt pain all over my body. I saw the pillow soaked in my blood.

"God," I thought, "he's going to kill me." I started to cry.

Then he came back into the room. Still naked he had a glass of beer in one hand. He looked at me and started to arouse himself with the other.

"So, you've woken up have you, have a good sleep?" He started to caress my neck. "You know, you're not bad looking for a queer boy." He let his hand wander all over my back, then onto my bum, caressing my cheeks. "Yes, not bad at all."

Then he poured the cold beer all over my back and buttocks. He bent over me and started to lick the beer off, his tongue searching and probing. Then I felt hint on top of me, rubbing his rock-hard penis over my back. He forced my legs even further apart as he tried to enter me. I begged him to find some cream, but he kept thrusting at me until finally he was there. The pain made me yell out. He hit me in the back taking the breath out of me. He pushed harder and deeper. The pain was awful. At last he gripped hold of me, I felt his body go taut and he climaxed. He collapsed on me kissing my neck then down, still kissing, where he had taken me. He was moaning that I was wonderful. I prayed that he had finished, but my prayers went unanswered. He raped me four or five times more that night – I lost count, I also lost consciousness.

When I did wake up I was on my own on the bed and I was untied. I felt as though my whole body had been beaten with a cricket bat. My head throbbed. I tried to lick my lips, and drew my tongue back in shock and horror – my lips were thick and clogged with congealed blood. I turned over on my back and pain shot through me like burning hot irons. I tried to sit up but I fell back onto the bed. I told myself that I must get up. I had to get out of this place. I felt sick.

I tried again to get up, this time with every muscle in me screaming in pain. But I made it, I sat up. I flinched when I saw a face in the dressing table mirror. I took me some time to realise it was me. My face was swollen and cut, my nipples had two huge red marks on them, the blood was everywhere, dried and black. It looked as though someone had poured black paint over me. My eyes found it difficult to focus. I heard a noise. I turned my head and saw Steve Shaw standing, still naked, in the doorway. He looked weird, almost as though he wasn't there at all. He had a strange faraway look in his eyes. When he saw me sitting there on the bed he winced. Then, as though he had suddenly remembered something, he seemed to pull himself together and the violence came back into his eyes.

"Right! Queer boy – pack up and get out, now!" I could tell by the way he slurred his words that he was by now very, very drunk. Either that or he had taken a drug or something. Either way, I knew that by now he was even more dangerous.

He lurched towards me and stood staring down on my naked bloodstained body.

"You pathetic creature. You human scum. Hold your hand out NOW." The command made me flinch but I did, yet again, do as I was ordered. He then placed a one pound note in my hand. "That's for services rendered. I have just paid you for the use of your lousy body. Now you're not only a queer you're also a male whore! You have five minutes to get out, and I mean five." Then he left the room. I looked at the money that he had paid me. I let him rape me for a pound – not only rape, me but nearly kill me, for one measly pound! I felt sick and that feeling made me think "Get out" – I had to get out. I dressed the best I could in the clothes that were lying about – some were his, some mine. Every movement sent pain shooting through me. I thought I would pass out but I kept telling myself that I wouldn't, that I had to get out, get out. "Hurry," I told myself. I grabbed my case and went out onto the landing as quietly as I could. I was shaking with fear by now lest he should hear me and the whole thing start again. I reached the top of the stairs. I had only taken about two or three steps down when I heard the lounge door open.

He was coming after me. God, he was following me. As I tried to run down the stairs I slipped and crashed to the bottom. My legs screamed at me in pain.

I got up and reached the front door. I could hear him on the staircase. The door wouldn't open! "Oh god please don't let me be locked in, please." I fumbled with the lock, at last the door opened. He was nearly down the stairs by now. I half fell, half ran down the path and out of the gate.

He too was running down the path, screaming at me. "Tell your fucking brother and you're dead. Do you hear me? Dead." He was at the gate now. I was running and stumbling down the road. I looked round to see how far away he was. He had stopped at the gate. As I looked at him, still naked, he screamed again at me: "You queer bastard. You filth." I turned and ran as fast as I could until my legs buckled under me. I lay on the pavement, gasping for air and drawing great lungfuls of cold fresh morning air into my sore, pain-ridden body. As I lay on the pavement I felt something in my hand. I opened my fist and looked down at the pound note he had given me. I yelled and threw the note into the gutter.

Then I got up and ran and ran. I reached a main road. Nobody was about. It was about five-thirty or so. I had no idea where I was or what way to go. I was confused, my head throbbed and my heart beat so fast I thought it might burst. I ran in what I thought was the right direction. I was stumbling and falling, hardly able to stay on my feet. My case felt like lead as I dragged it along. A lorry passed me then stopped fifty yards or so ahead of me. I saw it reverse, I felt my chest pumping, everything was spinning. I could hear people talking. I couldn't answer, I just wanted to sleep then I felt as though somebody or something was carrying me. Everything went black.

When I woke up my eyes wouldn't focus. I tried to move my head but pain soared through me. Then I heard someone speaking to me.

"All right ducks. Gawd, you didn't half give us a scare." My eyes got used to the light. I was in bed with crisp white sheets. I looked in the direction of the voice, the room was spinning. As it slowed down I saw Vi. I tried to raise myself up but she gently pushed me back down.

I tried to speak, "Where—" I began.

Vi interrupted. "Two of the boys found you a couple of days ago in the Hertford Road. Good job they were passing. Don's been in, so has the quack. You've got no bones broken but you 'ave 'ad a bad time. Don'll be in later. All you gotta do is rest 'ere."

I tried to say thank you but I couldn't. I went back to sleep.

I felt somebody gently pulling my arm.

"Bruv, bruv, it's me, Don." I opened my eyes to see my brother wiping his. He grinned. "'Ello boy, 'ow yer feeling? 'Oo did it to yer?"

I remembered what Steve Shaw had said, "If your precious brother finds out you're a queer, he'll kill you!" I looked at Don and said I didn't know.

"You sure? Don't you go protecting no one will yer, cos I'll find aht in the end."

"Two blokes jumped me. I didn't have time to see who they were." I was beginning to panic, and Don, I think, could sense it.

"All right bruv, all right, take it easy. No one's going to 'urt you, I promise." That calmed me down but I could see he didn't believe me. "Look "ere," He spoke again, his voice soft and kind." Eileen's sent you some fruit and flowers. Get some more rest, I'll see yer later, OK?"

It was about a week before I could leave Vi's. One of Dons mates came to collect me in a huge black American car and took me to the café. As I stepped from the car, the door held open by one of Don's friends, people passing in the street stopped to stare. I felt really important. As I walked into the café people called out, "'Ello Rick, 'ow are yer Rick?" Now I really did feel important. Don put his arm around my shoulder. Then he said, "Blimey, you get a better welcome than me." We both laughed. He asked me if I felt better. I told him "Yes" but although the flesh wounds had healed I still had horrendous nightmares that would not go away.

"They will bruv, they will," he told me reassuringly. "Come outside – I've got something to show you." He led the way around the counter and out the back door of the café. Behind the café was a small orchard, and in the orchard was a small touring caravan. We walked towards it.

As we got nearer a man opened the door of the van. Don went inside and beaconed me to follow. Once inside I blinked to get used to the half-light. The curtains were drawn and the light was off. It was quite small inside. Don moved out of the way and pointed to a heap in one corner of the caravan.

"Is 'e a mate of yours?"

I looked at the heap and it moved. I felt the colour drain from my face. The heap was a man. He had been very badly beaten. So much so that I had to look twice before I recognised Steve Shaw. I felt sick. His once handsome face was now a mess – his nose smashed almost flat, both of his eyes greeny-mauve colour – and his clothes were torn and ripped. Blood oozed from many cuts. I wanted to throw up.

Don was speaking to me but I was in a daze. "Is this geezer a mate of yours or not?"

I looked into Steve's eyes through a swollen mess. They were terrified pleading eyes, begging me to help. I thought of what he had done to me, how I had felt that night as he beat me and then raped me. "The bastard, he deserves all he gets," I thought, "I only wanted him but he nearly killed me. Now Don's going to kill him."

Don was getting impatient.

"Bruv, is this bloke a mate of yours?"

"No," I said, "I've never seen him before. I don't know him. What's happened to him?"

Don looked at me. Then pulled back the curtain, light streamed in. Steve put his bloodstained hands up to shield his eyes from the strong light.

"Put your 'ands down!" Don growled at Steve. "Look at 'im again. You sure you don't know 'im?"

I nodded. "Yes, I'm sure."

I had to lie. I hated Steve for what he had done, but lying there he looked so pathetic, so helpless, as indeed he was. He had taken a severe beating and to me, that was enough. I knew that if I identified him, my brother would see to it that he ended up in a concrete overcoat holding up one of the bridges on the M1 and I didn't want that on my conscience. I looked at Steve for the last time before I left the caravan and I felt only pity for him. Don wasn't fooled, he shrugged his shoulders and had the final word.

"Well lads, my young bruvver 'ere says 'e ain't 'is mate. Clean 'im up, give 'im a few quid, and get 'im away from 'ere. But if I see or even 'ear that 'e's been round 'ere again, 'e's dead." Then he turned to me "Come on bruv, I'll buy yer a cuppa."

I sat in the corner of the café, Don got two teas and sat

opposite me. "Why did you lie to me?"

I looked at him and I could feel the colour rising in my cheeks. "I didn't lie to you."

"Yes you did bruv, don't say anymore and make it worse, you told me you were kipping down wiv a mate, you only met the Shaw bloke just over a week ago, that means you 'ave been sleeping rough, and that makes me look a mug. 'Oo would let their kid bruvver sleep rough? Not me or Eileen, she'll do 'er nut when she finds aht."

"I didn't want to worry you, that's all."

"If you 'adnt wanted to worry me, you wouldn't 'ave found me after all this time, so don't talk shit, just tell me the truth." He put his hand on my arm, squeezed and continued. "The Doc that looked after you is a friend of mine – don't look so surprised! I've got mates in all walks of life. Anyway 'e told me in great detail what that bastard that you just let off the 'ook did to you. Now what I want to know is, why 'e did it? And why you lied to protect 'im? You told me you didn't know 'im. Yet Vi tells me you left 'ere wiv 'im the night before 'e did what 'e did. So I ask yer again, why did you lie?"

He sounded hurt and I knew he was, he had tried to avenge me and I had almost thrown it, or so he thought, back in his face. I looked into his eyes and said simply, "I just couldn't put him through any more – seeing him cowering in the corner like that. I just felt pity for him."

Don squeezed my arm again. His eyes were soft and kind. "Look," he said, "I saw you after 'e'd finished wiv you. 'E's lucky 'e's still got a prick. Now, why did 'e do it?" He opened a packet of Senior Service, took out two, lit them and passed one to me. "Tell me," he spoke quietly, "I'm your bruvver, your only bruvver, now tell me, please."

"I can't tell you. I can't. If I did you would kill me – never mind him. At the very least you would get up and walk away from me and leave me. Even he said you would. I can't tell you." The words came out in a streaming torrent, tears filling my eyes and splashing down my cheeks. I tried to hide them or brush them away, but Don wouldn't let me. He held my hand, then took the white handkerchief from his top pocket and wiped my tears away. That had the effect of making me cry even more.

"Let it all out bruv. Just let it all out. You'll feel better." When at last I did stop the floods of tears Don said, "Do you mean you can't tell me you're queer, is that it?"

I looked at him in shock disbelief, "HE told you. He said it?"

"'E didn't 'ave to. You're my bruvver, my own flesh and blood. I've known since you were about seven years old."

"Seven!"

"Well, I couldn't be sure but I 'ad a rough idea. As a nipper you was always soft and kind, fussy about yer clothes and about being tidy. Lots of fings like that. So why would I kill yer or even walk away eh? If it's any 'elp I know one or two REAL East End villains that are queer. Real 'ard nuts – oops I don't fink I should have said that!"

"Said what?"

"Real 'ard nuts. It's a gag – queer, 'ard nuts – come on!"

"Oh yes, I get it. I'm sorry."

"That's it, smile and stop saying sorry, you've got nuffink to be ashamed of."

"But I have," I protested, "I could go to prison."

"Only if you get caught, so don't get caught, just be careful."

"But if, as you say, I've got nothing to be ashamed of why, would they put me in prison? I don't know why I'm like it, I've tried to stop."

"I can't answer that bruv, I wish I could. But God made yer and that's that. You ain't the only one in the world, there's fahsands of 'em. Just make sure you meet a geezer wot feels the same way."

"But how will I know?"

"I can't answer that either. But I'm sure you will, somehow. Now listen to me," he placed a key on the table, "that's the key to that caravan out the back. Your case is in it wiv one or two new bits and pieces." I tried to speak but he wouldn't let me. "Don't say nothing yet. There's also an envelope wiv a few quid in it, on the envelope is the name and address of a factory. Go there first fing tomorrer – ask for Johnny Clark, he'll give yer a job. But you gotta work, if you ain't up to it he'll sack yer, right?" I nodded. "Stay in the van until you get on your feet. You can't stay there permanent OK?" I nodded again. "Just a couple of weeks or so. You eat 'ere." He tapped the table with his finger. "Every day, twice a day, got it?" This produced yet another nod from me. "It'll all go on my bill, so 'ave what you want. One of my mates will be 'ere at all times just to make sure you're OK. You won't even know who 'e is, but there'll always be somebody looking after you. That don't mean spying on yer – but just in case some smart arse tries it on, understand?" I told him I did. "Right – now come on and give us a smile." I tried to smile, but it wasn't a very good effort. "Gawd, if that's a smile then I'm a copper."

He laughed and so did I. I put my hand on his. "Thanks, Don."

"I don't want no fanks. I just want you not to feel ashamed of yourself. Now get in that van, 'ave a wash an' change, then you can buy me and Eileen a drink."

4 – BACK TO THE STOW

The job at the factory turned out to be night work for a company that made costume jewellery. It paid me nearly £27 per week, plus a bonus. I was rich! I worked a ten-hour shift, 9 p.m. until 7 a.m. five nights a week. My workmate was a boy about a year older than myself. He was huge, he must have weighed at least seventeen stone. He was also a wimp and a bore.

It was our job to put a film of colour onto the plastic beads, thus giving the beads an aurora borealis effect. To do this we would firstly string the beads onto 'jigs' then place the whole lot into a large cylindrical machine. Dry chemicals were then put onto the electric elements, the machine closed, and by a process of turning dials and pushing buttons an electric charge was passed through the chemicals, this caused a reaction and the result was a fine glaze of colour on the beads, which were then made up into necklaces and earrings.

The job was boring but, as I said, the pay was good. I didn't get on very well with Bob, my large workmate. He resented my being there. Before I joined the company, Bob had been the only one on the night shift doing this job, but the firm was getting busy, hence the need for another operator. He tried to treat me as something from the gutter and he never tired of telling me that he was in charge and how important the job was. I let him believe it, poor sod. He lived with his mother and father and was as mean as Scrooge. I did try hard at the beginning to make a friend of him but he didn't want to know. I would ask him to meet me for a drink on our day off, but he didn't drink – so I would suggest that we went to the pictures, but he went every week with his mum and dad. Well then, maybe he would like to go to the café and have something to eat and then play the pintables – but he didn't gamble and he could eat cheaper at home! So in the end I gave up.

The day shift always seemed a much brighter bunch. There were four of them including the overall section manager – a young guy about twenty-two, five foot ten, slim, fair-haired and very good looking. His name was Warren but everybody called him Bunny. To the women on the day shift, he was a sex symbol, they would chase after him at every possible moment and he would oblige whenever he could! As I was leaving one morning Bunny called me over. As I hardly knew him, he introduced himself, and we shook hands. He told me that since I had been on the night shift the quality of the work done on the night shift had improved 100%! I told him I was pleased to hear the news. Then he asked me if I would like to work on the day shift. He had another person he could put on nights. I told him that of course I would prefer days, if only because I was feeling the strain of working with Bob. He laughed at the mention of my tubby workmate and then he asked if that meant I would change. I told him I would, but the money on nights was more than the day shift pay.

"I understand that," he said smiling at me, "Suppose I make you my number two, that would give you a pay rise and you would be, in fact, earning more than you were on nights."

"Really?"

"Really," he smiled, "so will you come then?"

"Yes please, but there's just one more thing. Please don't think I'm being awkward," I said, "but I need a couple of days to look for a room or some digs."

I went on to tell him that I was living in a friend's caravan and that I did have to find somewhere else.

"Well in that case," said Bunny, "your problem is solved. My landlady has a spare room or rather a spare bed, so you could move in there."

"Where is there?" I asked.

"Walthamstow," came the reply.

"Walthamstow!!" I said it so loudly I made him jump.

"Why yes, do you know it?"

"Oh yes I know it, but I couldn't possibly move there, it's much too far. I would never be able to afford the fare."

"And I thought you were bright." He was grinning like the Cheshire Cat. "Have you forgotten that I will be living in the same house and that we will be on the same shift? I'll give you a lift in, I have a car. Or did you think I had wings and flew everywhere?"

"No of course not," and I laughed. Then I thought about what had happened to me and I began to feel nervous. "Look," I continued, "You don't know me from Adam. You know nothing about me."

"Look, I know you are a bloody good worker– true, you have only been here for a couple of weeks, but you've more than proved your worth. I can see that you are clean and tidy and although I have only really just met you I also think you're quite a nice person, will that satisfy you?"

"Well yes, but it's like I said, you know nothing of my background or anything else about me."

"All right," said Bunny, "have you robbed a bank lately?"

"No of course not," I said indignantly.

"Well, have you killed anyone lately?"

"No, but—" He interrupted me.

"But me no buts. I've made you an offer, now tell me yes or no."

I didn't wait to think. "Yes, yes please I'd love to live in Walthamstow."

"OK then," he winked, "I'll pick you up straight from night shift on Saturday morning. I have to come in for our three-month stock check, but it won't take long. Then I'll take you back to Walthamstow and you can meet Mr and Mrs Pearson and see your new digs. I'll have a word with them tonight and fix it all up. All you have to do is to remember to bring your suitcase and things, right?"

"Right." I shook his hand. "I'll see you Saturday then."

"I look forward to it" he replied as he shook my hand.

As I walked through the factory gates that morning it was a typical November day. Cold, grey and wet, very wet. But I didn't care, I felt good again. I was going back to the 'Stow' so that meant I would be able to see Alf again and I was going into digs with somebody I really liked. I had a job and money in my pocket. I had found my brother. It could have been spring, I felt so happy. The memories of the past few months would soon fade, I felt sure.

I thought a lot about Bunny that week. What was his sudden

interest in me? Bit shit, it was purely work, he was always chasing girls. He wasn't interested in me like Steve Shaw had been and for my part that was how I wanted it – good looking and easy to talk to as he was, I didn't want to get involved. So I decided to keep my distance. I would just work with him and travel with him but there it would have to end.

I told my brother. He seemed pleased and asked if I was sure. I told him I was he then said he would have his mate at the factory check out Bunny anyway. I asked him not to, explaining that if he did, people at the factory might find out about me and I didn't want that. I assured him that I would be all right.

"OK, if that's what you want," he said, "but keep in touch. No more sloping off."

I promised I would.

As I left the caravan that night, my case packed, I stopped and looked at the café. I didn't want to go in. I just stood there looking at the tumble-down café remembering all the villains, rogues and vagabonds who used the place and who had been so very good to me. I learnt something there that was to stay with me always – never to judge people on first sight. I remembered Vi and Fag End, Vi with her hands full of jewels and her mouth fall of foul language but her heart full of gold and Fag End Andy with the eternal cigarette end hanging from his lips. A rough diamond if ever there was one but a diamond with a soft centre. I walked away slowly. A new chapter of my life was about to begin.

The house in Ruby Road, Walthamstow was very like Anne's except that the caretakers, Mr and Mrs Pearson, lived in a small flat on the ground floor. The house was owned by a Jewish couple along with three or four other similar properties. The houses were all let in single or double rooms and every house had a married couple living in as caretakers. These couples lived rent-free but had to look after not only the house but the "families" as the owners, Mr and Mrs Stern insisted the lodgers were always called. I only met the Sterns once and from the moment I met them I knew that although they earnt a living – a very good living – from their properties, they did care about their "families" and gave value for money.

The house in Ruby Road was spotless. The bedrooms were decorated in bright cheerful wallpaper, the toilets and the bathroom were better than some hotels I have been in since. There was a dining room-cum-lounge with big comfy armchairs, a television and a large table with six chairs. We would all sit around this on Sundays and Mrs Pearson would cook lunch for all of us.

I shared my bedroom with a mixed-race bus driver (I couldn't get away from busmen!) and a milkman. Both were nice and easy to get on with but it seemed that I was forever waking up to hear someone coming or going. At first, I would jump up in bed, heart pounding, thinking I was about to be attacked but nobody did, thank God. Both of my roommates tried very hard not to wake me as they came and went.

Bunny shared a room with a bank clerk of about fifty who kept himself very much to himself. So much so in fact that he would hardly say "good morning" to anybody, even Bunny, who had lived in the same room with him for over a year!

Life for me had taken on a new meaning. The job was better now that I was on the day shift. Bunny took me backwards and forwards to work and we went out about twice a week for a drink or to the pictures. The rest of the week he would go out with his girlfriend and I would go out with one of the other lodgers –sorry, 'family' – or stay in.

Bunny's bank clerk roommate left the house for good at the end of November. He went to live with his sister who had been recently widowed. She lived somewhere in Essex I think – anyway he went never to be seen again. Bunny asked me if I would like to share his room. I told him I would because however much my roommates tried they still woke me up. Moving in with Bunny brought us naturally closer together. We went out more together and would spend hours talking about our plans. He talked about his girlfriend Kay and showed me photos of her. She was very pretty. He would tell me that he wanted to buy her a big house and for them to have lots of kids. He asked me about my girlfriends and I invented some telling him about bogus exploits but that backfired on me when he suggested that we all went out in a foursome. I had to make all manner of excuses – my girl was shy, or she was away, or even that she wasn't well. After a time, he stopped asking me about forming a foursome.

In that December I had a bad cold. Bunny told me to have a couple of days off work and stay in bed. He said he would fix things at work for me. After two days I felt a little better. On the third day, I was in need of some fresh air. I had been thinking about Alf for some time. Since my return to Walthamstow, I hadn't made any contact with him and I was feeling very guilty about it. He, after all, had no idea where I was and no way of contacting me, but the longer I left it the more worried I became – would he be pleased to hear from me? Or would he be hurt that I had left without a word and now tell me to piss off! Well, whatever the answer, I made up my mind I would go and see him.

I got the fresh air I needed. It was freezing cold as I stood at the ticket barrier of Wood Street Station. From where I was standing I could see right down the platform. I just hoped that Alf was at work or hadn't changed his job. The train Alf usually travelled on came into the station, belching black smoke and steam. Doors flew open long before the train came to a halt – people jumping and leaping from it as though any minute it might blow up.

As the crowds of passengers pushed and shoved their way through the barrier I caught a glimpse of Alf. His handsome face glum as he huddled into his black and grey raglan style overcoat trying to escape the bitter wind that blew down the long, exposed platform. As he got nearer I started to worry again about what sort of reception I was going to get but I needn't have had any cause for concern. As he neared the barrier he looked up and saw me, his face broke into a huge grin. As he passed though passed the ticket collector we rushed at each other, arms thrown around each other's necks, both saying things like "Hello you old sod", "Where the bloody hell have you been?", "You look great," and "So do you.". People passed us as though we were from another planet but we didn't care about anybody else for a while. We were both so pleased to be together again. After our hellos and greetings, one of us or both of us said, "Let's go for a drink."

We went across to the Railway pub. There we sat drinking and talking for nearly three hours. I felt so much better, my cold had all but disappeared and I felt as though a huge weight had been lifted from my shoulders. It was, of course, just the utter relief of knowing that I hadn't lost my best friend and how I wish he was still there, still my mate, still understanding.

Christmas came and went. I had sent cards home and to Don and Eileen. Alf bought me a pair of shoes and I bought him a pair of shoes! Bunny bought me a shirt, it must have cost a bomb. It was a mauvey colour with white polka dots and I loved it! I, in return, bought Bunny a cigarette case with a lighter attached. Christmas Day was spent with the Pearsons and the rest of the 'family', except Bunny who spent the whole Christmas (rather reluctantly I thought) at Kay's parents' home.

Boxing Day I spent with Alf in the Palmerston. It was like old times. All the old crowd were there – we got well and truly pissed and stayed on the stage for nearly an hour! You couldn't get us off! We were like chewing gum on the carpet but the crowd loved us. Mind you they were as drunk as us and that might have had something to do with it!

On New Year's Eve, the two of us were asked to join some of Alf's friends at work for drinks in a West End pub. Then onto see the New Year in, in Trafalgar Square. What a night!! Thousands of people crushing into the square – all in a happy, friendly mood. Singing and dancing (when they could find a space) and all of them as drunk as sacks. As I was standing there enjoying the atmosphere with the people pressing all around, I felt someone behind not only pressing against me but rubbing themselves against me. At first, I hardly noticed it but it gradually got worse. I thought I was dreaming or that I had too much to drink – a hand was now massaging my bum. I froze, I couldn't move, my head was swimming and I felt sick.

I felt my legs start to buckle under me.

Suddenly a man yelled with pain and fell on me from behind knocking me to the ground. I was petrified. Hands came down to me and lifted me up. Then I saw the reason for the yelling – Alf was punching three kinds of shit out of a man aged about thirty. He was dressed in a camel hair coat spattered in blood. He was quite good-looking. Alf kept hitting him, he was calling him everything, "Touch my mate would you, you dirty fucking queer." The words screamed through my head. I didn't know what was worse. Being assaulted by this creep or hearing Alf say that. Is that what he would think of me if he found out? Some of our friends pulled Alf off my attacker and he fled.

Alf took my arm and said gently, "You OK mate?"

I nodded, "Yes."

Still holding my arm, he led me out of the crowd. "You should have kicked him yourself, bleeding good job I saw him."

"I couldn't Alf, I just seemed to freeze on the spot, I was so scared. I didn't know who it was or what to do – but thanks for helping me."

"Thanks? I don't need thanks. You're my friend. Fucking queers – they should all be in nick or hung. Come on, don't let it ruin your night." He led me out of the crowd and into a bar. "Ruin my night," I thought, "ruin my night, it's ruined my life!" I had not only been groped but I had heard the person I thought most of in the world telling me that ALL queers should be hung or at least be in prison. What the hell would he say about me when – because surely it had to be when – he found out about me? His so-called best friend was one of those queers he hated so much. I tried hard to smile at everybody yelling "Happy New Year" but I felt empty.

Why did that bloke pick on me? Of all the hundreds, thousands of people in the square tonight, why me? Was it God punishing me for being what I was? Was it, perhaps, God letting me know what it would be like if my friends did find out about me? Or was it God telling me I had to change and change fast? My head was reeling. People were talking to me but I didn't hear a word of what they were saying. They thought I was drunk – I let them go on thinking. Friends were wishing me "Happy New Year" – the prospects of having one didn't seem very good.

New Year's Day and things hadn't improved. I had finally reached home at about six in the morning and I slept until late in the afternoon. Then I had a bath and was back in my room when Bunny came in. I was naked drying myself with a towel when he entered. When he saw me, he gave me a wolf whistle and said, "Oh, get you sexy. Have a good New Year?"

I let the towel drop and put on a pair of briefs. "Yes, not bad, got really pissed. You?"

"Oh, it was great. All the family and Kay of course. Christ, you look terrible. Fancy a hair of the dog?"

"Thanks for the compliment," I said icily, "and I don't think I could face a drink."

"Oh, come on Ricky. We haven't been out together all over Christmas. Anyway, it'll make you feel better and maybe we could have a meal as well."

The very thought of something to eat really made my stomach turn. "Oh," I groaned, "do you mind, I think I'm going to throw up. Anyway, I spent out over the holiday."

Bunny laughed, "Oh come on, my treat. I feel like going out and I don't want to go on my own. Apart from anything else I'd like to take you out."

I looked at him, "Oh OK you win, I'll pay you back when I get paid. Fair deal?"

"Deal." He said, and we slapped hands to seal it.

While he was in the bathroom, I searched through my wardrobe. "Oh shit, sod all to wear that's clean." Then I found a pair of jeans that I had bought before Christmas but had not yet worn. I took them from the bag and pulled them on. "Christ," I thought, "I'll need to grease my legs to get these on!" I pulled and struggled to get them on – at last the task was done and as I zipped them up I looked at myself in the mirror. "Jesus, it looks as though I've painted them on!" I told myself and what was worse (or better) was you could clearly see all I possessed! Which I may remind you reader, was quite a lot!!

I put on a chunky sweater, did my hair, and had another look at myself in the mirror. "Magic," I told myself as I stood there admiring the way the jeans showed up my long slender legs, neat round bum and my manhood off to perfection.

Bunny came back into the room. He took one look at me and said, "Christ, don't sit down in those tonight, will you?"

"Do they look all right?" I asked.

"They look great," he replied and gently but firmly slapped me on the bum.

As he did so he let his hand linger for a fraction of a second, not long, I admit, but long enough to send a tingle of excitement through my body. "Steady," I told myself, "remember, just good friends."

We didn't go to our local pub or even to the Palmerston. We drove instead out of London to Epping where Bunny said that he knew a nice little pub-restaurant. Epping was then a small sleepy country town, almost a village, but it was very well to do and very conservative in every meaning of the word. We found the pub – a charming Tudor building with a wealth of exposed beams covered with old copper pans and kettles, huntsman's horns and a motley of old farm implements, plus the usual collection of horse brasses.

The conversation around the bar was quiet and refined. Nobody pushed or shoved to get to the bar. Most of the men wore blazers with the old school tie or a cravat. While the women were dressed in tweeds and sensible shoes, nothing like what I had been used to – busty barmaids showing their tits off to full advantage, women dressed in semi-cocktail dresses, their hair bleached, hennaed or dyed black and wearing fur coats, some cheap, some not so cheap, the men in long Crombie overcoats with Slim Jim ties and light tan suede shoes or boots. East Enders like dressing up. Most had drab jobs and lived in drab houses or flats, rented from the local council or from private landlords – most of whom didn't give a damn about living conditions as long as the rent was paid. If it wasn't then out you went! In Walthamstow houses and flats were rented from the Warner Estates, rows and rows of the same boring green and cream dwellings. Not all East Enders worked in factories or on the docks. Some, of course, were "at it" – thieving or receiving stolen goods. A bit of a fiddle is all right to most East Enders as long as nobody gets hurt.

But here in Epping, they all looked to me to be dull and boring. They wouldn't have been seen dead in the East End and would have tut-tutted at the way of life. These were the sort of people who would be JPs and magistrates sitting in judgement over the so-called 'villains'. It's quite different to steal from a bank, for example, than it is for the bank, finance house or insurance company to charge exorbitant interest rates on loans or deals – or to be involved in dubious takeovers. All these would be regarded as good business sense by the good folk in this bar. I still call it stealing.

When we walked into the bar the hushed voices seemed to stop altogether. People looked at us – some even stared in disbelief. That these two persons should dare to invade their world. You could almost hear them saying "I say chaps, who the devil are those two people?" Me – I just stared back and I do mean stared back. I minced to the bar, really going over the top. When Bunny asked me what I would like to drink I spoke without thinking and said, in a very loud voice, "Oh the usual, a large gin and lime." Bunny nearly choked laughing. Me – I just sat on a bar stool with one leg across the other and smiled around the bar.

Bunny paid for the drinks and ordered a table for two from a barman who was as much a snob as the customers. We sat at the bar waiting for a table, me sipping my gin and lime – why that particular drink I'll never know, I had never tasted gin and lime in my life. As I took my first swig I too nearly choked. I don't know how I kept myself from falling off the stool but I did. I was determined not to let these prats in the bar get the better of me. I forced myself into composure. The gin had all but burnt my throat out. I looked at Bunny who had realised what had happened and was all but wetting himself in an effort not to laugh.

When finally we were informed that our table was ready, I asked the snooty barman in a very loud, even camp voice to "bring my drink through to the restaurant." Then I swished through the bar with Bunny following carrying a pint of light and bitter! People looked at us from behind menus or glanced in our direction and simply stared yet again. Of course, once again, I stared or glared back. By the time we reached the table, my gin and lime was waiting for me and that made my day. The rest of the diners had by now stopped talking – I think my jeans were having some effect, forks were at lips, but food was not being allowed to enter any mouths, it was wonderful!

When at last we had sat down and ordered Bunny looked across the table at me and said, "I've never laughed so much, you were brilliant, you should be on the stage, and to order a gin and lime like that was pure genius." I just laughed and agreed. "That's the ultimate in an old biddy's drink!"

The comment brought a fit of coughing on me. I had no idea gin and lime was an old woman's drink! But I wasn't going to tell him that! The food was good and although I had said that I didn't want to earlier, I was now very hungry and ate everything that was put in front of me. After the meal, we went back to the bar. I changed my drink order to halves of lager and we stayed until closing time.

The drive back into London was nice. The night was cold and clear. As we drove through Epping Forest in the little Austin A40, the moon silhouetting the trees making them look like huge men from Mars, their naked branches black against the night sky and the moon making the shadows of a thousand arms. But I was with Bunny – happy, contented and unafraid.

We were both happy – giggling and laughing at my antics in the pub. When we reached our room I shivered, feeling cold for the first time. Bunny put on the one bar electric fire, I turned off the light and we both got undressed with a fit of giggles as I tried to get my jeans off. He came across to help me, I pulled and he tugged my legs, finally, as they did come off he fell flat on his back. Again we both fell about laughing. Now jeanless and wearing only a pair of briefs, I pulled him up off the floor. As he stood up our naked bodies touched. We stopped giggling as we looked into each other's eyes and after what seemed to me like an hour, but could only have been a few seconds at the most, I said quietly, "Goodnight." I let go of his hands and got into bed.

As the ice-cold sheets touched my still naked body I yelled, "Jesus!"

"What's up?" he called.

"The bloody bed's freezing," I said, my teeth chattering with the cold.

"Shit, you're right," came the reply as he too got into the frozen sheets.

I wished him goodnight again, and he replied likewise.

I lay back on my pillow trying to get warm and my thoughts drifted back to the happenings of that night. I thought of our bodies touching only moments ago and I asked myself if he knew. I told myself it was impossible, it happened all too quickly. I wondered if he had noticed or felt the shudder of excitement that had rippled through me the moment our skins had touched. I thought of his slim body and tried to put it out of my mind. I looked around the room. The glow from the electric fire made me think of the drive through the forest – the fire glow gave off different images, they didn't move as the trees had seemed to move when they had been caught in the car headlights.

Then suddenly I did see something move, a shadow flickered across the room – or was I still pissed? The room spun in my drunken mind, then a cold hand touched me – I nearly jumped out of my skin and I yelled.

"Sssh!!" It was Bunny. "Do you want to wake the whole bloody house?"

"What's the matter?" I asked.

"Nothing's the matter except that I'm bloody freezing to death. So I thought I could get in with you. That way we can keep each other warm, what do you think?"

What did I think? My heart leapt. "I think I better say no," I told myself, "in fact, I HAVE to say no." Instead of which I said nothing but I pulled the bedclothes back and Bunny slipped into bed beside me.

"Oh, that's better." He said as he put his arm around me. We were lying face to face. I put my arm around him and agreed that it was much better.

We could see each other in the half-light. He let his hand run down my back, he caressed my bum and he kissed me. I flung myself on him with all the passion I could muster. His tongue searched out my lips again and probed deep into my throat. Then he kissed my eyes and my neck – his tongue darting in and out of my ear. All the while his hand, having found my erection, massaged between my legs making me writhe with pleasure. Then slowly he went further down my body, kissing every part of me. At last, I felt his tongue warm and soft in between my legs, his mouth found my hard prick that was throbbing with excitement and anticipation. As his mouth closed around it I moaned. Slowly at first, he worked his mouth, stopping when he thought he might lead me to an early climax, then again faster, then once more stopping. He did this until finally I could no longer control myself and I let my sperm find its way into his mouth. This made him even more excited and he turned his body around and my mouth then closed over his erection, just as he too released his sperm. I felt it warm and bitter in my mouth. We lay there each letting the other savour the bitter yet sweet taste.

Then he turned around again his moist mouth filling mine, and he whispered, "I want to feel you inside me, I want to feel a part of you, please cum inside me, please." Then he reached out of bed for a small tin.

"What's that?" I asked him.

"Only hand cream, don't worry." Then he spread the cream on my still hard prick. He lay face down on the bed and I applied the cream to him. I had never been the active partner before and was a bit of a loss as to what to do but soon my instinct told me and I found myself entering him.

"Please don't hurt me," he moaned as I felt his body stiffen under me. The same words I had said to Brian the very first time anybody had entered me. I reassured him and as I felt myself go deeper into him I could feel him squeeze his buttocks together drawing me yet still further into him. I thrust back and forth harder and faster, he called my name softly. I could feel the excitement in his body and to me, it was the most wonderful experience, I was making love to another man. I was inside another man, he wanted me and here I was, my body and my mind were on cloud nine. I could feel my sperm welling up inside waiting to be released. Faster and faster I went, deeper, still deeper until I felt the warm liquid leave my body with a jolt. I carried on for a few more strokes, not wanting to leave him and to make sure I gave him all of my love juices. When I was sure I collapsed on him taking deep breaths of air. As I lay there panting I caressed his neck and turned his face towards me and kissed him as I had never kissed anyone before. Then we fell asleep in each other's' arms, the perfect end to a perfect night.

That night changed my life sexually, at least. After that night I was never to be a passive lover again. When I awoke the next morning, Bunny was still in my arms his slim body tucked into mine. He woke up and smiled, we kissed gently. He looked at his watch, got out of bed, put his dressing gown on and left the bedroom. He came back later with tea and toast. He bent down and kissed me on the forehead. He said, "You have changed my life, I love you."

I held his hand and told him I loved him. Then I thought to myself that two lives had been changed that night, two lives changed not by filth or perversion, but by love for two people for each other. So how could that be wrong?

On the way to work that day he warned me that we had to be careful. We didn't dare show to much favour or affection for one another at work and he would still have to see his girlfriend each week. They had planned to marry and he would have to let her down gently. He didn't want to hurt her. I told him I should hope not! And for my part I would still see Alf when he was seeing Kay, at that moment he got angry.

"Why see Alf?" He asked me.

"Because he's my friend," came my reply.

"Is that ALL he is?" I could hear the jealousy in his voice.

"Yes of course." I snapped, "Don't be so stupid. He has been my friend for years, I've never slept with him and now I have you," I told him. "I don't want anybody else."

He apologised for being jealous. I was secretly pleased that he had been jealous. I asked him about Kay and told him I didn't get upset when he told me that he had to go on seeing her for the time being. He told me it was different, Kay being a girl, was no threat to our relationship. I didn't quite understand his logic, but I told him I did and also told him he had nothing to fear.

We both remarked how strange it was that a few short weeks ago we hardly knew each other and now here we were – not only together but in love.

It was his first relationship with someone of his own sex. He also told me that until he had met me he was like everybody else he knew, he hated 'queers' and he would join in with the other men in the factory in telling jokes about 'poofs'. Now here he was with me and he didn't feel a bit 'queer' – he only felt great.

He stressed that I was not yet eighteen and he was twenty-three, and if we were caught, he at least would go to prison and I would be sent to a remand home. It sent a chill through me – prison for loving me. All day everyday people were getting killed, murdered, raped and robbed and the people who committed those crimes would be sent to the same prison as Bunny if we were caught and Bunny's only crime would be loving me. Society (whatever that was) said it was wrong and if you did love another man you would be shut up in prison.

We did as we said. We kept our relationship under wraps around people we knew. We didn't know anybody else in the same situation and it was a strain. He kept seeing Kay and I kept seeing Alf. On those nights when we were apart, whoever got home first from their night out would get into the other one's bed, and then when he came home we would have a night of love. It was bliss.

One night before he was due to go and see Kay he said, "I might be late tonight love, very late."

"Oh yes why? You going to Gretna Green?" I asked.

"Don't be bloody daft. No, I'm going to tell Kay about us."

I looked at him. "Are you sure?"

"Yes, I'm quite sure. I love you and I want to be with you, not her. If I marry her my whole life will be a sham and I'll lose you and I couldn't bear that."

I kissed him and watched him go, I really had somebody who loved me, I felt ten feet tall.

That night I met Alf in the Palmerston. It was always good to see him. We had a good laugh and more than enough to drink. On the way home I thought about my secret life with Bunny and wondered what the average person in the street would think – I imagined they would be horrified. It was a strange feeling, there I was living with someone, someone who loved me and whom I loved in return yet I had to keep it to myself when I wanted everybody to know. It must, I thought, be the same for a man who had a mistress or a woman with a sugar daddy or a lover. Far from dampening my ardour, having to keep it quiet and secret seemed to add to the excitement – although at times it could and did make me, and I'm sure Bunny, feel cut-off and isolated.

When I reached home, Bunny was still out. I washed and climbed into his bed. I had been asleep about an hour I suppose when suddenly the bedroom light was switched on flooding the whole room in stark white light. I hid my eyes from the light and called out, "Bunny, is that you love?"

"You queer bastard," was the reply. It was a woman's voice. I froze, slowly opening my eyes. Standing in the doorway was a pretty blonde woman about twenty-three or four – I recognised her straight away as Kay, Bunny's girlfriend. Her photo was still on his bedside table.

"What the hell's going on?" I yelled as I jumped out of bed, forgetting that I was naked. When she saw my naked form, she flew at me screaming, "You filthy queer, you're even in his bed you bastard." I felt her long fingernails dig into my flesh ripping my arms and chest, blood trickled from the wounds.

I pushed her away. "What the fuck is going on?" I yelled at her again.

She was punching and kicking me. "He told me," she screamed, "he told me you wouldn't leave him alone, that you keep trying to make him do things with you that he doesn't want to do, well you're not going to have him. Do you hear me, he's mine, mine." Then she picked up a glass dish from the dressing table and threw it at me. I ducked as I felt it whizz past my ear.

"Enough," I thought, "Enough, piss off." I was screaming now, "Go on, piss off before I belt you, you cow. He loves me not you, now sod off or I will give you a bloody good slap." I stood there shaking, shaking with anger. I raised my arm to let her know that I meant what I said but she just stood there.

I walked towards her. "Alan," she said suddenly. At almost the same moment a tall blond guy, about twenty-five or so, came rushing into the room.

"Who?" was all I managed to say.

I saw his clenched fist coming towards me but I had no time to get out of the way. I just heard him say, "I'm her brother, you pervert." Then his fist crashed into the side of my head, knocking me across the room and the bed. The back of my head hit the wall with a sickening thud, then darkness.

When I came round, Mr and Mrs Pearson were fussing over me, she sponging my face with ice-cold water, him picking up broken glass.

"Who the 'ell were they?" It was Mr Pearson talking, "we 'eard a noise and thought it was them next door 'aving a bull and cow."

"It was only when we 'eard the front door slam," interrupted Mrs Pearson, "that we guessed it was here. Did you 'ave anybody back 'ere tonight?"

"No, no." I said quickly, "I was in bed, I don't know who they were."

"Well, it's queer to me," she said. For a moment I thought they knew. Then I realised that the word queer was often used in the East End to mean something that someone didn't understand or if someone was "queer" it could mean that they were unwell. I convinced them that I didn't know my attackers, at least I think I convinced them.

Mrs Pearson brought me up a cup of hot sweet tea, the Englishman's answer to everything in moments of stress or shock. "What, your wife or husband has just dropped dead! Oh, come and sit down and I'll make you a nice hot sweet cup of tea." Bombs could be dropping or the outbreak of another world war could be on the way, but it will be all right as long as you have a cup of hot sweet tea!

They left me after my reassuring them that I didn't want to call the police. I told them that I thought I was a case of mistaken identity.

I lay on my bed looking at the chaos. Clothes were piled up on the bed, books and bits and pieces were scattered all over the place. There was a bloodstain on the wall, I supposed, by the size of the bump on my head and the fact that it was so painful, that the blood was mine.

Kay's words kept ringing in my ears, "He told me – he told me – you wouldn't leave him alone – he told me—" Then I heard him saying to me, "I'm going to tell her tonight – I love you not her – my life would be a sham – I love you – my life would be a sham." The words spun around and around in my head.

I felt sick. I got up from the bed, his bed, and as I stood up I saw lying on the floor a letter addressed to me. It hadn't been there this morning or when I came home tonight. I picked it up and opened it. I sat back down on the bed as I read:

You trapped me. You made me do it. You're nothing but a pervert. Don't come to work, I'll make sure your cards are sent to you. People like you should be locked away.

Warren.

I read it over two or three times. Then I looked again at the signature: "Warren". He would never sign himself like that, unless on a business letter. He would never write to me like that. I got up and crossed to the dressing table, I picked up the Christmas card he had sent me. I looked at the message he had written, "Have a good one, love Bunny." The handwriting was completely different.

As I glanced around the room I saw the shirt he had bought me for Christmas – I picked it up and hugged it to me. Blood from her attack was still oozing from the wounds and it spread onto the fabric of the shirt. I got back into his bed and held the shirt close to me then I cried and cried until I cried myself to sleep.

I received my National Insurance cards, plus a month's pay and a week's holiday money. I could tell by the handwriting that Bunny had made the wage slip out himself. I also knew that I was not entitled to a month's money, only a week, so I counted my blessings. He had at least done that for me and that was all he did. I never saw or heard from him again. I only hope that he found happiness but I doubt it. His love for me couldn't just have been a phase he was going through – he just lacked the courage to live his life the way he wanted to. He was right when he said it would be living a sham and that I guess is just how he did live it.

He sent a letter to the Pearsons, asking them to send all his clothes on to his girlfriend's. He made some excuse that he was going abroad to work. I often wonder how his girlfriend coped with life. After all, marrying a man who she knew had slept and had sex with his workmate couldn't have been easy. Would she, for example, watch him in case his eyes wandered, not onto another girl, but another man? When he came home late from work would she wonder if the reason he gave was the truth? Her life would not be easy, I felt sorry for both of them.

The following weekend I had an invitation to an engagement party. It came via Alf, one of my old workmates was taking the plunge and he had asked Alf to make sure that I came along. I thought it a little ironic, to say the least, that I was going to such a party after the happenings of the previous weekend.

5 – THE JET SET?

It took me ages to get myself ready. I really wasn't in the mood for such an occasion. But once in Chelsea, I changed my mind. We all met in a very arty part of the Kings Road. James, the friend getting married, and his twin brother Jonathon had really gone to town – taking over a small restaurant and supplying their guests with mountains of food and drink. It was my first taste of the high life and after my affair, I needed something like this to cheer me up.

Most of the guests I knew, but some I didn't, they were friends of the twins, plus a few cousins. These guests were from a different world to the one that I lived in. They dressed in the latest fashion, had pots of money and really seemed to let nothing worry them. All they wanted to do was to have a good time and I for one didn't blame them.

I was introduced to the bride-to-be, a pretty girl called Jean. She had long soft brown hair that fell in cascades onto her slender shoulders, she wore a strapless bright yellow cocktail dress. Her skin was almost dark brown, probably from lots of expensive holidays abroad, I thought. It certainly went well with her dress. Her breasts were small, but perfect for her delicate frame.

As I stood there making small talk with her I wondered what she had seen in James, for although both twins were really nice guys, quiet and considerate, God had been less than kind to them as far as their looks were concerned. Both suffered from acute acne and both were short and a little overweight – but they did come from a very wealthy family, so perhaps that was some compensation!

The party was one of the best I had ever been to. I laughed and joked with my old friends and had a couple of dances with Jean. I was quite a good dancer and seemed to be in demand. I told lots of lies, of course, about my non-existent job and about my flat! Also about my many girlfriends. One of the friends I saw again was Kevin Brown. A small pretty blond youth, about eighteen years old, Kevin was a Mod and he looked great in his Italian style suit and long pointed hand-made winkle-picker shoes. I had always liked him but had never really had much chance to speak to him at work as we were in different departments, but here at the party, it seemed I was either talking to him or dancing with Jean. I know which I preferred!

The party ended in the early hours of the morning. Alf had chatted one of the rich young things up and she had agreed to drive us to the Embankment so that we could catch the all-night bus. Alf told her that he had smashed his sports car up the previous week, escaping only by a hair's breadth before it burst into flames – he was a bigger liar than me! I arranged to meet Kevin the following weekend in the World's End pub in Chelsea. Jean had heard me make the arrangement and said it was very near where she lived, and if she and James weren't doing anything they would pop in and join us for a drink.

Kevin was already in the pub by the time I arrived. He waved to me from a table and held up a large scotch to show me he had already bought me a drink. I pushed my way through to the table and we grinned at each other like a couple of Cheshire Cats. He was wearing yet another snappy Mod suit. We said our hellos and were just feeling relaxed in each other's company when in walked Jean, wearing a skin-tight floral dress, her hair piled up on top of her head – she really did look good. I was a bit disappointed that she had shown up before I had a real chance to talk to Kevin.

She saw us and waved, then made her way to our table. She walked like one of that group of girls discovered by such people as J Arthur Rank, the film mogul, and called starlets by the press. Although most of the girls couldn't act, all were beautiful. Some of them, of course, could act and proved to be very competent actresses indeed, Diana Dors and Maureen Swanson are two that spring to mind. As she walked her whole body swayed, she looked good and she knew it! When she reached our table, I said hello, and asked her where James was.

"Oh, he couldn't make it, so I thought if you two didn't mind I'd come anyway – unless of course, you two want to be alone."

It wasn't what she said but the way that she said it that made me wonder if she had some idea about one of us or, for all I knew, both of us. Either way, I'm sure I blushed. I know Kevin did.

"Of course not," he said, "what do you take us for?"

"Oo, I'm not sure I know ducky," she chortled, in a voice that was a send-up of everyone's idea of a queer, "but there's a lot of it about."

"Yeah well, that's as maybe, but there's not any around here," Kevin was not only embarrassed – now he was angry. I had no idea that he had such a temper, he was shaking with rage. I did my best to cool the situation by getting another round of drinks. The conversation was punctuated by long embarrassing periods of silence when all three of us would sit and stare into our drinks or look around the pub – anything but look at each other.

I asked Jean about the wedding – had they set a date? She replied that a date hadn't been fixed and what's more she didn't want to talk about it. Kevin was sinking more into his shell and getting more and more pissed by the minute. I decided to join him (in getting pissed I mean).

At closing time Jean suggested we all went back to her flat for a nightcap and something to eat. I didn't really fancy it but said yes for the want of a better suggestion. Kevin just shrugged his shoulders and followed on. The World's End stands in the poorer part of Chelsea, a Chelsea far away from the smart restaurants and boutiques, one of a mixture of council flats and rows of decrepit Victorian houses and small factories. We walked further and further into the Lots Road area. I guessed she didn't have a mansion flat, but when she walked up a few stairs to an end of terrace Victorian ruin, I was shocked, to say the least.

The smell of rotten food, stale sweat and cat piss hit me like a slap in the face. We went into the hallway where a battered pram and an old bike were parked at one side. The faded rose-patterned wallpaper was hanging from the crumbling plaster. In various places the dark brown paintwork was chipped and filthy.

The floor had the 'luxury' of being covered in lino – now worn so badly that the worst places were covered with offcuts from numerous scraps of other lino, making the floor into a patchwork of colours, with dirt and grime clogged in every conceivable nook and cranny.

"We'll go into the lounge," she said this as though she had just shown us into the hallway of some beautiful country house. We followed her through the first door on the left and into the front room.

"Lounge!" I said to myself, "Christ!" The mess in the middle of the wall facing us was, I supposed, the fireplace – coals and ashes had spewed out over the hearth. The coal scuttle was an old galvanised bucket, holding not only coals but all sorts of rubbish. On the other side of the room stood a grey and red bed-settee, so dirty that it was difficult to make out the colours. Two odd fireside chairs and a blue Formica kitchen table and chairs made up the rest of the furniture in the "lounge". The table was littered with coffee mugs, old newspapers, empty cigarette packets and half-empty sauce bottles. Plates with the remains of a meal, chop bones and burnt black chips set in thick white grease, completed the picture. The only covering on the floor, apart from yet more faded and worn lino, was a filthy ragwork rug, its pattern and its colour again long since forgotten. Piles of clothes and books littered the floor.

Poverty was nothing new to me, my own home as a child had been furnished with deckchairs for armchairs. We also had ragwork rugs, made by weaving scraps of cloth onto a piece of sacking – the rags were pushed through the sacking so that the two ends were on the same side. These ends were then tied into a knot so that they stayed put. Many, many homes in the East End had such rugs – indeed some were almost works of art, the maker inventing his or her own designs. It wasn't unusual to go visiting and see a member of the household sitting by the fire making such a rug, but however poor we and our neighbours had been, the small terraced houses were spotless. We as kids might have the arse of our trousers hanging out and few good clothes, but what we had was clean. I remember the pine table in our kitchen-cum-living room. It was so large that we would sit under it during the air raids of World War II. My mother, brother and sister all crushed together, but all feeling safe under our shelter. That table was scrubbed almost snow white.

The sight of Jean's home made both Kevin and me sober up very quickly. Suddenly Jean was talking. "I'll see what's in the kitchen, sit down and make yourselves at home! "She looked at us and smiled. "Won't be a jif." She turned and was gone. As the door closed behind her, Kevin and I just looked at the room then at each other.

"Christ, what a shithole." It was my voice that broke the silence. "She doesn't even know that it's a shithole, did you see the way she just breezed in as though it were the bloody Ritz or something?"

Kevin nodded. "Yes, let's piss off. I'll ruin this suit if I sit on one of those chairs!"

"We can't just walk out, put a newspaper on the chair then sit down." I remembered my mum's front room, bright and shining, and smelling of nothing more than love and Johnson's Wax. I looked around the room again and shuddered. The door opened and Jean came back into the room. "Mum's awake, she wants to meet you both." She smiled again and at that moment from somewhere out in the hallway we heard a yell of complaint from a throaty-voiced woman.

"Oh fuck! This bleeding lino's cold!" This was followed by a phlegmy cough and into the room, hopping and coughing like a demented rabbit with the flu, came Jean's mum. Her hair was dyed almost the colour of carrots, at least the ends were – the roots were iron grey. It was very frizzy and she had tied a scarf around it in what must have been a vain attempt to keep it under control. I guessed she was about fifty years old. She was wrapped in a dirty floral dressing gown and a fag hung from her lips.

"Nice to meet you, lads," she said half-coughing and half-spluttering, then wiping the back of her hand across her mouth, thus removing any trace of the mucus she may have coughed up. At the same time, taking the fag end from her lips she said, "No don't bother to get up. Oh Jean," she said with disdain, "you could have cleared the fucking table, what will they think of us!" As she spoke she waved the cigarette about, gripped in between two fingers stained almost black with nicotine, dropping ash everywhere.

"Clear the fucking thing yourself, you lazy old cow," was Jean's swift reply. I was stunned.

"I'll slap your mouth for you, my girl," yelled Carrot Head, "I'm your bleeding mother, so don't talk to me like that in front of your fancy men."

"Oh sod off Mum, and get them something to eat, you silly bitch." To my amazement, the old girl turned on her heel and went out of the door into God knows what mess, calling out as she went, "I won't be long boys, don't go away." Jean found a half-empty bottle of Scotch and a couple of dirty-looking glasses. I took one look at the glasses and drank from the bottle, Kevin did likewise. Jean then left the room again.

Kevin looked at me, his face screwed up in disgust, "What are we going to do?"

"What else?" was my reply, "I'm going to get pissed."

"Good idea," said Kevin, "at least if we're pissed it won't look so bad!" He took a long swig from the bottle and passed it to me.

When Jean came back she was wearing a housecoat and very little else, "There, isn't that better, I hate having too many clothes on, don't you?" We both nodded and I took another swig from the bottle.

"Has James met your Mum yet?" I asked her. Knowing the background he came from, I was curious to know what he had thought when he had seen the pigsty his fiancée lived in, and even more curious to know what he thought of his future mother-in-law.

"No, not yet, I want to surprise him."

"Oh, you will," I thought, "you most certainly will!"

The door suddenly burst open again and back into the room came Jean's witch of a mother carrying a tin tray with two plates on it. On the plates were what looked like slices of toast and what was piled on the toast was anybody's guess. "There, get that down you," she coughed as she put the tray down on the table, pushing all the other junk to one side as she did it. "Pilchards on toast with a bit of grated cheese. The cheese got a bit burnt while I was in the lav, but the pilchards are OK They're the best, I'll have you know, I nicked 'em from the hospital where I used to do a bit of cleaning. Well come on you two, don't let it get cold."

We both took yet another swig at the whisky, then got up and sat at the table. We each we took a deep breath and pushed some of the vile stuff down our throats, while the witch with the carrot hair beamed. "Nice?"

We both nodded a lying yes.

I was the first one to be sick. I rushed from the room following the directions I had been given. I found the lavatory and went inside. If I hadn't felt sick from the pilchards I most certainly would have done from the stench and the sight that greeted me. I thought I was going to die in that stinking lavatory and I think I should have done had it not been for Kevin banging on the door pleading to be let in. By now it was nearly three in the morning, and both Jean and her mother insisted that we stay the night. As we both felt like death, we agreed.

I was shown to a small bedroom, airless and furnished only with a single bed and a battered dressing table. The dressing table was thick with dust and littered with old nail varnish bottles, empty tins and tubes that had at one time been full of make-up. Some of the tubes still contained remnants of beige-coloured creams which had started to leak – the result being a sticky mess on the top of the dressing table. Clothes hung around the wall, their hangers hooked onto any available nail or on the picture rail.

I sat on the bed and looked around. The walls were covered in dowdy, faded, fawn and green wallpaper, stained with grease where the headboard on the bed was missing. A naked bulb glared from the light socket, showing up the cracked ceiling and the black cobwebs that filled the cornices. "Oh, sod it," I thought, it was a bed and I was too tired and felt too ill to care. I put the light out and lay on the bed fully clothed. I wasn't that pissed, there was no way I was going to get in the bed. I dreaded to think what family pets were waiting for a meal as they hid amongst the bed linen. The light came on again and Jean was in the room having discarded the housecoat she was now wearing only her black bra and panties – I remember wondering if they had been white when she bought them!

"All right, are we?" she inquired, "I just thought you might like some company. Do you know, I've just said to my mother that I think I like you better than James, isn't that strange?"

Strange! I was speechless, I nodded to her and as I did so she took off her bra to reveal two small, yet perfect breasts – the nipples of which I could see were hard with excitement.

I panicked inside. "Er-I know this isn't the time," I stammered, "but I want to throw up again." I jumped off the bed and rushed past her out of the bedroom and back into the foul-smelling lav. I almost laughed when I thought of her standing in the bedroom with an amazed look on her face. I say almost, because before I could laugh I really was throwing up again.

When I finished I rinsed my face under the tap and wiped it dry on my shirt rather than use the filthy towel that hung from a rusty nail on the back of the door. I decided not to go back into the bedroom from which I had just fled, so I made my way to the front room and Kevin.

As I opened the door and crept in I saw someone bending over Kevin. I stood rooted to the spot – then I reached out and switched on the light. I could hardly believe the sight that reached my eyes, Jean's mother –the witch – was chewing away at Kevin's manhood!! As the light went on she stopped her meal, spun round and called me an interfering bastard before rushing from the room. She was naked from the waist up and as she ran past me her long, flat, tired breasts flapped against her skin, making a noise like a seal clapping its flippers.

Kevin looked petrified. "Thank fuck you came in," he said, as he tucked his dick back into his trousers – I had to admit to myself that it did look appetising – "first I got rid of Jean by saying you fancied her—"

"Oh, thanks a lot," I interrupted, "That was very nice of you, I don't think!"

"I'm sorry," he continued, "But I didn't know what else to do, anyway then that old cow came in, at first I thought it was Jean trying her luck again, so I let her get on with it, I lay there with my eyes shut, then she spoke and I nearly shit myself! I couldn't get a peck on and she was cursing me when you arrived."

"I'm not surprised you couldn't get a lob on, who could with her?"

"What are we going to do now?" Kevin's voice was full of panic as he asked me the twenty-four-thousand-dollar question.

"Easy," was my reply, "move over."

"What for?"

"I'm going to sleep with you, and if they come back for Christ's sake cuddle me, that must put them off!"

He pulled back the bed covers as I took off my clothes. He looked at me, then grinned and said, "Let's cuddle anyway in case we don't hear them." I got into bed and put my arm around him, I felt his arm wrap around me and within seconds we were both fast asleep.

In the morning I woke to find Kevin still in my arms. I heard a noise in the room and sat up to see Jean's mum laying the table – by 'laying the table' I mean simply putting a cloth on it and a few knives and forks! She had also tidied the room up a bit.

When she saw me sitting up she said, "Sorry about last night luv, I didn't know you and 'im were – were – well, you know. I wouldn't have tried it, honest, 'e should have said. Its small wonder 'e couldn't get a bleeding hard-on. I nearly wore my fucking lips out!" She laughed and coughed her phlegmy cough. "Breakfast in ten minutes, OK?" Then she left the room.

I got out of bed and dressed, then I woke Kevin and told him what the old girl had said. He looked at me and grinned again, "Well, I'd rather have you any day, than either of them!"

"Just my bloody luck," I thought, "and I went to bloody sleep!"

Breakfast was a bit of a surprise – cornflakes followed by bacon and eggs all served up on clean plates and set on a fairly clean tablecloth. I asked where Jean was. "Oh, her ladyship never gets out of bed until two or three in the afternoon." was the reply.

We ate breakfast and said goodbye to the witch.

"You're always welcome in this house. I like gay boys, they don't want you just for your body, you can come back anytime." She coughed her cough and we tried to hide our amusement.

We said, "Yes we would both like to see you again." Then we ran down Ashburnham Road, laughing our heads off.

Three weeks later saw me walking down that same road. This time I was trying to get enough courage to knock on Jean's door. I hadn't been able to get another job and so I couldn't pay the rent. I didn't want to worry my brother again and I couldn't very well go home to my mother and father. I had packed my case said goodbye to Walthamstow and here I was. I hadn't planned to come here, I just ended up here. As I lugged my case past the house for the umpteenth time the door opened and Jean's mum came down the crumbling steps. She looked at me then started to walk past me.

I plucked up courage, "Hello fancy seeing you again."

She stopped and turned around looked at me, then smiled, "Well bless my soul, it's one of the fairies. Sorry luv, my manners are shocking. One of the gay boys I should have said. What brings you round here then?" She looked at my case.

"Oh, nothing," was my reply, then trying to sound casual, "I didn't realise you lived here – it seems different in the daylight."

"Is that a fact, well apart from some little sod smashing one of my windows with his ball," (she pointed at the pane of glass with a large jagged hole in it, covered from the inside with a piece of cardboard) "I can assure you nothing has changed but I can see it has with you. What's the matter, had a lovers' tiff? e thrown you out has 'e?"

I had to think who "he" was for a minute – of course, Kevin. "Yes, something like that," I lied (again).

"Well 'e's not much of a loss is 'e. I mean he didn't have much did 'e?" She laughed her phlegmy cough. "So I suppose you got no job and no home and what's more no money. Is that about right?"

"Yes," I nodded, "that's just right." She walked back up the steps again and took a key from the pocket of her cheap fur fabric coat.

"Come on then, come in. Now you're here you might as well stay."

I was given the small box room to sleep in. Jean and her mother shared the only other bedroom and if either of them had a 'guest' then the other would sleep on a camp bed in the kitchen. I unpacked my case and Mrs Smith (Jean's mum) called out that a cup of tea was waiting for me in the "lounge". I went into the front room, Mrs Smith or Smithy as I was to call her, was sitting at the Formica table pouring tea from a large brown teapot.

"I suppose you're skint." I nodded, I told her I wasn't only skint, I was flat broke.

"'Ere, get this cuppa down yer. I 'ave to go out – I won't be long."

She handed me a cup of tea, picked up her coat from where it lay on the settee and was gone. I sat at the blue table and drank my tea. I looked around the room – seeing it for the first time in daylight. It was a bit shabby, to say the least but it could, with thought and a bit of paint and paper – even with the pushbike parked in the hall – look quite nice, if a bit cluttered.

I helped myself to a second cup of tea and read the Daily Mirror, if you can read the Daily Mirror. The only thing I found at all to read and enjoy was the cartoon strip "The Flutters". I heard the front door slam and Smithy came back into the room, she had been gone about forty-five minutes at the most.

"All right? Had your tea?" She took her coat off and threw it back on the settee, then she rooted around in a large black plastic handbag and thrust some notes into my hand.

"'Ere, take this, pay me back when you can."

I looked into my hand and saw ten pounds, ten whole pounds! "But I can't, I can't take your money," I stammered, "it's not right."

"Who said it's not right? I earned that money. Anyway, it's just a loan till you get straight. Oh, sorry – on your feet I mean.

I laughed at her pun about getting straight. "But Smithy, I didn't come here to take your money, it's not my way."

"Now look 'ere young 'un, I've 'ad an 'ard life, I've 'ad two kids, although where my boy is God only knows. He left home two years ago, said 'e couldn't stand my way of life. All right, I understand that, but 'e could write couldn't 'e?"

I looked into her eyes and unlike her mouth which was hard, they were soft and brown and quickly filling with tears. I nodded and thought of my own mother.

"Well, 'e don't, I've 'ad to bring up the kids as best I can. I've 'ad no man to 'elp me. Well, only my 'clients' and they don't care about the kids – all they care about is their own requirements."

"Clients?" I thought, "requirements, Christ! She's a pro, an old brass, a prostitute! No, she can't be." I looked at her, she was still talking, the tears that had filled her eyes were now spreading onto her cheeks. I didn't hear a word she said. I just kept staring at her and thought, "Who for Christ sake would pay her? She's an old hag."

Suddenly she jabbed her finger into my ribs and I heard her clearly as she hissed, "What the bleedin' 'ell are you staring at?" Then, "Oh my Lord, you didn't know, you didn't know about me and Jean."

"Shit," I thought, "and Jean."

"What must you think of me, what sort of person must you take me for?"

"A real lady," I said surprising myself, "a real lady, anyone who cares that much for her kids is all right in my book. I just can't take your money Smithy, but I'll make a deal. Lend me the money and I'll do the flat up for you."

Her eyes lit up. "What, decorate this dump for me?"

"Yes, of course for you."

"Do you mean it?"

"Yes, I mean it." She got up and put her coat on again.

"You got a deal," she said.

"Well, where are you going?"

"Going? I've got to get enough tonight to pay for the paper and paint, I'm going—" she paused, "I'm going to work."

She really was a tart with a heart. I did as I said and decorated the whole flat. I found myself a job in a local factory, dipping metal in sulphuric acid all day. It was laborious work but the pay was OK. Out of my pay I bought settee cushions, curtains and a couple of rugs for the flat. Smithy was chuffed. Jean was not so pleased, she seemed to resent my being there. Not long after I moved in, James swiftly broke off their engagement and Jean blamed me. Why, I don't know, because I certainly didn't have anything to do with it.

Both she and Smithy started bringing clients home. I didn't really care, but I came home from work to find two or three men in the lounge or "waiting room" as Smithy called it and in a small flat it was a bit much.

On Saturdays I used to go to Stamford Bridge dog track. I would spend two or three quid and as a rule would come out winning, sometimes ten or twenty. I really loved the dogs. I would stand on the side of the track jumping up and down yelling my head off, "Come on four, come on you silly bastard," all on my own. I felt equal there. All those people and they all had the same chance as me, and when I won I really felt great. I had beaten them at their own game. It was a strange way to look at things.

One Saturday, when I was going to put a bet on at the Tote, the young guy in front of me was taking an age to explain his bet. The hare was due to run any second.

"Come on mate, hurry up, the hare's ready."

"I can't understand him," the girl behind the wire mesh said to me, "he's foreign."

"Stick it all on two for him and put a quid on for me."

"Will he mind?" she said.

"If he doesn't understand and he's foreign, he won't know, will he?"

"Suit yourself, love," she said, looking at the foreign guy, and smiling, "but if the last of the big spenders 'ere loses 'is shirt, DON'T blame me, you hear?" I laughed, took the tickets, gave the foreign bloke his, and went down towards the track. The lights dimmed, the race was about to start, the 'hare' went zooming around the track. As it came past the dog traps, the cry went up, "they're off!" As the dogs left their traps, mine got a good start, but they soon bunched up with mine in the middle. I always loved greyhound racing, still do, even though my mother would not have approved. My Dad was a gambler, and a bad one at that, he would study form for hours on end, buying all the racing papers he could get his hands on, but he seldom won. If he did my mother never knew. They would row about it, it did no good. My Dad always thought that one day he would hit the jackpot – he never did of course. With me it was different, I never expected to win, so I didn't gamble that much, I'd start with a couple of quid, and if I won I'd keep the winnings and play with the stake money again, but I would never spend anything I'd won, so I wasn't really the bookmaker's friend, unlike my father who, along, with many others was.

The dog I backed was still in the middle, bunched up with the rest, I jumped up and down yelling at the top of my voice, "come on TWO!" or whatever number it was that I had backed. I would lose all my shyness, I was completely unaware of what was going on around me, normally I wouldn't have said boo to a goose, but while the race was on, I'd go barmy (I've been told since, that I can be quite an embarrassment at a dog track, and I daresay at one or two other places!!)

My dog scraped home, and I must have looked like the cat that got the cream as I walked back to the pay window. All about me people were tearing up tickets, and throwing them on the floor in disgust, swearing as they did so, "bloody two dog, came from nowhere – did you see that two dog? cost me money 'e has." Unlucky punters were bemoaning their losses, or giving their mates the benefit of their own expertise, albeit a bit late: "You should have backed it each way like me mate, I don't take no chances."

Me, I was still grinning from ear to ear as I pushed my ticket through the window marked "Paying Only". It was then that I became aware of somebody at my side tugging at my sleeve. I turned and there was the foreigner I had helped (if unwittingly) earlier. "Yes, yes," he said, pushing his ticket into my face, "money, yes?" He too was grinning broadly.

"Oh yes," I laughed, as I took the ticket and pushed: it under the wire window with mine, "money you most certainly have," and I put a pile of notes in his hand, topping it up with a few shillings. "There you are, fifteen quid and a bit of shrapnel," a lot of money in the late 50s. He took the money, then he looked into my face and for the first time I had a good look at him. He was about my age, maybe a bit younger, blue eyes, fair skin and hair, straight pure white teeth, a brilliant smile, and oh so very good-looking. I just stared at him, my heart skipped a beat, in fact several beats. By this time people in the queue behind me started getting upset. "Oi! 'Urry up for gawd's sake – come on, get a move on." The foreigner took my arm and led me to the bar, I let myself be pulled along, but I got back my composure by the time we were at the bar. He was trying to order a drink without much success. I bought myself a large brandy and a light and bitter for my new-found friend, we found a table, and I tried to find out who he was. I was getting nowhere fast when we were joined at the table by a large middle-aged woman, she was very well dressed and spoke to the foreign bloke very rapidly in a language I had never heard. While they were talking they both kept glancing at me, pointing and laughing, I thought they were taking the piss, so I got up to leave – the woman put her hand out to stop me.

"Please, do not leave," she spoke very good English with a thick accent, "please do sit," she waved a gloved hand towards the chair. I sat down. "I am told you have been very kind, this young man is Imrech Ish, Hungarian."

"Hungarian?" I thought, "Hungarian?"

She interrupted my thoughts, "you look a little surprised, no?"

"No, I mean yes, I suppose I am a bit." This was after all 1958, and you didn't meet many foreigners in the ordinary way in England at that time.

"I have lived here for many years," she was saying, "Imrech only a short while, there has been some trouble at home for him, you understand?"

Trouble, I thought, some trouble. It was in 1956 that the Hungarian people rose up against their Russian masters, who ruled Hungary with the aid of a puppet government, that was until a brave man, Imre Nagy, took over as leader of the Hungarian people, he stood against the might of Russia. Students came onto the streets in support of Nagy, soon ordinary Hungarians also saw the chance of freedom, and they joined the students in a bid to rid themselves of the yoke of dictatorship. It was a brave and valiant attempt, that fight for freedom, but alas it failed, with the loss of hundreds of lives. I don't suppose anyone will know just how many. The Russians, faced with the will of an oppressed people, brought the full might and fury of the Red Army down to bear on the entire population. Tanks were brought onto the streets, all the people had were home-made weapons, plus sticks and stones and

Molotov cocktails, and a few light small arms. They fought hard, the outside world even thought they might win, or at least get some concessions, but the battle was lost almost before it had started, there was no way the Russians were going to lose face. Nagy was arrested, and the freedom fighters rounded up and imprisoned, or simply shot. Many of course fled their homeland, in fear of their lives, preferring to live in exile, rather than, under Russian rule. The young guy opposite me now was, I suspected, one of the latter.

"Christ!", I almost screamed, "were you in the uprising?"

"Please!" Miss Gross, put her hand to her mouth, "please, he cannot understand you, we do not talk of such things, he has been in this country only a very short time, wounds do not heal in such a short time, do you understand me?"

I felt myself redden, stupid bastard! I thought. "I'm sorry, it was tactless of me – please, I didn't mean to cause offence."

She smiled and Imrech smiled as well. "There is no need for you to apologise, but thank you anyway, you see there are not many Hungarians of Imrech's age here in London, he has not many friends here you see? so he comes here," she waved her still gloved hand around the room. "I can't say I approve," she sighed then smiled again, "but he has been through much, so why not. He told me that you were kind to him and that you made him laugh. Maybe you will meet him again next week, here in the bar yes?"

I was a bit taken aback. "Why yes, yes of course, I'll meet him here at this same table, if that's OK?" She spoke to Imrech in Hungarian of course, pointing to me then the table, and smiling all the time, he broke out in a huge grin, looked at me, then they both stood up, she held out her hand and I shook it.

"Thank you, you have made him very happy – oh, I don't even know your name."

"It's Ricky," I said. She told Imrech my name, he tried to pronounce it, and we all laughed.

"We must go, I shall not be here next week, but I hope to see you very soon." She walked away. Imrech put out his hand, I took it and squeezed it gently, he did the same, smiled and followed Miss Gross. As they got to the door he turned and waved, I waved back, he paused, then was gone, I sat down. "Bloody hell," I thought, "what a turn-up", then the negative thoughts started. "Bet he won't be here next week, it's all a wind-up." Then I thought, "Well, wind-up or not I'm going to be here," and I couldn't wait.

The following Saturday, just as I was leaving home, Smithy asked me where I was going. When I told her, she of course wanted to come with me, I made excuse after excuse as to why she couldn't or shouldn't come. She didn't say anything, she didn't have to, I could see the hurt in her eyes. I supposed she thought I was ashamed of her, that I didn't want to be seen with her, and to my shame that was partly true.

"Look Smithy, I don't know how long I'll be, I might even have to go somewhere after," she simply looked at me and nodded. I knew I had hurt her, why didn't I just tell her the truth? The truth was I was scared, scared that he wouldn't be there, then I'd go into a fit of depression and self-doubt and probably take it out on her. But of course, if he was there, I wouldn't want Smithy, or anybody else around to spoil it. Either way, she would come off badly. She sat down at the table and stared out of the window, she looked suddenly very old and frail. I went to the kitchen and made her a cup of tea. When I came back into the room with the tea, she was still sitting looking out of the window.

Without turning her head, she said, "I'm a silly old cow, I was young once," she looked up at me and laughed her phlegmy laugh. "I bet you find that 'ard to believe eh?" I put the tea down in front of her, and put my arms around her scrawny shoulders, then I kissed her lightly on her head.

"You're not a silly cow, and you're not that old, it's just that today I need some space, OK?"

As I left the flat I still wished I had told her the truth, at least then she would have been able to make up her own mind as to whether I was ashamed of her or not. All this argy-bargy had made me late. I ran through the turnstiles and raced up the steps to the bar. The table where we had arranged to meet was empty. My heart jumped, I looked at my watch, I was nearly forty minutes late. "Shit," I said out loud, I looked over at the bar and the other tables, there was no sign of him. Then I saw him, he was looking out of the huge windows overlooking the track, looking for me, I hoped! I went up behind him, "Hi," I almost whispered, "sorry I'm late, couldn't get a bus." He spun round so fast he spilt his beer all over me, he was trying to brush me down and speak all at the same time. I caught his hand, took the pint put it on a table, his blue eyes seemed to sparkle.

"You come, it's very good," he was shaking my hand with such force I thought he might shake it off. We sat down at the table, then I went to the bar and got more drinks, I really did need a large brandy. We spent the whole of that afternoon trying to understand each other, we had a few bets, but I couldn't concentrate on the racing – I couldn't keep my eyes off my new friend. I tried to ask him what his name was in English, he, of course, didn't understand what the hell I was talking about, so I told him I would call him Fred, which in retrospect was a bloody cheek. I just thought it easier to call him Fred, he didn't seem to mind, in fact, he thought it very funny, as he said "Fred" over and over again to himself. We left the dog track and went for a meal to a nice but cheap Italian restaurant in the Fulham Palace Road.

We sat at a window table, and just talked and ate, it was strange, because although his English wasn't very good, and my Hungarian non-existent, we seemed to have an empathy with each other. I found out that he worked at a factory, doing what I didn't know, then he told me about his family, mother, father, brothers and sisters, and that he didn't know when he would see them again. He wouldn't (or couldn't) talk about Hungary, or how he came to leave, and I didn't press the point. We left the restaurant and went to a pub not far from where Fred worked, once there he then started to ask me about my life, then came the question I dreaded most. "You have girlfriend?" he asked in a casual way, but as he did so he looked at me while taking a sip of his beer, his eyes fixing on mine. I felt myself flush, the colour seemed to rush to my cheeks, they felt red hot. As a kid I had a bad stammer and now this came back with a vengeance.

"Er-er no," was all I could get out.

"No me," he said, pointing to himself, and laughing "no me, it's good yes?"

"Oh yes," I said, "it's very good." Suddenly I started talking thirty-three to the dozen, stammering and stuttering like I hadn't done for a long while. My stammer had been the blight of my life, ever since I could remember, I had been cursed with it. I had tried very hard to lose it. Singing with jazz bands had helped, and over the last couple of years, I had learned how to speak without falling over words. It was hard work, it meant my slowing down my speech, and thinking of the next word before I said it, and trying only to use 'safe' words. One of the reasons for my childhood being so miserable was my stammer – other kids would laugh and taunt me, sometimes trying to make me say words that I couldn't get my tongue round. It didn't stop at other kids, adults could be just as cruel. School was a nightmare for me, and one teacher at the secondary school I went to after failing my eleven-plus, was to me then and still is now the most evil of the lot. His name was Peacock, he taught French, a thin man of about thirty with an angular face, dark eyes set back, thick black hair that kept falling over his eyes, making him keep flicking it back. His worst feature was his mouth, it was just a thin line on his long face, a thin wicked line that would suddenly gape open and out would pour words full of venom.

For reasons best known to himself, he hated me, and to show that hatred he would ask me a question right at the beginning of the lesson. "Right now, let me see – yes, yes you boy," – he never called me by name always "you boy" – he would then point a long bony finger at me, then shout "Stand up, boy!" He would then ask a question that I knew I wouldn't be able to answer, even before he asked it, I might even know the answer, but I knew it wouldn't ever come from my lips. My brain would swirl, I'd sweat, my heart beating so loudly I thought all the rest of the kids must surely be able to hear it. "Come on boy, get your brain in gear!" he would yell at the top of his thin whiny voice. The other kids would start to snigger, this seemed to urge him on. "Come on boy spit it out, you'll stand there for the whole lesson until you do answer."

I would pray that the ground would open up and swallow me, or I'd wish I could just die there and then, or better still that he would die. I hated him then and I still do to this very day, he was a sadistic bastard, but his sort are still around today, maybe even reading this, and laughing to themselves at the picture of my discomfort, or writing articles in the national newspapers, about people like me, calling us the "Gay Plague" and blaming us for all that's wrong in the world, instead of looking into their own thoughts and cleansing themselves of their own bitterness and bigotry.

The sad thing is that Peacock and those of his ilk are looked upon as pillars of society, men and women in positions of power in the Church, the media, politics, and the police. The very people, in fact, who should be putting their energy into understanding other people's views and lifestyles, and trying to educate people. I don't mean by this forcing folk to like certain other groups, or condoning wrongdoing, or making special laws for minority groups, I simply mean, educate people to understand others. I have never believed in demos or gay rights marches, most gays that I know live a quiet life with a partner, and regret the image of us that has been so eagerly used by the media to paint us all the same colour.

The bell in the pub rang time. I stopped gabbing. Fred looked nonplussed. "Sorry," I said meekly, he shrugged his shoulders and grinned, what I wanted to say to him was that I was glad he didn't have a girlfriend and that I wanted him to come back with me, but, now it was too late – the bell had gone and we were being asked to leave. We got up and went outside. It was getting cold and there was an awkward silence between us. Then he took my arm and said, "You come home, my house?" he squeezed my arm.

I put my arm around his shoulder and said "Yes." We walked back down the Fulham Palace Road until we came to a corner shop. Fred opened the door at the side of the shop and in we went. With him in the lead I followed, up and up and up until I thought I'd go dizzy, at last we reached the top. Fred opened the door of the attic flat. We walked straight into the bedsitting room, the ceiling went up in a point, rather like a pyramid. The only window was a fanlight in the ceiling, the walls and the ceiling were of featherboard painted cream. Because I was so tall I kept hitting my head on the sloping roof, which amused Fred. Against the only straight wall stood a green and brown moquette-covered settee, the rest of the furniture consisted of a wardrobe, a small chest of drawers and two fireside chairs, placed either side of an electric fire. Although nothing really matched, everything shone and was spotlessly clean.

"It's great, really nice."

"You like?" he said with some hesitation, "sure?"

"Very sure, is this all?" I asked him. At that, he took my arm and showed me the small kitchen and a bathroom, all gleaming, almost as if they had been expecting company. While Fred made coffee, I went back into the living room and sat in one of the fireside chairs. As I looked around the room, I could feel that something was missing but I couldn't think what.

He brought the coffee out and sat in the other chair, then he asked me a strange thing. "Please Ricky, you my friend, yes?"

I nodded. "Yes, of course."

He nodded back, "Then please to tell no people where I live."

"Well of course I won't," I said, "but is there a reason?" Then he went on to tell me, that he didn't really trust people. Not me! now he did trust me, but at first I could have been anybody, even an informer! An informer! what the hell was he talking about? This was England, land of the free. He assured me that I was the first person to come to his home, he trusted me but nobody else, not anybody, even other Hungarians. It seemed that some of those who had left Hungary as refugees were in fact informers, working for the Soviet-controlled regime back in Hungary. They tracked down freedom fighters and those who had given their support, then blackmailed them into going back to Hungary by threatening the lives and well-being of the families and loved ones they had left behind. Many people had gone back after being told of loved ones who were sick, or in need of their help. When they went back, they were never seen or heard of again.

It all sounded too far-fetched for words, he must be going a bit over the top I thought. I mean, informers, spies, I couldn't imagine it. I knew about Burgess and McClean, but that was different, they were spying and informing on their own country, not on students and sympathizers. Still, I listened while he told me all this, and you could sense the fear as he spoke, at one point I thought he would burst into tears, I got out of my chair and put my hand on his shoulder. "I'll make some tea," I said, then I thought, what a typical English thing to say. Someone is breaking their heart, feels that all is lost, thinks they may never see their family again, and I say I'll make some bloody tea! "Don't upset yourself, one day tell me all about it, you'll feel better then, but only tell it when you are ready."

I'm not sure if he understood any of what I had said, but he put his hand on mine and squeezed it firmly. After the umpteenth cup of coffee or tea, I said goodnight and left, as he showed me out he shook my hand, and I said I would see him the following week at the dogs. As he closed the door I wanted to bang on it and ask him to let me stay, but I lacked the nerve. I walked home, wrapped up in my thoughts.

I went on meeting Fred most Saturdays unless he or I had to work. My job was becoming more and more arduous and hating it didn't help. I started getting careless and came close to getting badly burnt by the caustic solution I was using. Sitting in the bar at the track, one Saturday afternoon, I was telling Fred about another narrow escape I had that morning with the caustic. He said it was very dangerous, and I said only if you didn't take care, he then asked why I did such a job, and I replied with only one word, "money."

"But you can earn money better no?"

"Well, it's not that easy," I said, "there's not much work for someone like me with no training."

Then he said matter-of-factly, "Come work with me." I looked at him. "Sure," he said, "why not, we have place for one."

"There's a vacancy at your place?" then I had to explain what the word vacancy meant, but it turned out that a bloke had left that Friday night after a row with his boss.

"So you come. I ask boss, yes?"

"Yes, oh yes, you ask boss," was my delighted reply, "that is if you don't mind, I mean if you think—" I was rambling again.

"Calm, keep calm," he laughed, "this is no problem." I went to the bar and got refills, when I came back we toasted my would-be new job, that I hadn't even got!

"When you work with me," he was saying, "means we go more places, yes?"

He was right. "Of course we can, many more places."

"That very good," he said, and we then both got very pissed.

Two or three days later I received a letter from the factory where Fred worked, asking me to go for an interview. I got dressed to the nines. Smithy asked where the hell I was going: "You look like a pox doctor's clerk in that lot."

"Well thanks for nothing, that coming from the Princess Margaret of Chelsea, really had me worried!" She coughed on her fag.

"I'm only taking the piss, you look very 'andsome. You meeting that bloke of yours?"

She caught me unawares. "Bloke," I said as casually as I could, "what bloke?"

"You must think I come up on the down train, you've been walking on air these past few weeks, and all you talk about is some geezer called Fred, now if Fred ain't a bloke, I'll show my arse in Woolworths"." She coughed again and cackled like an old hen.

"Well, you've shown it everywhere else, so why not Woolworths!"

She aimed a mangy slipper at me. "Go on, you cheeky young sod, go and see lover boy."

I found the factory, tucked down a side road in Fulham. The area was a mixture of terraced houses, shops and small factories and workshops. The factory I was looking for turned out to be a hodgepodge of small sheds, with a larger, more substantial building in the middle. I rubbed my hands over my clothes and walked through a pair of dilapidated wooden gates, which bore the words "Wilkinson and Gross" in faded paintwork. Underneath, it read, "Injection moulders." I had no idea what that was. I made my way to the main factory, a two-storey building, the noise from machines being my guide. As I entered the noise was deafening, I saw about a half a dozen machines, all of which looked different. They were manned by young guys about my age, some maybe a few years older. Nobody took any notice of me so I picked my way through, then I saw Fred. I yelled his name, but the noise of the machine drowned it out. I was almost on top of him when he spotted me. Beckoning me, he pointed to a door marked "Private" at the back of the workshop, I followed him through the door as it closed with a thud behind me the silence was deafening. "Christ," I said, "what a bloody din!"

"Din? what is din?" he asked me.

"That bloody noise!"

Smiling, he said, "you get used—"

"I bloody well hope," I said as he steered me down the corridor, with its cream-coloured walls covered with posters warning about the dangers of using machines without the guards being in place. We arrived at a door, with a polished wooden nameplate that proclaimed that this was the office of "M Gross". Fred tapped lightly on the door, and a voice from within bid us "enter." Fred led the way into the office. It was a complete contrast to the rest of the factory, the walls were wood-panelled, with bookcases on two walls, and a large polished wooden desk stood in front of the window. Behind the desk sat a middle-aged woman with neat hair, she was wearing a twinset and pearls. I blinked and looked at her again.

"Hello," she smiled, "so we meet again." It was the lady I had met at the dog track, the day I met Fred.

I babbled "Hello". she spoke to Fred in Hungarian, and he left the office.

"Please sit down," she pointed to a high back chair, "you look a little surprised to see me." I nodded. She then told me that she ran the factory with her elderly parents and that practically all the staff were Hungarian. It was, she said, their way of helping their fellow countrymen. Although most of the staff were Hungarian, Imrech was the only new arrival, the others being either born here or having been here for many years.

"Now it seems I have an Englishman that needs my help, you are English?" I nodded. "Imrech has told me many things about you, and your friendship." I must have looked a little alarmed. "Oh, don't worry, they were all good things," she reassured me. "He tells me you have a bad job. Well, there is a vacancy here for an injection moulder, have you done this?"

I shook my head. "'Fraid not."

She shrugged. "It's not a problem, you will learn. So now I hope I have made two people happy."

"Two?" I asked.

"Yes, firstly you, then your friend. You have a new job and he has been asking me for ages to find you something here, so now it is done." She rose from her chair. "It is good to see you again, I hope you are happy here." After hearing about the wages and the working conditions, I left the office. Fred was hanging about outside, when he saw my face, his lit up, we embraced very briefly, and he went back to work.

I started work there about a week later. Fred and I had celebrated my good fortune the previous Saturday by getting drunk then sobering up as usual at his place, and as usual, I left him and went back to Smithy's. Nothing had happened between us yet, and he showed no signs that anything would. It was making me uneasy, so I made my mind up that this would be just a straightforward friendship! I started comparing him to Alf. I'd loved Alf and lost him – or at least let him go – because I couldn't cope with him being straight. I was not about to make the same mistake twice, friendship was, after all, better than no relationship.

Getting to my new job was a bit of a problem, it meant a lot of mucking about on buses, and took quite a time. Then one day my problem was solved. My machine was so placed that Fred and I worked back to back. I was having trouble getting used to the work, my hands were soft, and pulling hot plastic off the moulds burnt them red raw. On this particular day, they were painful and I was having trouble getting an obstinate piece from the mould. Fred must have heard me cursing and did it for me, then he gave me some cream for my hands and bought me a cup of tea. As we stood there drinking our tea, he suddenly said, "You like to come and stay my house?"

"Sure," I said, "you want to go somewhere tonight?"

He half turned away, and lowered his eyes, then said quietly, "Not just tonight, you want to live at my house, with me?" My heart nearly skipped two beats.

"Move in with you? course I do!" I yelled this out, he turned round to face me, his finger on his lips.

"Ssh," he laughed, we looked around at the rest of the lads, and they were all either drinking tea or working, nobody had heard my outburst.

"So you mean it? you come live with me? we good friends?"

I took his arm. "Yes, I mean it, I will come, and yes we are VERY good friends."

After work that night, we went to the pub for a drink, then I told him about Smithy, and that I just couldn't move there and then, it wouldn't be fair, at first he didn't understand, had I changed my mind? What was so important about this woman? I tried to explain, I went through the whole thing, chattering away at what must have seemed breakneck speed for an Englishman to understand, let alone a Hungarian who had only been in the country a short while and whose English was not much better than my French – and I couldn't order a cup of tea in French! He just sat there nodding and looking as though he at least understood the gist of what I was saying. When I had finished, he said, "You must not hurt this lady." I thanked him for understanding, and he asked if I wanted him to come with me. I said that I didn't think it was a good idea, but I would like very much for the two of us to take Smithy out one night as a sort of thank you. He liked the idea very much – I think it gave some sort of reassurance that I was not keeping him in the background. Another reason for my not wanting him to come with me was simply that I knew it was going to be difficult making Smithy understand, and the sight of him would probably provoke language that would make a trooper blush!

By the time I got home that night I'd got cold feet, so I decided to tell her in the morning. I got up quite early and cooked a breakfast, and laid it out on a tray, then took it to her room. "Wot the bleeding 'ell's going on? Breakfast in bed? Something's wrong, you got bad news for me ain't yer? Who's dead? That's it, someone's died."

"Hey," I said. "will you give it a rest, I've only brought you breakfast for crying out loud."

She sniffed. "What time is it?"

I looked at my watch. "Nearly seven."

"Seven! in the morning?" I nodded. "Christ, I'm usually coming 'ome at this time, not getting up!"

"Just sit up and eat, will you?"

"Give me me bedjacket then." I didn't think I heard right.

"Bedjacket?"

"Yes, over there." She pointed to a heap of dirty washing, old magazines and God knows what else. I found an old cardigan, full of holes and smelling none too fresh. I held it up.

"This it?" She said it was, so I put it around her thin shoulders, and she started to eat. I was about to tell her my news, but the sight and sound of her, sloshing food around her mouth trying to eat without her false teeth was too much for me. I left her to it and went to work.

I came home that night with a bunch of flowers. "Is it my bleeding birthday? Breakfast this morning and now flowers, what's up? Come on, tell me." So I told her, she looked hurt, and then she cried, "Wot's the matter, ain't I good enough anymore?" She broke her heart, I put my arms around her, and drew her to me. She sobbed, "I thought I was yer mate."

"You are, and much much more, but I love this guy, and I want to be with him, please try to understand."

She pushed herself from me, tears were streaming down her cheeks. She took a grubby handkerchief from her pocket and wiped her eyes. "What must you think of me, silly old tart, I suppose," then she went into a fit of coughing. I lit a cigarette and gave it to her – it always seemed to help, don't ask me why, but it did – anyway, she stopped coughing.

"I really did like you being 'ere, yer know, better than me own son, you are, you treat me like I'm someone."

"But you are someone," I told her, then I put my arm around her again. "Look, if it wasn't for Fred, I wouldn't leave you, you must know that."

"Well bring 'im 'ere then." she sobbed again.

"It wouldn't work, and you know it," I spoke softly to her, "you are my mate, you have been great to me, and you mean the world to me. It's not the end, we'll still see each other. I'll bring Fred round and we can all go out for a drink or something, I'm not going to the ends of the earth, only to Fulham! Come on, cheer up, tell you what – how about you and me going out now, up West, yes that's it, we'll go up West, and have tea at Lyons Corner House."

"What – like this?" she wailed.

"No! get yourself made up, best frock and shoes the works," I steered her towards her bedroom, "and don't forget to put some drawers on! it's your day off!"

She turned around and laughed. "You saucy sod, bet you wished it was you, what was puttin' drawers on!"

"Gert yer!" I said and made to chase her. She squealed with delight and disappeared into the chaos that was her bedroom. When she finally reappeared, she looked every inch a lady. She wore a blue and white polka dot dress, with a large white shawl collar, a small white straw hat, navy shoes and gloves to match.

"Got it for Jean's wedding," she said, "but fuck 'er – she don't really care about me. You do."

"You look stunning," I said, "Jean should be proud of you, I know I am. Come on, let's hit the town!"

She took my arm and we sauntered along the road, I didn't have much money but I was determined to do things in style, so I hailed a cab and we headed for the West End. After a walk along Oxford Street, we went into Selfridges and I bought her a small cameo brooch. She made me pin it on her dress there and then, she stood in the store beaming as though I had just pinned the Koh-I-Noor diamond on her dress instead of a thirty-bob brooch.

Still grinning and admiring her new treasure, we went into Lyons Corner House and had tea while a string quartet played songs from the shows. Smithy loved every minute and drank it all in as though it were liquid gold. Nobody seeing her sitting there in that room in her new dress, sipping tea and swaying gently as the quartet played Ivor Novello tunes, would ever believe the sort of sordid grubby life she led, and I doubt many would care.

The following week I left Smithy. I bought her flowers and she held them to her as she stood waving and crying until I was out of sight. I felt sad. Smithy had been good to me and I would miss her. Soon, however, I was at Fred's door. As I rang the doorbell I was puffing and panting after lugging my cases up three floors. I waited but the door remained closed. I rang the doorbell again my heart beating a little faster now. Still Fred didn't answer, my heart was now pounding. I broke out into a cold sweat and now I was banging on the door calling his name. What the hell was wrong, where was he? "I know," I thought, as the tears came and I kept my finger on the bell push, "he has changed his mind, he doesn't want me to come after all, what should I do? I can't go back to Smithy, my stupid pride wouldn't let me, what then?" I banged and kicked at the door swearing and cussing, the tears stinging my eyes, then I stopped banging at the door and tried to calm myself down so that I could think clearly. I lit a Piccadilly No I, took a long draw on it, sat down on my case and tried to think, but my head was still in a whirl. Suddenly a hand grabbed at my shoulder: I nearly jumped out of my skin. As I yelled in fright I turned round to see Fred grinning down at me with a bunch of flowers held tightly in one hand.

"For you. I am sorry I was not here on time but I could not find flowers."

I stood up and thanked him as I took the flowers, I just hoped he couldn't see that I had been making a fool of myself. We went into the flat and I started to unpack as Fred fussed around. As I unpacked some mementoes I had collected over the years, a tankard, small bits of china and some framed photos, I suddenly realised what it was that was missing from Fred's flat – photos, there weren't any photos. I looked at him as he carefully put my things away. Here he was, twenty-three in a strange country, and although he knew a few fellow countrymen he was completely alone. I wanted to put my arms around him and tell him how I felt but I couldn't and what's more, I dared not.

After we had unpacked, we went out to the same Italian restaurant we went to for our first meal together and had ourselves a celebration dinner. We ate a lot and got drunk, not silly drunk but a mellow kind of drunk. By the time we got back to the flat, it was late and I was very tired what with the excitement of moving, saying goodbye to Smithy, finding him out and then the meal. I was ready to sleep on a clothesline!

Fred pulled the bed-settee down, put on some bed linen and said, "Sleep my friend, you need sleep." I thought that the bed converted into two single beds but this was a small double bed, I had wanted to sleep with him of course but I knew that if I did sooner or later I would make a move towards him and that would ruin everything he would hate me and throw me out.

"Oh God," I thought "what shall I do? Maybe he has a spare Put-U-Up in the kitchen. "Look," I stammered, "I can't take your bed, it's-it's—" I was stammering and stuttering, falling over words like lemmings falling over a cliff tumbling and stumbling in an endless stream.

"No! No! Ricky, please be calm, do not upset yourself", he put his hand on mine and led me to the bed, "please you rest, everything fine, you rest, I promise everything fine." Then he disappeared into the kitchen and I could hear him banging and clanging about.

"Jesus, now what have I done?" my tiredness having now vanished, "how can I live here like this? He is straight, he has to be, I should have kept my place at Smithy's or somewhere near Fred, but not here – it's going to cause too many problems." I undressed and got into bed, determined that the next day I would tell Fred and together we would sort it. I pulled the cord over the bed-head, the light went out and the moonlight streamed in through the little window in the roof above me. I lay there for about half an hour trying to think of the best way of approaching Fred in the morning, then I heard the kitchen door open and close. I looked towards it and saw Fred silhouetted in the moonlight. I half closed my eyes feigning sleep. He smiled, then slowly undressed putting his clothes on top of mine. He stood again and looked at me, then he pulled back the covers and got in beside me. My heart by this time was beating so loudly I wondered I hadn't woken up people in the next street! I was lying on my back, he lay on his side facing me, he was very still and so was I. All I could hear was the beating of my heart and his warm breath on my cheek. That's how we stayed for what seemed an eternity, then he swore softly and said something in Hungarian, then he was moving closer I felt his lips on my cheek and he gently kissed me and at the same time put his arm over me. I turned to face him, my eyes wide open in disbelief. He was shocked he pulled away and swore loudly this time. "You not angry I kiss you? You not hate me I kiss you?" I didn't say a word, I just put my arms around him and pulled him towards me my tongue searching for his mouth then we both exploded with emotion, half-laughing half-crying. We explored each other, him pouring out words of Hungarian, and me doing the same in English, neither of us understanding a word each other was saying but knowing only too well what each other meant. It was the start of a love affair I would cherish all my life, and it would not be until I was in my late forties that I would meet someone who would make me feel the same way only more so – that is, not just loved but needed and valued, but there and then it was something I had never before experienced.

The next few months were magical, we would go to work together but always had to be careful in case our secret came out. This was, after all, still only the 1950s and homosexuality was not talked about, let alone accepted by the man in the street or anybody else for that matter. It was just something that happened in the Sunday papers or the sort of thing that people made jokes about. I can't think of anybody I knew then who would have admitted to knowing a homosexual, let alone being friends with one, so once again I was to find myself making up stories about our conquests with women. Fred gladly went along with this – he feared that if we were ever found out he would be deported. That may sound a little over the top today, but then, well, we were both under twenty-one, and anything was possible.

So none of our workmates ever guessed that we were in fact lovers, and in truth instead of being out all night pulling birds, we spent most of our time at home drinking Hungarian Bull's Blood and making love on the Put-U-Up. Sometimes, of course, we would go out for a meal or to a pub. We had no gay friends, we didn't know any other people like ourselves, nor were we aware that even then London had dozens of gay pubs and clubs. As far as we were concerned, we were on our own, and it didn't matter somehow, it made what we had together more exciting, the 'forbidden fruit' (if you'll pardon the pun) syndrome I suppose. Anyway, we didn't need or even want anybody else to know in case they tried to spoil it or debase it, that's how we wanted things, we had our own private world and that's how we wanted to keep it. I'm not sure how either one of us would have reacted had we been found out or how we would have coped. Undoubtedly we would have lost our jobs – even Miss Gross would have had no choice but to sack us. She might or might not have wanted to, but the rest of the workforce would have made both our lives and hers a misery, and in all probability put us in some danger of attack. So by keeping it secret, we wouldn't have to face that problem, but it was something I was later to regret.

During those months Fred wrote repeatedly to Hungary trying to find news of his family, it was during this time that he told me some but by no means all of what he went through when the Russian tanks rolled into Budapest in 1956. When the government of Imre Nagy finally fell to the invading Russian Army, Fred was one of the thousands of Hungarians forced to flee for their lives. To stay would have meant certain death, he had led or been in raids on Russian tanks and Army patrols, throwing petrol bombs and stealing rifles and ammunition from dead and injured troops. He and his friends had fought hard and bitter battles in and around the university campus and in the streets of Budapest. Many of his friends died and his family fled Budapest. Fred stayed as long as he dared, finally he too left, travelling at night across country in a bid to escape to the West.

As he was telling me this I found it hard to comprehend. I had sat and watched this on television and movie newsreels and read about it in the press, but it didn't seem real. It was so far away, and simply looking or reading about such events can only give you a small insight at what is going on, not the full horror of bullets tearing through flesh and friends lying in dirt while their lifeblood seeps from their torn and shattered bodies. But now I could see it in Fred's eyes.

When Fred and a small group of friends finally made it to the border, they ran into a Russian border patrol. Two of his friends and a border guard died in the ensuing fight. Fred escaped but lost contact with the remaining survivors. It was months before he was able to get over the border, a Hungarian peasant family hid him until his final escape, clinging to the underside of a railway wagon.

After he had told me this, it made me wonder just how much pain and suffering the human body and mind can stand, and just what sort of people are they that can inflict that sort of brutality on someone and still sleep at night.

Some weeks later I was at my machine when Miss Gross came into the workshop and called Fred into her office, he came out about ten minutes later looking white and shaken. He said she wanted to see me, we both went back into her office, she was sitting behind her desk. She looked very upset, she spoke to Fred in Hungarian. He replied, sat down, and told me to do the same.

"I'm sorry to drag you away. Ricky" she spoke very softly. I knew by the sound of her voice that something was wrong very wrong, I looked at Fred, he just stared at the floor. I looked back at Miss Gross – the cheerful, bright woman had suddenly aged. "Imrech," she corrected herself, "Fred, as you will know, has been writing to Hungary for news of his family." I nodded. "Today I received this," she held up a letter, "it's from an aunt of his, with news that his mother is very sick and he should go to her, she says his mother is dying and his family needs him." My heart stopped. I grabbed Fred's hand out of sight of Miss Gross, his fingernails bit into my flesh.

"Where was the letter sent to?" I heard myself ask.

"To a Hungarian organisation here in London which looks after refugees, it is one of many such letters received each week."

"But is it true?" I asked. "Is his mother really ill? how can we be sure?" Fred's grip on my hand tightened even more, there was a long pause. Then she shook her head slowly.

"This we do not know, it may be so, maybe not. We cannot tell for certain." Once again there was silence. It was Fred who broke it, speaking in his native tongue, tears streaming down his face. Miss Gross, her eyes now filled with tears said, "He is afraid, but it could be true, he must go back, he fears she may die."

Then I just lost it. "NO! NO! HE CAN'T GO BACK! HE CAN'T! I WON'T LET HIM!" I yelled at the top of my voice. Fred put his arms around me, and Miss Gross came from behind her desk. She too put her hand on my arm and then spoke very softy to Fred. He got up from the chair and I could feel him pulling me up.

"You must be strong for your friend, Ricky, he will need you of all people to be strong." I looked at her and nodded. "Please take him home now. I will get you a taxi and I will see you later."

She called the cab, and we went home, him holding my hand, me just numb, but I remembered what she had said and I knew it was right. I did have to be strong for his sake not for mine, so I tried to jolly him up by saying things like, "By the time you get back I'll have the flat redecorated" and other stupid things too inane to mention. We got back to the flat. I made him some coffee and put in the last drop of brandy we had, he drank the coffee and I made him lay down. He slept until about eight o'clock when Miss Gross arrived.

"How is he?" she asked the question as though she already

knew the answer.

"Shattered – just shattered. He's hardly said a word, he will come back, won't he?"

She took my arm and kissed me on the cheek.

"I hope so, I really do hope so."

"Don't you know for sure? I mean you must know, he has to come back, he has to." I was starting to get almost hysterical.

"Ricky!" she was shaking me, "Ricky! you must stay calm. There is no way of my knowing the answer. Imrech must do what he thinks is best, and we have to support him, OK?"

I knew she was right of course, and I nodded my agreement, but I felt a huge black cloud of despair descend on me.

Two days later I packed his case. I had bought him a new one and we had been shopping together and got him some new clothes, we also bought some things for his family: a cardigan for his mum, a blouse for his sister and so on. I put a framed photo of the two of us, taken at work by one of the other guys, into the case pocket. He took it out and looked at it then at me.

"I come back I promise, I come back very soon, everything all right, promise," then he took the oval gold ring set with a cornelian from his finger and put it on mine. "We always together," then he held me close and we kissed and hugged, the tears now out of control. There was a knock on the door: it was Miss Gross, she was going to drive us to London airport. The journey to the airport was made in silence. Fred and I sat in the back of the little Morris Minor, our hands clasped together so tightly they ached, and my stomach was in knots. I could not believe what was happening – last week we hadn't a care in the world, now we were in the middle of a nightmare and our world was caving in on us. At the airport, everything seemed to be done at a rush, and almost before I knew it he was about to go into the departure lounge. He embraced Miss Gross and spoke to her in Hungarian, she looked at me, her eyes filling with tears, and nodded to him. Then he grinned at me and put both his arms around me and said softly, "Soon I will be home with you, there will be nobody else. I love you." We kissed right there and then – a very bold thing to do now, but then unheard of – but it didn't matter to us.

"I love you," I said, "please ring me when you arrive and write, please write."

He promised he would, then his last call came.

"And you'd better bring me back a stick of Hungarian rock, you bastard."

"Rock? what is rock?"

Miss Gross laughed and explained to him, he smiled and touched the ring he had given me, I took the gold chain I wore around my neck and put it round his, I kissed him again and said, "Don't be away too long." He smiled and as the tears welled up in his eyes he turned on his heel and was gone. I was never to see or hear from him again, but I will never forget him.

I went back and forth to work every day hoping for a letter of some news of Fred. Miss Gross was very kind to me, so were the other blokes at work. I don't know whether they had guessed our secret and felt sorry for us both or what, but they certainly did their best to get me out of myself, but I wouldn't respond and in the end they stopped trying. I just felt so empty, I wouldn't even go to the dog track, in fact I never went to Stamford Bridge again. The weeks and then months went by and I withdrew more and more into myself, so much so that by now I hardly spoke to anybody, and the only time I went out apart from work was to go to the off-licence for another bottle of Bull's Blood.

After one particularly heavy night, I must have looked awful. I certainly felt it. When I got to work Miss Gross called me into her office. "Ricky, this has to stop. Just look at yourself – do you think Fred would want you to do this to yourself? Well, do you?"

I couldn't look at her, she got up from behind her desk and came and put her arms around me. That was it, I broke down. I was sobbing uncontrollably and she let me get it all out, then she went to a cabinet and produced a bottle of brandy. She poured me a large one then poured one for herself, "Just sip it," she said quietly, "just sip it."

I did as she said and sipped the brandy. I asked her if I could smoke, she pushed an ashtray in front of me I lit the cigarette and inhaled deeply. I looked up at her kindly round face. She too was visibly upset and I was not making things any easier for either of us. I pulled myself together. Steady now, I said "He's not coming back, is he? Please don't say yes if it's not true, I couldn't bear that."

"And you know as well as I that I cannot answer that question. These are difficult times and Fred knew when he went back the sort of risk he was taking, but you know that he couldn't have lived with himself until he knew the truth. I know you understand that, he said you would, he also asked me to say to you that even if it was a trick just to get him back and that if that means he can never come back here again, he will never forget you, he told me you gave him something that will live with him forever. But you must go on with your life, Ricky, for his sake and yours – he said all these things."

I looked at her and knew it was the truth. "I miss him."

"I know you do, I also know he misses you, and you must not let him down. He would be so unhappy to see you like this."

She was right I thought. I got up and finished my drink then I held out my hand and shook hers. "Thank you, I will leave here, I hope you don't mind. I will leave London, make a fresh start."

"Where will you go?"

"I don't know. Cornwall maybe, I have an aunt there, I'll leave you her address in case you hear anything. I hope you understand?"

"Yes, yes, of course I do and I am sorry you are going. I am going to miss you, you are a very special person – Fred was right. If you come in on Friday I will have your money made ready for you. I want you now to have the rest of the week off and we will say our goodbyes on Friday." She got up and opened the door.

"Until Friday then."

6 – THE CORNISH EXPERIENCE

I had packed all of Fred's things into boxes and left them with Miss Gross. She, in turn, had paid me the money she said was due, in fact she gave me some overtime money that was due, but then she paid me a bonus – in all it amounted to fifty pounds! A vast sum to me then in 1958 and now I was on the Cornish Express wondering why the hell I was there! I had an aunt living in Cornwall – well she was not my real aunt, but the sister of my step-grandmother, and I had only met her once and that had been at her sister's funeral. I had been very upset at the death of my grandmother, a lovely old lady who I used to visit whenever I could, taking with me bags of groceries when I could afford it, because even at fifteen I knew she was quite poor. She always thanked me and told me I should not waste my money, then she would put them away in the cupboard in her tiny flat in Walthamstow. I used to think I was helping to keep the old duck alive. It was only when I found all my bits of shopping still unopened in the cupboard and the sideboard cupboard full of empty Guinness bottles that I knew I was wasting my time!

She was one of life's characters and when she died I was heartbroken. I was even more shocked when I arrived at her flat with my Mum and Dad for the funeral, only to find it being taken apart by her own relations, all looking for the fortune she never had. They were ripping her mattress and pillows apart, rooting through her clothes and turning out cupboards. I was devastated. My mother tried to stop it, only to be told she was only her stepdaughter, and to mind her own business! This from people I had never met – my grandmother would talk about them sometimes but they didn't bother with her while she was alive. Then her sister arrived, the woman I was to call Aunt Bess. When she saw the mess, she blew her top and ordered them all out of the flat. Then she and my parents cleaned the place up as best they could before the funeral directors arrived. I took to her in an instant and she to me, but I had not seen her since that day and she had no idea that I was on my way to see her. I thought of writing to see if I could come down, but it would mean telling her all about my family problems and she loved my mother, so I did not know what her reaction would be. Rather than just being rejected out of hand, I thought that if I could see her first I might be able to put my side of the story, even though I had no idea how to tell a seventy-nine-year-old woman that I was a queer. I use that word because that is the way we were described in those days, and of course we still are by some people even today.

The journey down seemed to take forever finally we pulled into Wadebridge. I grabbed my luggage and stepped onto the platform. It was May and there weren't that many people getting off the train. I gave my ticket to the collector and asked him the way to my aunt's. To my surprise and relief, because my bags were heavy, I found she lived just over the railway crossing.

I looked up at the house. It was at the start of a terrace of grey stone-built houses, all with neat curtains and bright paintwork; they were large four-bedroom places. I walked up the short path and pressed the large brass bell-push at the side of the bright blue door. Through the stained-glass panels in the door, I could see movement. I was quite nervous as the door opened slowly, then a tiny woman in a black-and-white patterned dress, black cardigan and thick black stockings appeared. She was old, with thin wisps of pure white hair tied at the back in a bun, it was not my Aunt Bess. My heart fell into my stomach the old lady smiled and said something I did not understand., I tried to explain who I was and what I wanted, but my stammer came back with a vengeance. I must have appeared like a gibbering idiot to the poor woman. I was just about to give up when the old lady turned and called out something to somebody inside the house, then I heard somebody clip-clopping down the stairs. Suddenly the door opened wider and there stood Aunt Bess.

"Who is it, Mrs Gill?" then she saw me." Well bless my giddy aunt! What are you doing here?"

"What indeed?" I thought. What indeed.

After her initial shock, she threw her arms around my neck and covered my face with big wet sloppy kisses. She smelled of lavender water with a hint of Guinness, and memories of my grandmother came flooding back. She quickly explained to the beaming Mrs Gill who I was, then she ushered me upstairs. As we climbed the staircase she told me Mrs Gill owned the house and she just had the top flat and she was sorry it was in a mess but why didn't I write and say I was coming, and was my Mum OK and when did I last eat and what the bloody hell was I doing there anyway? She sat me down in her cluttered living room, it was just how your elderly aunt's or your grandmother's home should be: all chintz curtains and cushion covers, lace chair-backs and doilies, photos of family and friends all over the place, and the walls covered in pictures of people and chocolate box scenes. Then she scurried away to the kitchen to make us some tea, calling out all manner of questions as she did so but giving no time to answer one before another one was asked. Finally, she came back into the living room carrying a tray laden with teapot, cups and saucers, milk and sugar bowls and a plate of homemade cakes. She put the tray down and poured the tea then went over to the sideboard to fetch some small plates. "Might as well get the best ones out now you're here, no expense spared see," she said as she put a couple of the cakes on a plate and handed them to me. "Well go on then, eat up. I made them for the WI but they will have to go without. Family first eh lad?"

As I munched the cakes and drank tea she chatted away. I nodded and smiled as I tried to answer the endless questions. Looking at her, she was much older than I had imagined, I thought about eighty, a wiry tough old bird who had worked hard to bring up her family. After her husband was killed in the First World War she had come to Cornwall to be cook-housekeeper in one of the large county houses. Her children had all left home and were living in London, she said they had asked her to go with them, but she loved Cornwall and Wadebridge so much she stayed.

Tough old bird or not, I decided it would not be right to burden a woman of her age with my personal problems. Although a warm and hospitable lady who loved to laugh, she was from an age and background where everyone knew their place and station in life, and good grief, if my own mother couldn't understand, how could I expect this grand old lady to?

So I told her I had quit my job and wanted to travel about a bit before I settled down. Jobs were easy to get in those days so my aunt did not think it very odd. After I had been there for about two weeks, although I liked it, Wadebridge was a small market town so I decided to move on for two reasons really. Firstly, I needed to earn some money as my fifty pounds was shrinking fast, and I didn't really want to work on a farm which was about all the work there was in Wadebridge. Secondly, Aunt Bess was spending a lot of time trying to marry me off to one of the local girls. Which girl did not matter to her, she just thought I "needed a nice young lady." Still, she understood when I said I wanted to go to a bigger town and so I moved to Newquay on the coast. I fell in love with the place the moment I first saw it, surrounded by nearly pure white sandy beaches, the sea deep blue and crystal clear, it was like being in heaven. It was the end of May and already it was quite warm, I felt so wonderful, so free, and for the first time for a long while I felt alive again. I slept on the beach for the first couple of nights not wanting to spend what little money I had left. On the third day, I got a job in an amusement arcade, in fact the only amusement arcade in the town. All I had to do was give change and open the machines if any of the little balls got stuck. There were no such things as video games then, just pinball machines, a few simple one-armed bandits and a grab-a-prize crane that would pick up a soft toy if you were very lucky. The walls were filled with penny-in-the-slot machines, we also had a jukebox, a big beautiful garish monster of a thing, and a rifle range where you fired real .22 bullets. I hadn't a clue about mechanics but I told the boss I did and got the job. I soon picked up what was what – when a machine did go wrong, it was usually for the same reason, so once you remembered each machine's quirks it was easy.

I got digs on the outskirts of the town on a vast council estate with a lovely old couple, I called her Mum. A short plump little woman, she and her husband had moved to Newquay before the war. Their children, like those of my aunt, had left home, so they let a room for a bit of income and I suspected company.

Gradually I made friends with the local people, it was difficult at first as they didn't have a very high opinion of Londoners. The locals said they would come down in the summer months and treat them with contempt. I was later, to my shame, to find this was true, not of all Londoners of course but of a few mindless beer-swilling yobbos. But I was accepted and had a great time at beach parties and dances and evenings in the local pubs.

As the summer season began so the town filled up with holidaymakers. This also meant that seasonal staff flocked to the town to fill the many holiday jobs created by the tourists. A few came from London and the North of England but most of them came from Ireland. They worked as kitchen porters, waiters and barmen. They worked long hours and spent their leisure time getting drunk and chasing girls and usually catching them. Once you got to know them they were a great bunch, but the local boys didn't like them very much, they complained that they stole their girlfriends. And some of the local people said they were too noisy and drank too much, which may have been true but at that time they worked hard as I have said and were grossly underpaid in the main so I didn't blame them at all for that, they would however sometimes clash with the RAF boys, stationed just outside Newquay with RAF Coastal Command. It was difficult for me as I had made friends with all of these groups, but it was only now and then we would have a flare-up – and then it was always worse than it looked.

One of the local girls became my closest friend. Her name was Cherry, she was a tall well-built girl with a very pretty face, and was always smiling. She worked for her mother, who owned the largest ladies' hair salon in town. Cherry was a real tomboy with a zest for life. The fact that I was living so far out of town became a problem – I always had to get the last bus or walk the four miles home. Cherry's mother owned a couple of holiday chalets at the back of the town, one had been her first salon. I doubt that now they would be allowed to be used as salons, let alone holiday lets. Built of sheet asbestos with outside toilets, they were tucked away behind a row of houses. The Retreat, the smaller of the two became vacant, and Cherry persuaded her mother to let me rent it. It boasted a kitchen, a bedsitting room, a tiny bathroom and the toilet outside. I adored it – soon I had put up new curtains, redecorated, and generally tarted the place up. It was my very first home of my own, my own little palace. Cherry thought I had gone a little over the top in my refurbishing– she said it was "like a tart's boudoir." I laughed it off but it made me a bit nervous. Then I took in a stray dog, a black Labrador cross that I called Satch after Louis Armstrong, one of my jazz idols.

My days were full and I started to lose my stammer again. I felt at home, even safe, but my nights were empty. I always came home alone, and I still longed to see or hear from Fred. I had phoned Miss Gross but she had no news for me. I gave her my address and she promised to write the moment she had any, but as you know now, she never did write.

I had plenty of offers of night-time company, but they were all from girls! It was getting to be a problem, people were beginning to talk. Some of the Irish lads started to ask me if I was a "steamer", their term for a queer, so to cut down the gossip I started to date a local girl, Julie. She was about my age and very sophisticated (or very full of herself, depending on your point of view). She looked upon our 'romance' as a bit of a coup – she had won where others had failed. I felt a bit mean about the whole thing, but I thought it couldn't do any real harm. I would take her out and wine and dine her and give her a good time, and I was quite fond of her – the trouble was, she wanted more of me than I could give. I was getting in deeper and deeper: she wanted sex. I kept telling her that I respected her and that I wanted it to be right, but it was wearing thin, so I decided that I would speak to Cherry.

I was to meet her in one of the quieter pubs at the back of the town away from people we knew, I was early and the pub nearly empty. I bought a couple of drinks and sat at a table in the corner. I lit a cigarette and tried to work out in my mind what I was going to say. Cherry came into the pub like a whirlwind as usual, she seldom just walked anywhere, she was always in a rush. She waved to people she knew, and she knew everybody. Then she saw me in the corner and waved. I waved back and pointed to the drink I had bought her, she grinned and came over. She was breathless, "Sorry I'm late, last minute bloody customer, this mine?" she pointed to the glass. I was about to say yes but she beat me to it. "Oh ta," she picked up the glass of lager, took a huge gulp and downed it in one. Then she burped. "Oh," she giggled, "manners, come on, drink up, it's my round." I swallowed the remains of my brandy and tonic, she took the glass from my hand and went up to the bar. By the time she came back I was a bundle of nerves and puffing on yet another cigarette, she put down the drinks and helped herself to one of my cigs, then she flopped down into her chair with a thud.

"So where is Julie tonight?" You could tell by her tone she didn't give a toss where she was. Julie was her cousin and they did not get on at all well together. "Washing her hair, I hope it all falls out," she said with some venom.

"Leave it out Cherry, but it's about her I wanted to talk to you."

"So that's why you wanted to meet in this dump. Oh Christ, don't tell me you got her in the club? You silly sod."

"Hold on, hold on! I haven't touched her, I swear, and that's the problem."

"You dirty bugger! Give her a chance, don't rush it."

I stubbed the cigarette out. "You don't understand, it's not like that."

"Well, what is it like, is she frigid? I always thought she was—" she paused, "well, you know – a bit – not easy but available."

"Oh, like you, you mean!"

"Cheeky sod," she laughed and swallowed another mouthful of lager, "so what is the matter with her then?"

"Not a thing that I know of, I'm the one with the problem, not her."

Her brows knitted together. "So that's why you haven't been with anyone since you arrived, have you been to see a doctor?"

"A doctor? what bloody good will that do?"

"Well, I don't know – maybe he could give you an injection or something."

"And what good will a fucking injection do?"

"Ssh! Keep your voice down, I don't know, how did you catch it?"

"Catch what?"

"VD, what else?"

"I haven't got VD, or crabs or the fucking clap! I'm a fucking queer for crying out loud," I looked about me to see if anybody had heard my outburst – they hadn't. I looked back at Cherry, half-afraid of what I would see in her face.

"What did you say?" her face was still and unsmiling, it showed no emotion at all.

"I'm a poof." I looked away, half-expecting to rush away from the table and out of the pub.

"Oh shit, you poor sod."

"What?"

"I didn't mean that the way it sounded, I meant what you must have been going through all this time, just pretending."

"You-you-you—" I started to stammer again, I felt stupid, "you don't mind?"

"You silly bugger, why should I mind? Who else knows?"

"Nobody, please don't tell anybody else, please, they will make my life hell. Please."

"OK, OK," she put her hands on mine and squeezed, "is that what you're scared of, other people finding out?" I nodded. "Does Julie know?"

"Not yet, but if I don't do something soon she will, and you know what a big mouth she's got."

"No, tell me!" she laughed a dirty laugh.

"Oh shut up, that's not even funny, we haven't done anything, the thing is what can I do?"

She thought for a moment then said, "Get a drink in, I think I've got an idea." I got the drinks and came back.

"Well, what's this bright idea then?"

She took the drink from the tray, had a mouthful and said, "You'll have to get a new girlfriend."

"Another girlfriend? That will make it twice as bad."

"Not," she grinned, "if I was the new girlfriend."

"You!"

"Don't panic, I don't want your body, you're too skinny anyway."

"Oh thanks."

"Don't mention it. If you drop Julie for me, all I have to do is tell all the others how great you are in bed, and nobody will ever know the truth about you. Clever eh?"

I was near to tears as I looked at her. "You'd do that for me – why?"

"Cos we're mates, dickhead," she squeezed my hands again, "come on, what do you say, no strings," now her pretty face was glowing, "will you stop worrying?"

"But what about you? Boys will think you're with me and you'll miss out."

"Look, I don't mind. I'm not likely to suddenly fall madly in love, anyway – I've had all those I fancy!" she laughed, "I bet I've even had a few that you fancy! So stop worrying, if I want it I'll get it, I always have done." I looked at her. "Terrible ain't I?"

I shook my head. "No, you're not terrible at all – you are truly wonderful."

"Oh shut up, you'll make me blush," she stood up, "come on then my lover, where are you taking me tonight?"

"Let's get drunk."

"Good idea," she said, "and tomorrow I'm going to tell Julie to get her hands off my man!"

Cherry proved to be a great friend.

It was hard work during the summer season, but after work or on our days off we all had a ball (at times Cherry had more than one!) but every night I slept on my own, and every night I thought of Fred. I missed seeing him, touching him and I missed the love we had shared. There were times, of course, when I ached for someone to put his arms around me, and had somebody approached me I have no doubt I would have been a willing partner, but as for me making that first move – no way! I was scared for a start. I really believed I was the only homosexual in Newquay, out of all those thousands of people I was the only one, or so I thought at the time. Now I know different, I dare say there were quite a few like me, alone and bewildered and leading a double life, and the strain of trying to keep that dreadful secret from your family and friends getting more and more difficult, with the frustration reaching bursting point at times. Even Cherry didn't know of anybody like me, and as I have already said, she knew everybody.

It wasn't that I didn't fancy anybody. I did, one or two of the hotel workers, a few of the RAF guys and a couple of the local lads, but I wouldn't let any of them get close to me. In fact, I would ignore those I really liked, in case I got careless with my emotions and they got suspicious of my intentions.

Meeting them all in the pubs and cafés could also be a strain. The conversation always got round to sex and as usual everyone had to brag about their latest conquest, or if there were girls present it would be dirty joke time. I could handle the "who pulled the best bird" part, because I was with Cherry and they all knew that I was "getting it", well they all thought that anyway. Some did try to get me to try other girls but I always said I wanted to be faithful. I was jeered at the first few times I said it but they got used to it in the end. Joke time was a different matter – it was always "There was this fucking queer" or "this old bender". I always laughed, of course, and usually I would laugh the loudest.

Sometimes I would see Cherry looking at me during one of these sessions and I could feel her cringing for me. I don't know why, but for some reason, the queer gags were always made to sound that much more disgusting, unless it was just me and my guilty conscience.

Soon the summer was over. The crowds left, hotels and cafés closed, as did most of Newquay. The town returned to being a quiet little seaside place once more. A few of the Irish lads decided to stay on for the winter, they said there was nothing for them to do in Ireland and there was always the chance they might find a winter job here. I was glad, they were good company. A truce seemed to have been drawn between all three groups – the RAF, the locals and the Irish guys – with only the local girls left in town, everybody seemed to know who was with who and respected that.

The trouble now was that there was nothing to do apart from drinking and hanging about the Double Decker Grill, a small café next to the bus station. This, of course, meant that at times things got a bit rowdy, and this in turn upset some of the older local people. They complained about hooligans hanging around street corners and the noise. Of course, none of them wanted to address the problem, all they would say, using that old hackneyed phrase, was "It would never have been allowed in my day," and that was a great help. It made me bloody angry – these so-called "hooligans" had worked long and hard all summer, and they had helped to make a few people very rich. Now there was no work and very little money, what did they expect them to do?

Some of the local boys got a rock and roll band together and they were very good. Rock and roll was the thing, with people like Bill Haley, Billy Fury, Elvis and Cliff Richard, young people filled dance halls and jived their hearts out. Newquay then had only one ballroom – apart from those in the posh hotels – and that was for the "Quick Quick Slow" brigade, but I found a village hall just outside the town. The village council agreed that I could rent it every Saturday night for five pounds! But I had to clean it up and pay for any redecoration I wanted. I agreed, I bought some cheap paint and slapped it on the walls, put up some red lampshades, and the Off-Beat Club was ready for business. I booked the local band and the first Saturday night we were packed. Cherry ran the snack bar, we had no liquor licence but nobody cared, they got drunk on the music and the atmosphere. Soon I was booking bands from out of town, bands with a following. I got the local bus company to run a service to the club so that our customers wouldn't have to pay for taxis. It was a great success and we ran for two years, I even made stars of a couple of hotel workers – one boy and one girl – by getting them to sing with the bands. It didn't do my name any harm either, I became quite a local personality.

Some nights, after a party or a good night at the club, I would ask some of the boys round to the Retreat, and we would drink and play cards until the early hours when we would all crash out. Gradually it became the thing, if you were stuck in town or fed up, to go round to Rick's. Even Satch brought home a friend one night.

I was late home one warm sticky night. When I got there Satch was nowhere to be found. I searched for him but without any luck. Finally, I gave up – I was worn out. I pulled out the Put-U-Up (yes, another one) and made the bed, but I left the back door open for Satch. At about four in the morning I felt him jump on my bed, he licked my face and I gave him a quick cuddle. About ten minutes later the bed suddenly tipped on end, nearly throwing me to the floor, then something wet hit me in the face. I yelled, Satch barked, I grabbed for the bedside light and turned it on. What met my eyes nearly gave me heart failure. Standing over me was a huge St Bernard, its tongue hanging from the side of its mouth like a roll of wet carpet and dribbling all over me! I pushed it off me and put the bed to rights, then I made both of them sleep in the kitchen. In the morning I told Satch to take his friend home and not to bring him back, and he did. I never saw the St Bernard again!

A week or so later I was in bed, and at about two in the morning I heard somebody tapping on my door. Getting up and putting on my red silk dressing gown, I opened the door slightly, only to see Sean, one of the Irish guys, standing there.

"Oh Jesus, thank heaven for that I found the right place."

"Sean! it's two o'clock, what's wrong?"

He laughed. "Sure, if I was to tell you that I'd be here half the night so I would, the truth is I nearly got caught in a young lady's bedroom by her old feller, I had to jump out of the window. If he had caught me he would have killed me." We both laughed.

"Come in," I opened the door wider and he came into the room. He was quite small with dark, almost black hair. He was also very good-looking and had the girls eating out of his hand. He was, of course, being Irish, full of the blarney, and he had a reputation for being aggressive – he would punch first and ask questions later. He looked around.

"It's a nice place you have here, so you have, would you mind if I dossed down here for the night? Your man might still be out looking for me and you wouldn't be wanting my funeral on your conscience, now would you?"

"No," I laughed, "I would not, of course you can stay." I made him some coffee and was about to unfold a small spare bed that doubled for a side table when he said:

"Now why do you want to give yourself all that trouble of pulling out another bed, when the one you have is big enough for the both of us, or do you think I might spoil your fine sheets?"

"Don't be daft – if you don't mind sharing, I'm sure I don't." I had said it but I was not at all happy about it. My mind raced back to Steve Shaw, I could feel my chest tighten, I started to shake. I tried to stop myself by tidying up – anything just to keep busy.

"Well, I don't know about you, but I've had it. Do you mind if I call it a day?"

"No, help yourself," I said pointing to the bed. I kept busy, but I could see him undressing – soon he was down to his underpants. They were red and very tight, his body was slim but muscular and his skin was golden from days lying on the beaches during the summer. He saw me looking at him and he grinned.

"Do I just leave my clothes here?" He pointed to a chair.

"Y-y-yes," I stammered, "anywhere." I turned round quickly in case he saw my face, which I knew by now would be bright red. I waited until he was in bed before I turned back round. He was lying on his side, facing outwards. I turned off the lights and undressed in the dark, dropping my clothes anywhere. When I was down to my underpants I climbed into bed. I lay on the edge of the bed for fear I would touch him and give him a reason for lashing out. I was too scared to sleep in case I did something in the night without realising. Then suddenly I felt him turn over, then I could feel his body touching mine he was pressing himself into me. He had an erection, he pushed it against my buttocks. I lay there rigid with fear, then he put his arm over me and pulled me onto my back. In an instant he was laying on top of me, kissing me. "Sean," I whispered, thinking he might be asleep, "Sean, it's me, Ricky."

"I fucking well hope so, I've waited for this for a long while, so

I have." Then he went down on me, pulling at my underpants, his mouth searching for my cock. He found it, hard and pulsating. I felt his mouth close over it. I lay there like that for some time, then I felt myself ejaculate. He gulped and came back up to me, his lips now pressed onto mine, his tongue searching my mouth. It had been nearly eight months since I had had any sex, now I was bursting with passion. I rolled over on to him and undressed him. Turning my body, I put my mouth around his cock, it was large and thick. As I pushed it further into my mouth I could feel him doing the same. I felt him climax, the warm bittersweet cum gushing into my mouth. I swallowed he moaned, I turned around and found his mouth. I kissed him very gently, he responded. I held him in my arms for some time, then I said softly, "I want to take you the whole way – can I?" He tightened his arms around me and whispered, "Yes."

I released him and gently kissed his body all over at the same time turning him onto his face. I gently spread his legs, then I kissed and caressed his buttocks, all the time my tongue probing and searching, He moaned softly. I reached into the bedside cabinet for some lubrication, put some on myself and some on him, then I penetrated him. I felt his body go rigid – he yelled, I soothed him and went in further, gently at first then gradually faster and faster. He called my name, I went faster, then faster still until we both climaxed. We both lay there breathless, my heart was pounding. After a while I withdrew, he cuddled up and we both fell asleep. We stayed in bed until late afternoon hardly speaking but we made love again twice.

It wasn't until he left looking rather sheepish that I suddenly began to feel guilty. The guilt turned into a feeling almost of remorse. I felt dirty and cheap. I thought of Fred again in Hungary, maybe even in prison or worse. I shuddered, then I thought about Sean. I had enjoyed the sex, I had enjoyed his body and the warmth I got from it. I found it difficult to put the Sean I had slept with and the Sean I knew from the street into the same slot. One was warm and loving, the other hard and violent. I knew I wasn't in love with him – although it would have been an easy thing to do, it would also be a dangerous thing to do. I couldn't see Sean giving up his mates or even telling his mates about me, but I did know one thing – I was not the only homosexual in Newquay. I was also amazed at the way Sean had kept it under wraps all this time.

Maybe, I thought, just maybe that's why sometimes he is so violent – the frustration makes him lash out.

I had a bath and changed the bed linen, it made me feel better. Then I phoned Cherry, we met for a drink and I told her what had happened, but not who with, even if I had told her that she would never have believed me. So I just told her what it was like and how I felt. She said it was only natural that I felt some guilt, but I couldn't stay celibate for the rest of my life, and wherever Fred was, she felt sure that he would not want me to be alone. "You loved each other, right?"

"Yes, we did, we didn't only love each other we were in love with one another, if that makes sense?" She said it did.

"Now put yourself in his place, if it were you who for whatever reason couldn't get back to him, would you want him to be lonely and unhappy? Wouldn't you want him to remember what you had together, and wouldn't you want him to go on living, with you always being a part of him, well wouldn't you?"

I looked at her and I couldn't believe that such a flippant and sometimes brash even vulgar girl could have said something so beautiful. I put my arms around her and kissed her on the cheek. "I love you, you tart."

She kissed me back. "Feel better?"

"Yes, I do, thanks to you."

"Well just remember you are only human –now tell me who he was."

I laughed and shook my head. "No way!".

"Bastard," she said and kissed me again.

I would see Sean with his friends in the pubs and cafés, and although we always acknowledged each other with a nod of the head or a grin, we never gave the impression of being close friends. He kept his old image going by sleeping with the prettiest girls and acting tough, but although we didn't say much in public, he did visit me late at night at least half a dozen times after our fling.

The club did so well on Saturday nights that I gave up working in the arcade and spent some of my time putting on rock and roll gigs in other towns – just small dances and not that often, but I was beginning to enjoy being in show business.

The RAF boys were good punters at the Off-Beat and I got to know and like many of them as mates, but there was one in particular who I felt attracted to. His name was Terry, he came from south London and was a year or two older than I. He was not a career airman, he had been called up to do his National Service (two years in the armed forces for all boys when they were eighteen, I just missed it) and he chose the RAF as an easy option. He – along with some other lads – was to find out that the RAF was no place for the timid or the workshy! They, as many of them told me, had their fair share of square-bashing to do as well as weapons training, and all the rest and more a soldier would have to do, but it wasn't all work, they did have a lot of good times.

Terry was unofficially engaged to a local girl, the daughter of a solicitor I think, but to see the way he behaved you wouldn't have believed it. He could usually be seen in his car packed with his cronies, cruising the town and chatting up the local 'birds'. His girlfriend never seemed to mind, merely saying, if anybody asked her, "Oh well, boys will be boys," but it seemed to work – they got on very well with each other.

It was Christmas 1959 and I for one was not looking forward to it.

On Christmas Eve Cherry and I went to the Central Hotel. It was packed mostly with our friends or people we knew. We all had a great time, most of us got legless. At closing time, as we were all wishing each other Merry Christmas and kissing all and sundry, Lyn, Terry's girlfriend, asked me if Terry could stay with me that night, as he was too drunk to drive and he didn't get on with her parents. I said it would be OK and as some of them were coming back to my place anyway, Cherry said she would drive his car. We all piled into the car. I'll never know how she managed to drive but drive she did. She parked the car at the bottom of the lane leading to the Retreat, and people never seemed to stop getting out! There must have been seven or eight of us in that car. The party went on until about four in the morning, then people drifted off until finally only Terry and I were left. I was too drunk and too tired to pull the bed down, so I just flopped out on the couch. Terry meanwhile had collapsed into an armchair and was in the arms of Morpheus.

I woke up on Christmas Day with a head like lead and my body stiff from sleeping in an awkward position. I pulled myself up and looked around the room. I had forgotten all about Terry and got quite a start when I saw him slumped in the armchair. The room was full of that after-party stench of stale beer and cigarette smoke. I opened the door to let in some fresh air and stood in the open doorway taking in great gulps of the stuff, it was almost springlike outside. I came back in and went into the kitchen. The sight that greeted me was even more revolting, empty Party Seven cans lying on the draining board – one had fallen on its side and the contents spilled out onto the floor making a dark sticky mess – glasses half or part full of beer and other concoctions were everywhere, some with used cigarette ends now partly disintegrated floating about in them. If there is anything likely to made me heave it's drinking glasses with soggy fag ends in them! I rushed outside to the lavatory. When I came back I set about cleaning up. When I had finished Terry was still fast asleep, so I made some coffee. Still he slept, so as it was Christmas I cooked Christmas dinner. It was only a chicken but in those days chicken was something of a luxury. When the meal was almost ready I woke Terry. "Where the fuck am I?" he slurred.

"At my place. Merry Christmas – want some dinner?"

"Oh bloody hell, Christmas!" he said as he realised what day it was, "Merry Christmas! Yeah, I'd love some dinner, I'm starving. Got a bath?" I showed him the bathroom and gave him some fresh towels, while he bathed I finished cooking the meal and laid the table. I had intended to have Christmas Day on my own, like I said I was not looking forward to it. I found it always brought back too many memories of past Christmases with my Mum and Dad and Fred and even Smithy, and I thought it best if I just stayed on my own with my thoughts. Cherry and other friends had asked me to spend the day with them but I had declined with a polite but firm no.

As I was putting the finishing touches to the table Terry came from the bathroom, naked except for a small towel around his waist. "Oh, I needed that – thanks," he looked stunning. He was slim, about five feet eight or nine, his body was firm and lithe. He stood there, his hair wet and dark falling over his face. "You ain't got a clean shirt or something I could borrow, have yer?"

"Su-su-su-sure," shit! I was stammering yet again. I squeezed past him and got some clothes from my closet next to the bathroom. As I was getting the clothes he turned to watch me.

"It's really nice of you to go to all this trouble, Rick, ta."

"No tr–tr–trouble," I said as I handed him the clothes. He took them with both hands, the towel falling to the floor. For an instant he was naked, I tried not to look at him but I found myself drawn like a magnet. He was looking at the clothes, I was looking at his body and his manhood. He had a semi-erection and his prick was long and slightly darker than the rest of his skin. I bent down to pick up the towel. As I did so he turned and went into the bedsitting room, but as he turned his dick swung, my face was almost level with it and it nearly hit me in the mouth, just touching my chin!

He turned to face me again and looking down at me now on my knees said, "Sorry Rick, didn't see you there, you all right?" and I couldn't speak. I just nodded then managed to croak "Fine". He turned away again, and I just stayed there looking at his back. His waist was quite narrow and his buttocks were firm. I wanted to run into the room after him and bury my face into them, but I pulled myself together and got the meal ready. When I carried it into the other room he was fully dressed and sitting at the table.

"Grub up," I tried to say it nonchalantly, hoping that he had not noticed my behaviour.

After dinner we played cards, he told me he should have gone home for Christmas, but it was too late now and did I mind if he stayed with me?

"Mind! Why should I mind? Be my guest, stay as long as you like."

That night I pulled the bed down and without mentioning that I had a spare bed said to him. "Don't mind sharing, do you?"

"Soppy sod, course not."

Oh God! I could hardly contain myself as I got undressed and jumped into bed. He got in almost at the same time that I did. I turned off the light. "Goodnight," I said.

"Night Rick," came the reply.

I lay perfectly still almost shaking with expectation. I felt him move, then turn over. My heart was in my mouth. Then I could hear him breathing softly, it got heavier and heavier. I couldn't believe it – the bastard was asleep!!

I turned over and was now facing his back. I got as close as I dared, I could feel the warmth from his body. It reminded me of Alf and the time we spent in Wales, but this wasn't Alf and we were not in Wales, this was Terry and I just wanted to be close to him. I moved nearer until I was just touching him and then contented I fell asleep.

Terry stayed at the Retreat for a further two days, then he had to go back on duty. On each of those last two nights he did the same thing, he would get into bed, turn on his side and go straight to sleep. It was frustrating but at least I had been close to him. It sounds absurd, I know, but I desperately wanted and craved for someone to love. I had plenty of friends, of course, and Cherry was great, but even when I was surrounded by friends inside of me was a huge void, a nagging empty space. When it got really bad I would go into black moods and deep depressions, and I would ask myself why I had to carry this burden, what had I done that was so bad. Was God punishing me? If so, what for? And when I saw couples together, holding hands, kissing and laughing, I would get full of resentment. I knew that was unreasonable, but I was in torment. I didn't know what was going to happen to me, I was frightened of the future and longed for the past. I suppose I felt sorry for myself at times but if I did it was not from choice. I would force myself out of the moods, do mad things, make people laugh, anything to get out of the blackness, and I would tell myself that one day, one day, maybe tomorrow, I would find what I was looking for and I would be able to face the future. I put out of my mind the old saying that tomorrow never comes. I knew it would, it had to or else why was I here?

Spring came and went, and the town started to come to life again. Hotels reopened, shops and guest houses got fresh coats of paint and the town buzzed with excitement. Soon the crowds arrived and the Summer Season had begun. I was asked to go back to the arcade – the club was doing well, and with the holidaymakers here it would, I hoped, do even better – but I had much too much time on my hands and I enjoyed the bustle of the arcade and chatting to the customers, so I agreed to go back.

Nothing very much happened that season, Sean came round a couple of nights and we had sex and it did help to make me feel like a real person and I think it helped him too. I said nothing much happened, nor did it, except for one night at the club. The usual crowd had turned up and were enjoying themselves when a crowd from London arrived. They were a bit over the top but they were on holiday, so I let them in and for a little while everything was OK. Then one of them grabbed one of the local girls and asked what she was doing with her "Swede Basher" of a boyfriend. The boy, a local, kept his cool and told the visitor to lay off, and before anybody could stop him the holidaymaker swung a punch at the local lad and all hell broke loose. I had a couple of stewards in the club and with their help I stopped the fight and threw them all out, which with hindsight was the wrong thing to do – no sooner were they in the car park than they started again. I rushed outside right in the middle of a hail of bottles and bricks, ducking and diving to avoid the missiles. I tried to part the two groups. I knew the local lads wouldn't harm me, so I tried to reason with the Londoners, trying to convince them we were soulmates, but they were having none of it. Cherry came out, saw what I was trying to do, screamed and ran back into the club. Sean was inside with some of his mates. Cherry yelled at him that I was getting murdered outside and before you could say "Punch Up" he charged into the car park. He saw me trying to plead with a guy about six feet tall and built like a brick shithouse, ran up to me push me to one side and landed the bloke one punch and knocked him clean out. By this time the rest of the lads and about a dozen RAF lads were right behind Sean, and Terry was among them. Soon fists were flying all over the place. Cherry came back out to warn me that someone had phoned the police.

That was all I needed. The sergeant at Newquay was not a fan of the club. He had made a forecast that it would lead to trouble, and even though this was the first incident since we had opened I knew it would spell doom for the Off-Beat. I looked around. It was like a battleground – the white painted walls were spattered with blood, broken bottles were everywhere and people were holding cut heads, arms and legs. I called out as loud as I could that the police were on the way. There were two buses in the car park, the drivers were standing watching the fight. I begged them to get back in their buses and get those fighting out. I didn't have time to argue, I stuffed some pound notes in their hands and they jumped back into their cabs. I then grabbed Sean and told him to get them all onto the buses. While he and Terry and the rest were doing that, I ran to Cherry and told her to get some of the girls together and to wash the blood from the walls.

As she was doing this we could hear the police cars bells ringing, leaving Newquay – we had about five minutes. The boys had got all the fighters on the buses. I jumped on each bus and told them to shut up and sing as loud as they could or else we would all be nicked. When I think about it now it still makes me laugh – blokes that a few moments ago were going to kill each other were now to be seen with their arms around each other's necks, singing at the tops of their voices. As the buses pulled out, the police cars drove in, screeching to a halt. The police spilt out of the two cars ready for World War Three, and all they saw were two coach loads of happy people singing to their hearts' content, and Cherry and a couple of the girls and some RAF guys scrubbing walls. "Come on you lot," I yelled at the wall cleaners, "I want to start repainting in the morning," then I turned to face the police sergeant. "And what brings you up here, Sergeant?"

"You know perfectly well what! A brawl! A fight!"

"Where?" I said, full of innocence. He pushed past me and went into the club – the band was playing and the few people left were all dancing.

"Very quiet tonight, Sergeant – that's why I've got 'em outside washing walls. Got to keep them busy, you know."

He grunted something, called his men together and left. He gave us a couple of surprise visits after that, but could never find anything wrong much, to his disgust. I didn't understand the mentality of the man, the club kept the kids off the street and gave no cause for concern, you would have thought he would have been pleased. Strange man.

Apart from Sean's occasional visits, other people still came to the Retreat to spend the night if and when they needed to. Terry stayed more than the others. I thought it strange that neither he nor any of the others ever ran into Sean. I was told by Sean some time later that he would creep around to the Chalet and if he heard voices or recognised any of the cars parked nearby, he would quietly slip away.

Terry was by now almost making the place his second home, sometimes arriving when I was in bed. He would just open the front door (I never kept it locked unless I was out) and say, "It's only me," then he would make himself a drink, come to bed and go straight to sleep. Even the dog didn't bark when Terry came round, he got so used to him. I did find it all a bit frustrating, yet at the same time, I was always so pleased to see him. He was not my boyfriend, I couldn't even touch him, but he was there and I could look at him – and when some mornings he would walk around the place completely naked, I could watch him, albeit slyly.

Although I didn't really mind people staying, I was getting to resent it a bit, apart from Sean who at least let me get rid of my pent-up emotions. Most of the others, especially Terry, were using the place like a bed and breakfast, and unintentionally they were compounding my situation. They didn't know my situation, of course, so I couldn't tell them, but I began to realise that by keeping on teasing myself and fantasising about some of them, I would never learn to live with my "problem". I simply had to put a stop to it all, and then and only then would I be able to cope. So I made my mind up, I would tell them enough is enough, but not Sean – I thought about it but decided that he needed me as much as I needed him. I couldn't just tell him that was that, for fear of what effect that sort of rejection would have had on him, I knew how I would have felt.

A couple of nights later I got my chance. I was in bed when I heard the door open and heard Satch's tail banging against the wall as he greeted Terry. "It's only me," he said quietly and went into the kitchen. Then he called out and asked me if I wanted a drink. I said I would, he came in a few moments later, put on the bedside light and handed me a glass. "What's this?" I asked him, as I screwed up my eyes against the sudden light and took the glass from his hand.

"Brandy and tonic. I got it right, didn't I?"

"Yes, you did, but usually I get coffee, so what's with the brandy?"

"Just thought you might like it – a change is as good as a rest so they say."

Tell me about it I thought as I sat up in the bed. "And they are right – cheers," I took a swig of the drink, "oh nice one."

"Cheers," he said, "here's to – well, to us," and he clinked his glass against mine.

We had a few more while he sat on the edge of the bed telling me about his day and asking me about mine, then he undressed and lay on the bed in just his underpants. How the hell was I going to tell him now! "Er, thanks for the drink Terry, now piss off!" I couldn't, I just couldn't. Just looking at him next to me was getting me sexually aroused. He just kept on talking about this and that (but not, unfortunately, the other!) I wasn't really listening, I was drinking him in and trying to visualise what it would be like making love with him.

Finally, he put the light out and got into bed. I had my back to him as always and I could hear him breathing as usual, then I felt him turn over. I lay there waiting for him to go to sleep so that I could get close to him. Suddenly I felt his hand on my back, I jumped. "It's OK– it's all right," he said quietly. He sounded nervous – there was a tremor in his voice. He moved his hand down and into my underpants, then he gently caressed my bum, he moved his hand around and felt for my dick, he found it hard and erect. He moaned, I just lay there letting him explore me – I couldn't move. I thought if I did he may stop. Then he was pulling and tugging at my pants trying to get them off, I helped him and he turned me to face him. "Oh Rick, you don't know how long I've waited for this to happen, do you mind?"

"Mind?" I thought, "do I mind?" I was ecstatic. I shook my head and said "no." He put his hand back down to my bum and pulled me into him, kissing me, not just a kiss but a kiss full of passion and feeling. He looked at me, kissed me again, his tongue in my mouth and mine in his, pressing harder and harder. He looked at me again.

"Do you have any idea of just how many nights I've laid there next to you, making out I was asleep, and feeling you next to me, praying you would touch me? It's been driving me crazy."

I was speechless. I could only look at him,

"What's – up don't you want this?" he said, quickly pulling his hand away, "I'm sorry, really sorry," now he was pulling himself further away. Quickly I put my hand on his lips.

"Calm down, calm down." I took my hand from his lips and rubbed his brow, "I felt the same way, I have been lying here since the very first time you slept with me waiting for you to touch me. I was scared to make the first move in case – well, in case you belted me."

"All that time! Christ! Never mind, we're here now, that's all that counts," his hand went down my back and in between my buttocks. I felt his fingers probing my bum and he pulled me close to him again. We held each other, it was as though each thought the other might disappear.

"Why didn't you tell me?" I asked him.

"Oh come on," he laughed," what could I say, I didn't even know why I felt like that about you, I just knew that I wanted you. I felt like a freak, but now you're here all I want to do is make love to you and look after you – can I?"

"Yes, oh yes." I went down on him and took his dick in my

mouth. As I closed my mouth around it he climaxed, I lay there not letting go until he pulled me up, kissed me and laid me on my back and with his hand brought me to a climax. And as soon as I did he took my dick in his mouth gradually, and still with my dick in his mouth he manoeuvred me onto my stomach. Then he spread my legs and let his tongue probe my bum. Slowly he pulled himself up on me, his own dick hard and throbbing now between my buttocks, he was kissing me on the back of my neck and rubbing his cock slowly up and down my bum. I reached out and fumbled to find some lubricating jelly, nearly pulling the bedside table over but, I found it and passed it to him asking to put some on me. I felt him working into me, spreading in between the cheeks of my bum, then I felt his dick. Slowly, very slowly, he pushed harder and harder. I caught my breath – it was painful at first, but I didn't tell him, I wanted him to go further and further in. At last, I could feel his pubic hair on my bum, he lay there for a while so that I got used to his dick being there. I squeezed my buttocks together as hard as I could to let him know I didn't want him to leave, then he began to withdraw and thrust back in, slowly at first, out then in again. Then he went faster. I responded by going with his movements. I heard him moaning, we both were helping each other, faster and faster, then I climaxed. Almost at the same time, he made one final hard push, moaned with pleasure and collapsed into my back, once again kissing my neck and calling my name. Tomorrow was here and I was very much in love.

For the next couple of days, Terry and I hardly left the chalet. That's not to say we spent the whole time in bed, a great deal of it, yes, but by no means all of it. It sounds sloppy, I suppose, but a lot of the time was spent just looking into each other's eyes, laughing together and hugging each other and of course talking – lots and lots of talking about us other people and our future.

One of the first things we discussed was about how careful we would have to be from now on. We had both gone to great lengths to keep our sexuality a secret before we found each other, now it would be even harder to stop people getting suspicious. I told him about Cherry – he was shocked, then pleased that at least she was not a problem. He was not so sure about Lyn, though. He had already been making excuses as to why he didn't want sex (shades of Julie, I thought) and now he had to make sure she didn't put two and two together and come up with the right answer. He, like me with Julie, had not wanted to deceive her, but he felt he had little choice. It was not just a matter of being a coward and not facing up to things. Other people had to be considered: his family and friends, even his livelihood. One complaint about him to the RAF would have meant him being faced with a court-martial, then prison, and finally the ignominy of being thrown out, with the reason clearly written on his discharge papers, which is a terrible price to pay for merely loving somebody.

So we both knew we would have to take extra care outside of the chalet. An over-affectionate look, our hands lingering for too long as we shook each other's hand, even just being too close to each other or singing each other's praises were all things our friends would pick up on. I hear people say, "Well if they were friends, why worry?" but it was not that black and white. Homosexuality was not generally talked about, especially among the working class. If it did exist, well, then it was something the upper classes did! if that sounds as though I'm trying to be humorous, I'm not, it's just the way things were. Today it's all so different. Here I am, in my seventies, I live in a very small community and my neighbours accept me with no questions or sniggers. I am asked to all sorts of functions, from family parties and weddings to show business dinners. But in the fifties that would not have been the case. I would undoubtedly have found myself ostracised by society and, as I have said before, the police could and would have brought a prosecution against me. Even today some of the more bigoted police still try to entrap gay men in public toilets with the excuse that they might be trying to pervert minors, which is claptrap. The average homosexual, like the average heterosexual, has absolutely no interest at all in minors. Paedophiles, however, do have that interest, but just as the average heterosexual loathes paedophiles, so the average homosexual shares that feeling of disgust.

Admitting you are homosexual is still a problem for some people today, but at least in this day and age, there are books with advice on how to cope, magazines telling you where you can meet people with similar views, plus clubs and pubs, hotels and restaurants, all catering for homosexual people. But in the 1950s there was nothing – nothing except secrecy and the hope that you might meet someone, who would, in turn, introduce you to somebody else and so on until you had built up a circle of friends whom you could trust. But even then, the vast majority of homosexuals had to keep that secret from their families and workmates – not an easy thing to do.

Terry went back to camp and I re-entered the world, but with a completely different outlook on life. I had arranged to meet Cherry at the Central. When I sat down at her table she looked at me and said, "Christ! what's happened to you?"

"What do you mean, what's happened?"

"You look like the cat that got the cream and the bleedin' fish cakes!"

"I'm happy that's all – I'm always happy."

"Bollocks! Most of the time, yes – but not like this, so come on, give!"

So I told her all about this wonderful guy who had changed my life, missing out the more intimate details of course, but then came the question I dreaded.

"Well, who is he?"

I didn't want to tell her but at the same time I did, I needed to tell her, so I took a deep breath and said "Terry." She looked puzzled so I tried again "Terry, you silly cow. Terry from St Mawgan RAF. Terry."

The look on her face turned to utter amazement and she yelled "What, Lyn's boyfriend?" She said it so loudly I thought Terry must have heard back at the RAF camp.

"Sssh!" I hissed, "don't tell the fucking world for Christ's sake." She looked at me, her face was glowing and she was grinning from ear to ear.

"Terry!" she said at last, "I can't believe it, you and him –he's so handsome." I nodded and was now grinning with her.

"Are you winding me up?"

"No – why would I do that? You asked me and I told you."

"But what about Lyn?"

"Well," I replied, "she could be a problem." I had stopped grinning now and so had she. "It's getting a bit like me and Julie, and if she blabs, well—" Then I told her about the court-martial if the RAF found out, and when I had finished she looked at me and said, "Why is it that nothing you do is simple and straightforward?"

I shrugged. "I don't know –the point is, what's to do?"

"We-e-ell," she was beaming again, "I could always drop you and get myself another boyfriend!"

It was my turn to yell now. "What!!"

"Well," she continued, "he has got a nice car and he is good-looking and a girl's got a right to change her mind, hasn't she?"

Then the penny dropped. "Hang on, do you mean to say you would do the same for him as you have done for me?"

"Oh, go to the top of the class! Anything to stop you from driving yourself mad, and anyway, can you think of a better idea?" I had to admit that I couldn't. "Well, that's settled then."

"Thanks – yes, settled as long as he agrees, and I'm sure he will, but what about you? Your name's going to be mud, especially with the other girls."

"Fuck 'em – just you think what the boys will say – they'll all wonder what it is that I've got that Lyn and Julie haven't. And with a bit of luck, they'll all want to find out!" We both roared laughing.

The next day the three of us met. I didn't tell Terry the reason for the meeting, as far as he thought it was just a social drink. I did tell him that I had confided in Cherry about us. He was, quite naturally, concerned, and was not looking forward to the meeting, which took place in one of the better hotels – we thought we would have less of a chance of meeting any of our friends there.

We were first arriving, he looked decidedly nervous and when Cherry appeared I think he wished the ground would open up and swallow him. It was understandable of course, he had known Cherry almost since he was stationed at St Mawgan, and all that time he had led her to believe he was some sort of randy womaniser. Instead, he was – well – queer!

"Hi, you two."

Terry looked at the floor and mumbled "Hi." I made frantic signs to Cherry and kept mouthing "he is embarrassed." Being Cherry, she cottoned on in an instant. "Have you ordered yet"? she asked matter-of-factly.

"No, we were waiting for you, do you want your usual?"

"I'm not sitting in here with a pint of bleeding lager! I want a lady's drink. Terry, be a love, as you're the only man among us get me something to compliment me in my present surroundings," she said, with a sweep of her hand around the bar.

"Good idea," I replied, "get her a pint of lager with a cherry in it!"

"Bastard!" she said and she thumped me. But it broke the ice, and when he came back with the drinks she proposed a toast. "To you both – I'm so pleased for you – I hope you have a long and loving life together, and thank you both for trusting me enough to let me share your happiness." Terry relaxed now, sure that she was truly on our side and that she would keep our secret.

"Well, when Rick told me he had told you I nearly died, but now I'm really pleased you know it helps to make it – well, more natural. I nearly said normal!" he gagged and we all laughed.

"And why not? It's your lives." She looked at me. "Have you asked him yet?"

"Not yet, give me a chance."

Terry looked puzzled. "Oi you two! I'm here, you know. Ask me what?"

"Well don't get mad at me but we always share things, Cherry and I, and she wondered if you would be her boyfriend as well?"

The look on his face would have turned milk sour, he turned to me then to her then looked back at me. "She wants what?" He turned to her. "Look, I like you a lot, but you want to share me with Ricky? Are you out of your fucking mind? NO!"

Cherry and I cracked up. He was so serious, he really believed it, then he saw the joke and laughed with us. "Shit pots! You had me going there for a moment."

Then I told him the reason for the meeting, and what Cherry had proposed. He was overwhelmed. He kissed her and thanked her and tears rolled down his cheeks. Soon we were all in floods until Cherry said, "Oh come on, let's stop the snivelling, this is a wedding, not a wake!"

Cherry, true to her word as ever, made a play for Terry in public, she and Lyn had a tremendous row, while Terry protested his innocence and I sat on the side-lines looking hurt. It was a performance worthy of an Oscar, and it did the trick. Lyn gave up Terry. He, in turn, said he couldn't make any commitment to Cherry until the dust had settled, and I had to put up with friends saying how sorry they were and what a bitch Cherry was.

It all blew over, however, and Terry, unattached as far as the rest of the world was concerned carried on cruising about town with his mates, chatting up the birds, and he got quite expert in putting them off, either by being rude or plain gross. Even his mates at the camp were telling him he would never get another girlfriend the way he was treating them. He would shrug and say, "I'm just being myself", and leave it at that.

Cherry and I were able to continue what friends now believed to be a platonic relationship, but they would still sometimes say to me, "How can you bear to be friends with her after what she did to you?" I would have loved to have said, "After what she has done for me, I'd do anything in the world for her," but I never did of course.

Summer passed by and Terry was due to leave the RAF after completing his National Service. In order to lessen the impact of moving in with me Terry had been telling his mates for months that he was thinking of staying in Newquay when he left the services. Most thought him mad, some envied him. "What will you do, stuck down here in winter?" was the general question. "Become a bleeding fisherman, out all bloody hours, or work on a farm up to your elbow in cow shit for the rest of your life!" He just smiled at them and said he thought he might open up a small car repair shop, after all, he knew something about cars – he had worked in a garage after leaving school.

When asked where he would live, he told them that I was willing to put him up until he got himself sorted. Nobody gave this a second thought – we were friends, after all. One or two people told me I should charge him rent – I assured them that I would make him pay in full!

Christmas was on us once again and Terry asked me if I would like to go to Plymouth for a spot of shopping. I jumped at the chance, as much as I loved Newquay, it was not the best place in the world to buy Christmas presents, and Plymouth, although a long way away, was a very big city. It promised bright lights, the lot. He booked us into the Astor hotel on Plymouth Hoe, telling the receptionist that we were brothers and didn't mind sharing. The city was all I had hoped for. After being almost wiped from the face of the earth by German bombers during World War Two, it was now like the phoenix rising from the ashes. Although it still had a lot of bomb damage, new shops and roads were springing up in the city centre, department stores full of goods, Christmas lights all over the place, it was great. After dinner, we went for a walk and found ourselves down near the dock area. We found a pub and could hear the sound of laughter so in we went.

The place was packed – mainly with men, the few women that were there were made up to the nines. It reminded me of The Palmerston in Walthamstow. At the far end of the bar was a small stage with a piano player sitting at an old upright and a drummer next to him. Standing at the mike belting out a song was an overdressed woman in a scarlet evening gown covered in sequins. Her hair was bottle blond and she was very heavily made-up. When she finished her song, she went into a string of jokes, all with double entendre. The audience loved it, us included. We got some drinks and got a bit closer to the stage, she really was brassy. Slowly it began to dawn on us – and I'm not sure which one of us saw the light first – it was no lady, it was a bloke! I was watching my first female impersonator at work and I thought he was magic. He had the audience eating out of the palm of his hand. Then we both took a closer look at the people watching the show. They were as I have said nearly all male – they were also nearly all homosexual. Looking back, it must have been the fact that some were holding hands, or the added fact that there seemed to be an abundance of silk shirts and chiffon scarves! But joy, oh joy, they were all so relaxed and having such a great time with people of their own ilk. I had never seen so many homosexuals in my life – I didn't know that there were this many in the whole country, let alone in one city! Once we got used to the place and its atmosphere we both relaxed. Terry had his arm around my shoulder and I got close in to him, something I never ever thought I would be able to do in public, but I did realise that once we were back outside the pub it would be back to 'normal' for us, and I daresay for the vast majority of the others too, but in there it was bliss.

On the way back to the hotel Terry said to me "You could do that."

"Do what?"

"Dress up like that bloke in the pub."

I stopped walking and looked at him. "Wear a dress! what the fuck for?"

"Well to earn money for a start. You're always cracking jokes when you put the bands on in the club. Think of the crowds you would pull if you did it like him."

"Have you lost your bleeding marbles or what? Do that? In the club? In Newquay! I'd be run out of fucking town with you close at my heels." I shook my head in disbelief. "I don't believe you just said that."

"What do you mean, run out of town? He wasn't tonight, was he? They loved him."

"I know they did but did you or did you not see the audience? they were – well, they were – all like us – queer."

He laughed," I know that, you plum, but there were some straight people there."

"Oh well," I mocked, "that's all right then. I can just see it now at the Off-Beat, I'll be on stage dressed like Charley's fucking Aunt, and you and Cherry will be in the audience! because we are the only two queers in Newquay!! Well, bollocks to that – not me – no way!"

"All right, all right, you've made your point. But," he persisted "do it without the dress. Start telling more jokes as you put the bands on, start taking the piss like that bloke did." I looked at him. "I mean it," he took my arm gently, "you could do it. You're very funny on stage, just do longer – at least have a try."

And so I did. Each time I went on stage at the club I started to do longer, cracking gags and sending the audience up, and much to my surprise they loved it.

A couple of weeks later Terry very casually told me he had met someone from St Austell (a nearby town) who had a small pub and had heard about me. "And he wants you to do his place."

"What, put a band in? Well, how small is this pub?"

"Not a band! He wants you to appear."

"Me!!"

"Yes, you."

"Terry," he could tell by the tone in my voice that I was not happy, "I can't. I may be all right in front of those people at the club, but they all know me."

He smiled. "They'll pay you a fiver."

"How much?"

"Five quid for twenty minutes' work."

"I don't know." Five pounds was a lot of money then, but I was very unsure – although tempted.

"Look," he said trying to reassure me, "nobody will know you there and I'll be with you, and so what if you don't do very well? You'll still get paid and at least you would have tried it. Anyway, I know you will do well, I keep telling you – you're very funny on stage. You make people laugh."

"Do I?" I knew he believed in me and he was always telling me so, But – and it was a big but – did I believe it? The answer was, no, I didn't.

"Look," he said, putting his arms around me, "if you won't do it for yourself, then please do it for me – please!" Well, I couldn't say no to him, and it was nice to have someone with that amount of faith in me – so I agreed to do it.

The day arrived, and Cherry arrived too. Terry had told her as soon as I had agreed to do the job, and the two of them had been working my 'act' out, and planning amongst themselves what I was going to do and what I was going to wear. Anyone would have thought I was going to do a TV show, not appear in some back-street pub. Still, I was pleased they were doing the planning. I was far too scared to think, never mind plan!

We found the pub and Terry went in to "smooth the way," whatever that was supposed to mean. As he disappeared into the pub I could see the windows were plastered with posters proclaiming my appearance there tonight.

"Fuck! Look!" I nudged Cherry.

"Oh sod you! That hurt,' she cried, nudging me back with twice the power, "I saw them – see, fame at last. Stop getting yourself all worked up." Terry came back out of the pub and beckoned us.

"Upstairs," he pointed "they have got a dressing room for you. I'll unpack the car."

"Unpack what? I'll go on in what I'm wearing."

"You can't," said Cherry, and pushed me upstairs.

I was shown upstairs and into a small tatty bedroom, with a single bed along one wall, a small dressing table in one corner with a cracked mirror and, a couple of chairs. So this was it, was it, my 'dressing room'? Well, I thought, at least I'm starting from the bottom! Terry came in, struggling with two suitcases and another box. "What the bloody hell have you brought? I'm only doing twenty minutes! Not a sodding summer season!!"

Cherry looked at Terry and said quickly, "I'll go get some drinks" and she quickly disappeared. Terry and I went over the act. I kept saying I shouldn't be there, he kept telling me I would be fine. At last, Cherry brought the drinks back, and she must have read my mind because she brought me two large ones.

"Oh great, ta," I said taking one of the drinks, "I'm going to need this." She looked at Terry again and said, "I'll unpack," then she grabbed one of the cases, opened it up and took out a long powder-blue taffeta dress with flounces of blue tulle around the bottom. The top was covered in dark blue and silver sequins. I was speechless as I stared first at Terry then at Cherry then back at the dress.

"NO! NO! NO!" I screamed, "I'm not wearing that fucking thing – no way!!"

"But—"

"Don't fucking but me Terry! What are you trying to do to me?" I got up from the chair. "I'm leaving NOW!"

Terry held my arm. "You can't go."

"Why? If I want to go I will."

"We can't go, any of us," said Cherry, "I got the drinks on tick!"

"Well," I turned to Terry, "pay for them!"

"I can't," he said sheepishly, "I don't have any money on me."

I looked at Cherry. She just shrugged, and I knew I hadn't any money – I thought that Terry had brought some. "All right, I'll go on, but not in THAT," I said, pointing to the dress.

Terry put his arms around me. "Trust me – you do love me, don't you?"

"You know I love you, but—" He cut me short.

"Well then, if you love me you must surely know by now that I feel the same towards you, and that I would never do anything to hurt or embarrass you. I know you can do this," he picked up the dress, "not only do it, but do it well. So please just try it out and if it doesn't work – then I promise I'll never ask you to do it again."

I looked into his eyes and I could see the love and the confidence he had in me shining out. I thought, "Well, he is giving all that, the least I can do is to show him that it's justified," so I gave in.

Cherry, with a huge sigh of relief, dived into the other cases and produced a blonde wig, shoes, make-up, the lot! Terry gave me a hug and then told me that he and Cherry had taken my measurements from my other clothes and that she had worked like crazy to get it all ready. She did my make-up and brushed out the wig, then they both pushed, pulled and coaxed me into the dress and finally the shoes – high stiletto silver evening sandals.

"Stand up and look in the mirror," Terry was saying as he helped me to my feet. "Well?"

It was not me, that big blonde tart that stared back at me through the mirror, mouth open and eyes heavy with false lashes staring back at me.

"You look brilliant," Cherry said, hugging me so tight that I nearly stopped breathing. She also said, "Well?"

"Give me a gin and tonic and make it a large one!" was my reply. I remembered hearing once that appearance was half the battle, and as I stared at myself in that mirror I knew I could win the other half. Suddenly from nowhere, my confidence told me that, providing I didn't panic, Terry was right – I could do it.

Then I could hear Terry saying, "But you don't even like gin," and I remembered those gin and limes I had with Bunny and how good I had felt at that bar.

"Only with lime," I heard myself say, "I like it with tonic." Poor Terry was the one in the flap now. He rushed out and came back moments later with a large gin and tonic with ice and, for some reason, no lemon.

"Here," he pushed the glass into my hand, "I hope you know what you're drinking – for Christ sake don't get pissed – not yet anyway."

"Stop it, you're making me even more nervous, "I put the glass to my lips and drank, in fact, I drank the lot! "Oh boy! did I need that! right, lead me to my public!" We all laughed, but it did help calm me down, and to this day before I go on stage I always have a large G and T. Ice, no lemon!

They both relaxed, and went over the act with me until there was a knock on the door and a voice calling out "Is 'e ready? We'll 'ave a bleedin' riot soon if 'e don't appear before long!"

"Shit!" My legs turned to jelly. Terry called out, "Right, we're on our way! Come on," he said, once again pulling me to my feet, "your public really are waiting." I hobbled down the stairs in my high heels, nearly breaking my ankle in the process, then we were outside the function room door. Terry opened the door and let them know I was ready, then came a roll on the drums and a voice saying "Well, it's cabaret time and here he is – Mister Ricky Greene!" Terry opened the door even wider and pushed me gently but firmly into the room. At the same time, I heard him say:

"You can do it – go on, kill 'em!"

When I got into the room it was packed. I thought there must have been at least a thousand people in there – but in truth, it was probably more like eighty! I could feel my heart pounding, I was petrified – all those people – it was so unreal. Then I saw that they were all smiling and laughing – then I heard them oohing and aahing, and they were clapping –yes, they were clapping me! I made my way to the tiny stage, the pianist and drummer were bashing out a tune and "playing me on". I started to relax and soon I too was smiling, beaming in fact. I reached the stage and tried to step up but I couldn't – the bloody dress was too tight. I started to panic, then I tried again, still I couldn't do it. I could feel the sweat begin to run down between my shoulder blades. What the fuck was I going to do? Then I saw a young guy standing very close to me, he was laughing with the rest of them. I wasn't sure if he was laughing at me or at my predicament, but I suddenly yelled to him, "Well don't just stand there, handsome, give a girl a hand!" I put out my hand and the guy, still smiling, helped me up onto the stage and the audience loved it – and I hadn't done anything! Yet there they were, clapping and cheering! So I started to tell gags, and ten minutes turned into twenty minutes and twenty into forty before I had finished the act and made my way back to the dressing room. As I walked through the crowds to calls of "more!", people patted me on the back telling me I was great or good or whatever. At last, I reached the door and went into the corridor to be met by Terry, who threw his arms around me.

"What did I tell you? I said you could do it! They loved you, and so do I!" He swung me around, kissing me as he did so. "Oh," he laughed, "I've just kissed a woman!"

"Bastard!" I was laughing with him, "put me down and let's get back up to the dressing room so that I can get this fucking frock off!" When we reached the room all three of us were talking at once. I felt as though I had just wowed the audience at the London Palladium, and if I had I couldn't have been happier or felt more exhilarated than I did that night. I got changed and we all went down to the bar as we walked into the room it took a few moments before people recognised me but when they did they gave me another round of applause – it was great! The landlord of the pub came over and said "Brilliant – brilliant – that entrance you did making out you couldn't get on the stage – so funny – brilliant." I looked at the other two, who sat with bemused looks on their faces, then I grinned and said, "Thank you, it always gets a laugh!"

I left the pub drunk but very happy – and with a return booking – and he had upped the fee to six guineas. If anybody had told me that night that I would still be climbing in and out of drag over fifty years later – admittedly now only for panto – I never would have believed them.

It was now spring 1961. I had done a few out-of-town gigs as a female impersonator and had still been able to keep my private life a secret. By now Terry was repairing cars and we were doing quite well, then he had to go to London to collect some tools from the family home. He said he would be away for three days. The days came and went and on the fourth day, I started to worry. Cherry turned up to see if he could do something to her car. When I told her he wasn't back and I was worried, she said that in all probability he had stopped off somewhere to visit friends or he had broken down.

"But he wouldn't just visit someone – he would know I would worry. Anyway, if he had he would have phoned."

"Well, he could hardly phone you, since you're not on the phone and anyway he may have forgotten my number." I could sense that she was trying hard to look on the bright side, she stayed with me that night. We hardly slept a wink, we spent most of the time drinking endless cups of tea and coffee. Then, at about half past seven in the morning, there was a knock at the door. I nearly jumped out of my skin. I looked at Cherry, she got up and opened the door and I heard her say "Come in" and in came two of Terry's mates from the RAF camp. I smiled at them but something in their faces told me all was not well. I felt my stomach tie its self in knots as I asked, "What's wrong, what's the matter?"

Mark and Pete were both career airmen. Mark was a short, stocky guy from Manchester and when I asked the question he shuffled his feet about, looking uncomfortable, and nodded to Pete. I looked straight at Pete. "Just tell me what's wrong," I spoke very quietly to him, I could see he was in some distress. He was a tall, slim, handsome bloke, dark-skinned with a mop of jet black hair, but now his face was pale, almost white and he was shaking, he looked at me his eyes filling with tears and said softly:

"There has been an accident," the tears were now streaming down his face and he croaked, "Terry's dead." I watched him close his eyes as the tears became uncontrollable. I was numb. The silence for a split second was almost unbearable, then it was broken by a scream. It was Cherry, she grabbed me but I couldn't say anything. I could see Pete's lips moving but I couldn't hear anything. I was aware, yet not aware. Mark came over and took Cherry, who was by now sobbing uncontrollably, then I could feel hands – strong hands – on my shoulders. squeezing me gently as though trying to give comfort but not quite knowing what to do. I just stood there with Pete's voice ringing in my ears: "Terry's dead, Terry's dead." It would not stop. I looked into Pete's face looking for a sign that this might all be some bad dream. His eyes told me that it was for real. Then I collapsed.

I don't know how long I passed out for, but when I came to I was lying on the bed. Cherry was sitting on the edge of the bed holding and stroking my hand. I felt something cold on my forehead. I looked up to see Pete, his handsome face now puffed and tear-stained, sponging my face with a cold cloth. He said to Cherry, "We must get a doctor," I shook my head and told him "No, no doctor," then I tried to sit up, but I felt so weak.

"Stay there." It was Pete. He pulled the pillows from the other side of the bed and put them behind my back.

"How did you find out?" I asked him.

"We had a phone call from his brother. I'm not sure how it happened but I think he skidded. He died in hospital the next day." He just looked at me and the tears came again.

They stayed with me all that day and night. Pete told me that he had guessed about me and Terry, and that Terry was constantly talking about me and only seemed to be happy if I were around. Pete hadn't said anything to the other lads and he didn't think they knew. I asked him if he had ever told Terry his thoughts. He said no, he had wanted to but he didn't know how to approach the subject, and anyway it was none of his business. He liked Terry as a mate and that was that, but he wasn't sure how the others would take it if they found out. I asked him not to tell them. I also had to ask when the funeral would be. He said he didn't know as there would have to be an inquest, but he would let me know. Then he said, "I don't want to pry, but do his folks know about you and him," I could feel his awkwardness, "what I mean is—"

I interrupted him. "Do they know he was homosexual? No, they didn't, and as far as I know, they know nothing of me either – and that's how it has to stay, there has been enough pain without me inflicting more."

"But the funeral?" Cherry said,

"I can't go. Pete, will you go?"

"Of course."

"And be sure to let him know that I wanted to be there."

He smiled "Sure, you know I will.

The days slipped into weeks and I didn't leave the Retreat. Cherry came by every day to bring me food which I didn't eat and to replace the gin which I did drink.

"You have to stop this – pull yourself together," she would say almost every day, "pull yourself together." It sounded as though I were some sort of self-assembly kit. I didn't pull myself together, in fact I was falling apart, and poor Cherry was watching me do it. Try as she might, there was nothing she could do to stop me. I refused to see anybody or talk to anybody – people did come round, but I just kept the curtains closed and let them bang at the door until they got fed up and left. Gradually Cherry's daily visits got shorter from a few hours each day to barely a few minutes. But I didn't care, that's what I wanted – to be left alone, just me and Satch and my thoughts. I didn't even cry very much – the odd tear now and again – I just drank, and thought of what Terry and I had planned to do with our lives. He wanted a proper garage and workshops, and I wanted my own nightclub, and we were going to call the club The Green Cockatoo, God knows why but that's the name we chose, and Terry wanted me to star in the cabaret – we had such plans, we would spend hours talking about them. Now – nothing, just emptiness – unless I stayed indoors. Then I could be left with my thoughts and make my dreams come true for a little while at least. I would sober up and try to look forward, but I couldn't or didn't want to, I don't know which, so I would pour another drink.

Cherry kept the club going for as long as she could. She would bring me the bills and I would tell her that I'd pay them later but I didn't – so in the end she had to close it. "I had to shut the club last night. The rent's long overdue and the drinks man wouldn't leave anything until he got his money. I'm sorry Ricky, I did try."

"Fuck him and fuck the club," was all that I could say. I didn't want to say it, I loved the club – the trouble was I hated life and I hated living. I just wanted to be with Terry – but I lacked the courage to do anything about it.

Now the weeks turned into months and my money was running out. Cherry said to me one day that I would have to cut down on my drinking or there would be nothing left. So I did – I cut out the tonic and drank the gin neat, and instead of Gordon's I got her to get the cheapest she could find. She argued with me and said that was the end. She refused to go on helping me to slowly kill myself. I told her if she didn't help somebody else would. I didn't want to put her through all this, but by this time I was like somebody trapped in quicksand: the more I fought to free myself, the further I sank, so in the end I just let it take me down slowly.

One day the door burst open. It was Cherry and she had someone with her. I was in my now usual state but I heard her say, "See what I mean? Just look at him and the place." I didn't hear the rest of the conversation just some hushed voices then the door slammed shut. "Good," I thought, "they've fucked off." Then I heard someone go into the kitchen, and a few moments later return. The next thing I knew I was soaking wet and spluttering for air.

"Wake up, you stupid bastard! Just look at the state you're in!"

I blinked the freezing cold water out of my eyes and tried to focus on the person behind the voice. Then I recognised Pete, he looked distressed and angry all at the same.

"Yes, it's me. I've been away on a course. But just look at you! What the fuck are you trying to do, you selfish sod? Poor Cherry's nearly out of her mind with worry and all you can do is drink. What would Terry say if he could see you like this? He'd have a fit." I just looked at him, I tried to speak but the words wouldn't come. "Look at this place, it's disgusting, Ricky – and look at yourself – you look like a tramp." He went to the windows and pulled back the curtains the sunlight streamed in hurting my eyes. "Now will you look? Go on Rick, take a look at how you're living." I opened my eyes slowly to get accustomed to the light. I looked round the room. It was littered with filthy clothes, ashtrays were piled high and what hadn't gone in them was all over the furniture. The floor was covered with empty gin bottles and cigarette packets. Dust covered everything. I looked at the bed I was lying on. It was a disgrace, the linen was grey, not white and stained with Christ knows what. I felt so ashamed. I looked at Pete he came up to the bed and put his arms around me, and I wept like I have never wept before.

"It's all right, it's all right," he said gently, "you should have done this a long while ago. Cry as long as you like." And I did. He helped me up and sat me in the armchair, went into the kitchen and made me some coffee. When he came back he was smiling. "Feel better?" He handed me the coffee, my first in seven weeks.

"I feel so ashamed."

"Then don't. Cherry's told me a bit about you and I know it

can't have been easy for you." I was about to say, "You can't possibly know what I have gone through" when he said, "My brother's queer – sorry, homosexual – that's how I guessed about you and Terry, and I know what he went through, it nearly killed him. Fortunately, my parents have stood by him – they don't understand – but they are not condemning him. It took me and my Dad some time to come to terms with it but it's – well, its fine now. I'll stand by you and so will Cherry, but you will have to help us, OK?"

"Yes, OK."

He took my hand and squeezed it. "Promise?"

"I promise."

I did get a grip on myself and tried to get my life back into some order, but it didn't happen overnight. Gradually I started going out, but everywhere I went I could see Terry – any car like his, any RAF uniform, all brought memories flooding back. If I were sitting in a pub or a café thinking about him and about us, and somebody came and spoke to me, even if it were only to say, "Nice to see you again," I began to resent the intrusion. I tried not to show my resentment by smiling and talking small talk and I supposed it must have worked. Even Cherry would say "Oh, it's great seeing you back to your old self", but I wasn't. I was determined, however, not to let her or anybody else see that – nobody likes a misery, not for long anyhow. I had at least learned that. So whatever I was suffering on the inside, I would keep it to myself and try my hardest to put up a false front to let the world believe I was happy. I worked hard at it so hard I didn't even notice that my twenty-first birthday had come and gone until I realised that it was the end of June 1961. It didn't bother me. I was glad in a way that nobody had remembered it, I don't think I could have faced a party – it would have pushed my resolve to appear happy to the limits.

By now I was broke. I had no interest in the club. It remained closed, and I owed money for rent and other bills, so I went back to my old boss and he gave me a job in his small arcade. Only two of us worked there. My colleague was an older man, Norman, an ex-farmworker now retired, a small man, stooped from spending years doing back-breaking work on the land. He lived alone and had never married, much, I think, to his regret – he had spent much of his life looking after his parents. He was a nice man, quiet and amiable. The arcade was open until ten o'clock at night, so one week I would work days, the next the evening shift. Slowly, I got back on my feet, but somehow Newquay just was not the same anymore. I felt like a stranger and I hated going back to the Retreat every night on my own. I wasn't sleeping at all well and found myself sitting up half the night, playing melancholy music and being very tempted to open another bottle.

At the end of September, I met Cherry for a drink one night and dropped the bombshell. "I'm leaving. I can't stay here anymore."

"You can't just leave! Why, what's wrong? You're OK now, so why go?"

It was very difficult for me, trying to explain the way I felt, but I told her I had to go. She was upset and cried. I felt so wretched doing this to her but I had to do it. I gave her a letter for Pete, asking him to understand (and I'm sure he did), then I asked her to look after my things until I could send for them.

"What about Satch?" she asked me. "You can't take him, can you?"

"No." then I explained that the people in the next chalet had said they would look after him, they loved him as much as I did. I had thought very seriously about taking him with me, but as I had no idea where I was going, it wouldn't have been fair to him – he loved the beaches and the freedom he had, so I had to say goodbye to him. I know that non-dog-lovers will think I'm crazy, but he knew I was going and for the two days before I left he wouldn't leave my side. I asked Cherry not to tell anybody I was leaving – I didn't want any fuss or any awkward questions. I didn't even tell my boss on the day of my departure. I walked to the bus station with a few things in a brown carrier bag. As I passed the main arcade I handed my keys to one of the guys and simply said that I was going away for a few days. At the bus station I got on the first bus out, and as it drove along the front away from Newquay, I didn't even look back.

7 – OUT OF THE FRYING PAN

As the bus lumbered along the coast road, I had a sudden panic attack. "What the hell was I doing, leaving my friends? Where was I going?" I almost got off the bus at the next stop but I forced myself to stay put. The further we went, the more relaxed I became, then I counted up what money I had – it amounted to a little over fifteen pounds. "Shit!" I thought, "I'm going to have to be careful." So where could I go? I thought about Mum and Dad, I wondered what they would say if I turned up on the doorstep. I tried to imagine it, then I thought about how long it had been since I had seen them or even written to them –I decided I couldn't face them. Aunt Bess – what about Aunt Bess? But again, no – though I had written to her and sent cards, she was far too old for me to want to give her any worries. So where should I go? Then I thought of Terry and our trip to Plymouth. "That's the place, plenty of work, new people." Plymouth it would be. I got off the bus in St Austell and went to a café for a cup of tea. As I went to pay for the tea, I put my hand in my pocket and I was gripped with a sudden fear – I couldn't find my money! I'd had two five-pound notes, five one-pound notes, a ten-shilling note and some change. The woman behind the counter gave me an exasperated look and held out her hand for her money. By this time I was in a cold sweat. Then, in my inside pocket, I felt the crinkle of paper money. I grabbed it and pulled my hand out. When I looked, I had found the five ones and the ten-shilling note but not the fivers. "The bus! I must have dropped them on the bus!" I raced from the café with the woman yelling after me. When I reached the bus station I asked an inspector if the bus from Newquay was still there – he told me it had gone on its journey. I then asked if anybody had handed in two five-pound notes – not that he was aware of, he told me, but try the office. They also said no, but if I left my name and address they would send it on if it were found, so I left my name and Cherry's address and went back onto the street. Now I really was in trouble, and I couldn't dare waste or lose any more money, so I would have to walk to Plymouth. Was this, I wondered, some kind of omen? Should I turn back? No – Plymouth I had said, so Plymouth it would be.

The fact that Plymouth was over fifty miles away seemed to have escaped me, or at least didn't daunt me. I thought of my trip to Wales with Alf and was confident that the walk to Plymouth wouldn't be a problem. No sooner had I left the outskirts of St Austell, it started to rain and my problems began. The fine mist of rain soon turned into a downpour. I tried to shelter under trees and hedges but I still got drenched. I tried thumbing lifts, but as the night closed in, the traffic on the narrow country roads became sparse.

Thoroughly soaked, cold and tired, I found a barn, wrapped myself in some old rags and slept a fitful sleep. The next morning, stiff with cold, I looked out from the barn and the rain was still falling. Back now to the fine mist and so it went on. After nearly three days I finally reached my destination.

I must have look one hell of a sight as I got to the outskirts of Plymouth – unshaven, dirty and still carrying my carrier bag. I waited at a bus stop and treated myself to a ride. I went to the main railway station, made my way to the Gents' lavatory and treated myself again, this time to a wash and brush up. After a cup of tea and some toast at the station buffet, I set about finding somewhere to live. It took me sometime before I found a bed and breakfast in North Street. By this time, I was soaked again and almost shivering with the cold. I rang the bell and the door was opened by a short plump lady wearing glasses. She was about thirty-five and had a smile from ear to ear, she spoke with a wonderful Devonshire accent. "Yes, m'dear?"

"I'm looking for somewhere to stay," I tried to sound cheerful and hoped I didn't look too much of a mess. She beamed at me.

"Well, now you've found somewhere m'dear, so come in out of the cold before you catch your death." I walked past her and into the hall. It smelt of home cooking and warmth and love. I could hear children squealing in a distant room. "Well, I'm Mrs Webb m'dear, and who might you be?" I told her my name and she ushered me into the kitchen at the back of the house. This was where the children were, three of them aged from about four to about nine, two boys and a girl. When I walked into the room they all looked up at me, then they gathered around me asking questions: Who was I? Where did I come from? How old was I? Just kids being curious. Mrs Webb shushed them out of the kitchen, telling them not to ask so many questions and not to be so rude. I laughed and said I didn't mind, and how nice they were. She beamed again. "That's kind of you to say so. Now, you take those wet things off, and let's dry you out." I handed her my coat and took my wet shoes off, praying there were no holes in my socks. There weren't, thank goodness, but my socks were soaking, so she asked for those as well. She spread all the things around the Aga, told me to sit down at the big pine table and then she made me a cup of steaming hot tea. "Well now m'dear, where are you staying at present?"

I was going to weave a better picture of myself, but I was tired and hungry, so I said "Nowhere. I've just left Newquay – well, three days ago. Broken romance." I don't know why I said that, maybe to stop any more questions, I don't know.

"Well, never you mind m'dear, I understand. Now, about money, 'tis awful but I have to ask."

"Oh – well, I've got this," I answered, as I dug into my pockets, pulled out the crumpled notes and put them on the table. She cooed at them, then at me.

"Well that won't last you very long, will it? I charge nearly as much as that for a week." She must have seen my face fall, because she added quickly, "that's with all meals of course m'dear – and I usually charge a week in advance." she added almost apologetically.

"Ah well, in that case," I got to my feet, "I'm sorry if I have wasted your time, Mrs Webb, but I have no job you see, and I thought that I-I-I—" Shit! I was stammering again.

"Now you sit back down in that chair," she got up and went over to the stove. "I'll make some more tea. I said," she carried on talking as she made the tea, "that I usually charge a week in advance, but I know you can't afford that – you're a decent chap, I can tell, so I'm going to trust you, right? Now drink this, and stop worrying so." She put a fresh cup of tea in front of me.

"Thank you, Mrs Webb, – I don't know what to say."

"You have just said it m'dear. What you need now is a good hot bath, something to eat and a good night's sleep. Then tomorrow you can go down to the Labour Exchange and sign on the dole, then start looking for a job. How does that sound?"

"Fine, just fine. I won't let you down."

She beamed again "I know that. Now let me show you your room," she picked up my carrier bag. "I'll take your luggage, shall I?" We both laughed and she led me up the stairs, pointing out the bathroom as we went. She opened the door on a bright room, with a double bed covered in a gold candlewick bedspread and topped with a gold brocade eiderdown. There was a large wardrobe, a dressing table and a chest of drawers. Either side of the bed were side tables with lamps, and on the floor a thick flowery patterned carpet that nearly matched the curtains. Everything was spotless.

"Will this suit you, Ricky?" I heard her say.

"It's-it's very nice. Y-y-yes, thank you."

"Good. Now, I'm going to run you a bath. You'll find clean towels in the bathroom, and behind the door you will also find my husband's old dressing gown – you can borrow that, he won't mind. Then I'll call you when dinner is ready and you can meet the rest of the family."

I thanked her again and she left. I looked around the room again and thought how lucky I had been, then I had my bath – oh, it was bliss! I felt clean and warm and safe again. I cleaned the bath, went back to my room and pulled the bedclothes down, and climbed into freshly starched crisp white sheets. "Just for five minutes, "I told myself, and the next thing I remember is Mrs Webb calling me for breakfast!

That day after breakfast I went to the Labour Exchange and signed on. Then I made my way to the docks and found the pub that Terry and I had gone to on our trip. It was lunchtime when I entered the pub, and it was empty, apart from one old lady sitting at a corner table. She was wearing a heavy top-coat and a floral headscarf and was huddled over what looked like a glass of stout. She didn't look up at me as I went to the bar. The barman didn't look up either. He was standing at one end of the bar, his elbows resting on the bar while he read a racing paper. I coughed. He looked up, plainly annoyed at being disturbed, then he slowly put the paper down and came down to where I was standing, a cigarette hanging from the side of his mouth. He didn't speak, just made a "What the fuck do you want?" gesture with his head. I asked for a Mackeson. He reached under the counter, brought up a bottle, opened it, took a glass from the rack over the bar and poured a small amount of the beer into it. Then he pushed the glass and the bottle towards me, mumbling the price as he did so. I, in turn, put a ten-shilling note on the counter and waited for my change. He picked up the note and shook his head with disdain, as if to say, "Couldn't you find anything smaller?" Then he slammed my change down in front of me and went back to his paper. A far cry, I thought to myself, from the happy friendly atmosphere we had met the last time I was in the pub. I took my drink to a table, sat down. took a sip of the stout and looked around the bar. Now in daylight, the place looked shabby, seedy, even. The carpet was worn and stained with – well, I dreaded to think with what! The wallpaper. painted a garish red, was hanging off in places.

When we had come in that night, the place was full of colour – lights gleamed around the stage and sparkled on the backdrop, it was like a West End nightclub. But now, with the torn and patched stage curtains hanging limply to one side of the stage, and the backdrop nothing more than a few sheets of silver paper pinned to the wall, it looked – sad. And it made me feel the same, it was almost as though that whole night hadn't happened, or that it was as seedy as this pub now was. I shivered and drank my drink. Some workmen came in, their overalls covered in paint and plaster. They were swearing and laughing. The old woman still sat staring into her glass. I got up and left and never went back.

I stayed at Mrs Webb's for six weeks until I found a job. It hadn't been as easy as I had expected: there were jobs to be had, but I had no qualifications, so when the man at the Labour Exchange offered me a live-in job as a breakfast and veg cook, I jumped at the chance. "You can cook, I suppose?" he said, not really caring if I could or couldn't as long as I went for the interview. "Yes of course!" I replied indignantly. Imagine my shock when I found out that the job was at the Astor Hotel on the Hoe! As I went into the back entrance of the hotel to be interviewed by the chef, I thought of the irony of the situation and hoped nobody recognised me from my last visit. The chef was a tall greying Maltese man of about fifty. He asked me some simple basics about cooking and I got the job. I went home and told Mrs Webb, and although she said she would be sorry to see me go, she was pleased I had found something at last.

My room was not in the main hotel as I had thought, but in the annexe just around the corner. It was right at the top of a dilapidated house that had once been a small hotel. My room, in fact, was one of two in the attic. When the porter who came with me to show me the room pushed open the door, my heart sank. To say it was a dump was an understatement. It was large, with a single bed, a wardrobe with one door missing, and an old mock leather armchair – ripped and with the stuffing sticking out in dirty grey tufts. In one corner was a filthy hand basin. The rest of the 'furnishings' consisted of a table and two chairs. In the middle of the room, laying on top of the filthy lino that covered the whole floor, was an even filthier worn and stained piece of carpet. I was stunned. "Not the Ritz, is it," the porter said. I didn't bother to answer him. "Oh, one more thing" he added, "don't leave anything of value in here."

"Why?"

"Look at your door," was his reply, before he vanished down the dusty staircase.

I looked at the door– the lock had been broken. Then I looked at the door frame – the wood was splintered. I went over to the door across the landing. That too had been smashed, and the tenant had put a padlock on to keep out thieves. I went back into my room and thought of the Retreat and of my room at Mrs Webb's, and I wept.

My day's work at the Astor started at six o'clock in the morning. When I arrived at the kitchen the first morning, I hadn't a clue of what to do. I looked into cupboards and the pantry and waited for someone to ask me for something. Then a small mousy woman about thirty years old arrived. She looked up at me. her plain face smiling out under a mass of light brown frizzy hair. She was about five feet tall.

"Oh hello, you waiting for somebody?"

"Well yes, yes I am, my name's Ricky, and you are?"

"Tilly, the kitchen maid" she giggled

"Well, what do I do, Tilly?"

She started opening fridge doors and lighting two huge gas grills "Just cook the breakfasts when the waitresses ask for 'em. I'll help you." And she went on to show me the ropes, which entailed cooking endless sausages and bacon, scrambling eggs, and adding more to a large pan of congealed porridge, picking out any lumps as it was stirred. I soon got the hang of it. After breakfast, Tilly would set about washing the pots, and I would cut up cabbage, peel carrots and pull the poultry. I had watched my Dad clean out a chicken, so I knew what to do, which seemed to impress the chef.

I enjoyed working there even though the hours were long. After we had finished lunches, Chef would go home, but I had to stay and prepare for dinner, so I would finish work around about four o'clock, making it a ten-hour day, six days a week. But on the day before my day off, I would have to prepare the vegetables for the following day! So by the time I finished, I needed the day off in order to recover! I was quite unused to working such long hours, so when I finished work I would go back to my room, read a little, then sleep. I kept myself very much to myself. I had only been there a few days – and was in bed – when, about midnight, I heard a crash of thunder and rain lashing against the window. I pulled the clothes up around my chin, and suddenly felt water on my face! I leapt out of bed and turned the light on, only to see the rain pouring through the ceiling right over my bed. I quickly pulled the bed to a dry spot and put a bowl under the leaking roof, then I pulled off the wet top sheet and got back into bed. I had hardly been there for more than five minutes when the same thing happened again – and kept on happening. I moved my bed five times that night, finally finding a dry spot – but then I couldn't sleep. The pitter-patter of the water dripping into bowls, cups and tins nearly drove me mad. The next morning, after I had cooked the breakfasts, I went to the hotel manager to report my leaking roof. He was a small squat Greek man, about forty. I told him what had happened the night before then he said, "So you find a dry place?"

"Yes, eventually."

"That's good, that's good," he nodded his head, pleased, I thought, that I had at least been able to keep reasonably dry. Wrong!! He looked up and quite calmly and pointedly said, "The room is free, you understand, free? So, no more complaints, eh? Now go back to your work." He turned on his heel and left me standing there in complete disbelief. I went back to the kitchen and never mentioned it again, but I could hardly forget it. The "dry spot" was right in the middle of the room, so it looked a little strange, to say the least, but Christmas was nearly here and I needed the job.

With the money I was earning I bought some new clothes, amongst which was a beautiful brown suit with small cloth-covered buttons at the cuffs and at the bottom of the side seams on the trousers, the jacket was lined with gold satin. I loved that suit – some nights I would come home from work and put the suit on, together with my new shoes and shirt and tie, then stand in front of the mottled, stained mirror on the wardrobe door, looking at myself and dream of meeting somebody. I was desperately lonely by this time, but putting on my suit gave me some hope – stupid I know, but it kept me sane. Loneliness is the most desperate thing. If you have a broken arm or leg or a bad cold, people can see it, and understand it, but people can't see inside of you at the nagging gnawing pain for which there is no pill. They can't understand the longing for someone to hold you, to kiss you, to want you. Some people, of course, can cope with it, I can to a certain extent, but only by fooling myself – only by making out it doesn't matter, by pretending that right now I don't want anybody, but deep down, aching to love and be loved.

b

Christmas was nearly here. I had a card from Cherry, she wanted to know when I was coming back – people kept asking her, she said. She told me Satch was fine, and if I wasn't coming back, what should she do with my things? I wrote back telling her to get rid of all my things – they all brought back memories, and although I could never forget, I could not face being reminded every day of what might have been. As much as I loved her and my friends in Newquay, I was trying very hard to make a new life for myself, so I would never be going back. I had to go forward.

Tilly, Chef and Mrs Webb all gave me cards, so I had four – quite good I thought, certainly an improvement on my twenty-first anyway. I had to work Christmas Day. Chef opened some wine and all three of us got pissed, but we managed to serve the lunch without mishap until it came time for the Christmas pudding. These were in a large upright steamer. Tilly stood in front of it holding a large tray and swaying ever so slightly. I opened the steamer and a rush of steam burst out into the kitchen covering Tilly.

"Oops," she yelled, giggling, "that nearly poached my tits then!" We were all three of us laughing as I took the puddings from the steamer and put them onto Tilly's tray. As I was about to put the last one on, she moved slightly and I dropped it onto the floor, spilling hot Christmas pud onto the red stone tiles. Tilly went to move out of the way, stepped in the wrong direction, slipped and threw the remaining puddings up in the air. She fell and the puddings followed her crashing and spilling all over the place. I thought "Shit! Chef will go mad," but when I looked at him he was all but on the floor himself, nearly crying with laughter. By this time we could hear the waitresses calling for the pudding.

"What are we going to do, Chef?" I yelled in panic.

"Stay there," he said, still laughing, then he took a large saucepan full of custard from the stove and put it on the floor next to the spilt puddings. Handing me a serving spoon, he said "Well, don't just stand there, dish up!" and so I did.

It was now February and very cold. My room being directly under the roof, it was particularly cold, and I had no heating whatsoever in the room. I had no choice, I would have to speak to the manager again. I had a word with Chef first, and he said it was wrong to expect me to live like that and I should speak to the manager. So I went to his office. He sat and listened to me, then he exploded, his face contorted in its anger. "Why you always make trouble, every time you come to me you want to make trouble."

"But," I protested, "it's not summer, it's February, and it's really cold in my room. I only want a small heater!"

"How many times I have to tell you," he stormed, "room is free! Now get back to your work, you lazy bugger, or I kick you out!" I was astonished. I walked out of the office and into the reception hall. He followed me out and continued shouting, "I don't want you coming with no more complaints!"

"The bastard, the arrogant fucking bastard!" I thought. "Me! Lazy! Ten hours a fucking day, six days a week –the shit!" Then I turned to face him. I was shaking with temper. "What did you call me?" I said slowly and quietly. "You got the cheek to call me lazy?" Now I was yelling, hotel guests were staring, the whole of the reception area came to a standstill. "I'm not lazy, you fat little ball of shit! Well, you can shove your job up your greasy fat arse. Get some other poor bastard to work sixty hours a fucking week for you, and live in that hovel you call a room!" and with that, I picked up a large vase full of flowers from the reception desk and threw it at him. He saw it coming and ducked. The girl on the reception screamed then grinned at me as the vase smashed into the wall behind him showering him with water, flowers and bits of porcelain. "Now," I shouted, "you can fucking sue me!" and I stormed out. He was almost dancing with rage, and yelling threats at me that I would never be able to work in hotels again, and that I had better be out my room at once or he was calling the police! He was still yelling as I walked through the doors and past the doorman, who whispered, "Good for you, about time someone told the little sod." Once in the street, I ran to the annexe and up to my room. "It would be just like him," I thought, "to call the police just to get his revenge." So I quickly packed my things into my new suitcase. "Thank God this is Saturday and I got paid yesterday," I thought as I was about to leave the room. Then I looked around, put the case down and took a broom from the corner of the room. I climbed onto the table and smashed the handle through the rotten ceiling, pulled the table around the room and did the same thing twice more, finally leaving three large holes with daylight clearly visible. "Now," I shouted at the top of my voice, "you will have to fix the fucking roof!"

Before I knew it, I was at the railway station. I looked up at the train departure board and saw Bristol. I bought a single ticket and found a seat. As the train pulled slowly out of the station I began to wonder what the hell I was doing – why was I running away yet again?

I arrived at Temple Meads Station, Bristol, at about three in the afternoon, and once again I found myself looking for somewhere to live. I had my wages and some savings so I knew I would be all right for a few weeks if I were careful. I bought a local paper, and after numerous phone calls found two address I could view. They were both in the Fishponds area of the city, so I treated myself to a taxi and was soon on my way. As the cab nosed its way around the streets I felt my stomach tie in knots again as I wondered what hand fate would deal me this time. "Please God," I thought, "let me find some peace here."

The first 'flat' turned out to be a poky little attic room at the top of a large grey stone house. It boasted a fitted kitchen – well, the old gas cooker was certainly fitted, in fact, I don't suppose it had moved for about fifty years, and neither had the old sink with its piece of old curtain wrapped around it like a skirt, hiding pipes behind its dirty folds – and a cupboard containing the 'Cooking Utensils', two chipped enamel saucepans and an old frying pan. It reminded me of my hovel in Plymouth, so I said very politely I would let them know. Why I didn't just tell them the place was a disgrace, not fit for a pig to live in, I'll never know. The next address was a similar grey granite Victorian villa but this time the flat was a ground floor bedsitting room, with a view over the garden. It had its own bathroom and a small kitchen. The furniture was old but very good and well looked after. For a bed, there was a large Put-U-Up. All in all, a very nice clean flat, so I took it and moved in there and then. After I had unpacked, I went for a walk to explore my new city and I liked what I saw – large granite buildings, small alleys filled with antique shops, then in contrast whole areas of new buildings, department stores and shops. I saw the famous Old Vic Theatre and the Hippodrome (which I was to play many years later). The only thing I did find hard work was the fact that I was either walking up a hill or down one! "But I'll get used to that," I told myself.

It took me about a week to find a job, and when I did it was only a short walk from my new home. I was now a trainee manager for Dolcis, the shoe people. I had passed the shop and saw the position advertised in the window. The manager, a small dapper man of about sixty with snow-white hair and a rose in his buttonhole, interviewed me and took me on there and then. It was only a small shop and employed just two other staff. One was an elderly woman with a blue rinse and a sharp tongue, she seemed to resent anybody else coming into her territory. The other was a timid girl who could do nothing right for Blue Rinse – she was about eighteen and rather spotty, poor thing, but very nice. I think she fancied me, but thankfully in those days familiarity was not encouraged among the staff, and both Blue Rinse and the girl had to accord me the courtesy of addressing me as Mister, and not use my Christian name. This had the effect of making me a little distant – and to that end, I was truly thankful. It didn't please Blue Rinse, she would nearly choke as she addressed me, and always stressed the word in an attempt to show her displeasure at calling someone of my inexperience "Mister". I would retaliate by smiling broadly at her and using her Christian name, "Thank you, Mabel," that would irritate her even more – silly cow.

The timid girl (whose name I have forgotten) would ask me during tea break, or at a time when things were quiet, what I had done the night before. My usual reply was "I stayed in and read a book," or "I went to the pictures." One morning she asked me the same question as usual, and I had given my usual reply, when she added, "Don't you ever go dancing or to a pub?"

"Well – to a pub sometimes – but I'm not much for dancing."

"Oh," she said with some disappointment showing in her voice, then she brightened up. "What pubs do you go in then?"

"Any," I said, "if I fancy a drink and I'm near a pub I go in – that is, if it looks all right – some are a bit, well – a bit rough!"

"I know what you mean," she proceeded to name some of the pubs she went in, and on what nights. I made a mental note of them so that I could avoid them. Then she continued, "And don't ever go in the Spotted Dog on a Saturday or Sunday."

I looked at her blankly. "Why ever not?"

"It's full of queers!" she said in hushed tones, lest Blue Rinse should hear. What had been a boring mundane conversation now sounded distinctly interesting! But I had no idea where this pub was, and I had to find out without arousing her suspicions.

"What?" I exclaimed, "are you sure? What, in Bristol! Oh, that's too bad – how did you find out?"

She, pleased that we were getting friendly, could hardly contain herself. "My boyfriend told me," she gushed.

"Your boyfriend!" I said. She realised her mistake and could have kicked herself.

"No, no," she corrected herself, "my ex-boyfriend. I'm not with him anymore."

"I should hope not, if he goes into pubs like that!" I might just as well have smacked her between the eyes, as the realisation of what I had said sank in.

"Oh, he's not like that," she said in his defence, "he just went in one night for a drink," then she added quickly, "but he didn't stay – he wanted to beat them up!"

"Good for him," I said, and thought, "The bastard!" but still I didn't know where the bloody pub was! "Well, thanks for telling me, I'll stay well away from it. It's the one by the Hippodrome, isn't it?" I asked casually.

"No, silly! Down near the centre – you know!" I didn't, but she then proceeded to give me full directions.

"Oh, that one!" I cried in mock surprise," Well I'll definitely stay away from there, and," I added, "once again, thanks for the warning." Oh God! I could hardly wait for Saturday night!

At last, the day arrived and all day long I wondered what it would be like. Maybe like the pub in Plymouth when Terry and I went there first, packed with other men – men like me! And maybe a female impersonator as well – or perhaps it would be quieter with more class. And who knows, maybe I would meet someone. I could feel the excitement course through my veins. The day seemed to drag on endlessly. Finally, we were closed, and as we were all preparing to go home the timid girl said to me, "Going out tonight, Mr Greene?"

Blue Rinse gave her a cold stare. "You shouldn't ask personal questions, learn to mind your own business, my girl!"

Timid blushed and lowered her head, then mumbled, "I didn't mean any harm."

"That's all right," I said brightly, "I don't mind. There is no great mystery to my life, as a matter of fact, I shall be staying in. There's a programme on the radio I want to hear," then I had a sudden thought. "Oh shit! I hope she doesn't ask what bloody programme!"

"What, on Saturday night? I never stay in on Saturday nights!" she wailed.

"Or any other night I shouldn't wonder," said Blue Rinse, "the state you come to work in, half asleep. Now stop asking silly questions and get off home!" She turned to me, "Good night!" then pushed the girl out of the staff room. "Come on, if I miss my bus because of you —", she went on nagging the poor girl all the way to the door, but she had saved me from any more questions and for that I was very thankful.

I had rushed home, bathed and splashed myself all over with Old Spice, before putting on my brown suit and my Italian-style shoes. Then I looked at myself in the mirror. "Oh yes, very nice, I even fancy myself! Well then, look out Bristol, here I come!" The pub was quite easy to find. I looked at my watch – it was eight o'clock. I walked past the pub at first. "Supposing," I thought, "that everybody knows about it, and someone sees me go in –and tells my boss!" I walked back past it again but now I had a different worry. "Maybe it's the wrong pub or they're not like me – look at the way I'm dressed!" I looked down at my brown suit and Italian shoes. "I look like a queer in this lot! I can't go in – I just can't." So I walked past yet again, and I did this about six times before I held my breath and pushed the door as hard as I could. Bang! "Shit!" I cursed, the bloody door opened outward. I pulled it open this time and went into the pub. All those already inside turned to stare and see who the noisy bastard was. I say all those in the pub – at a quick count that amounted to about seven, including three bar staff! I made my way to the bar, looking anywhere but at anybody else! I ordered a drink and slunk away into a corner. After a while, I casually glanced around me. It was just a pub, a bit scruffy but not bad. The other people in the bar were middle-aged men, all standing on their own sipping at their drinks and doing what I was doing – looking around. A couple of them caught my eye and smiled. I quickly stared down at the table as I felt my cheeks flush red. My heart was pounding, I couldn't do this, I wasn't me. I felt awkward and embarrassed. I quickly emptied my glass, got up and left the pub. Once outside I ran – and I ran – but from what, I didn't know. I just kept running until I found another pub, packed with all sorts of people, young, old, men, women, all laughing and talking and generally enjoying themselves. I found a seat at the corner of the bar and quietly got drunk.

Because of the students, Bristol seemed quite a lively place, and I was beginning to enjoy it in a quiet way. I would go into the pubs and cafés used by the students, mainly because I felt safe in their company. Many of them were quite mad and completely over the top. I didn't know any of them but I felt able to blend in – I didn't feel as though I stuck out like a sore thumb. Some of them, of course, were a complete pain in the arse – hooray Henrys who upset the general public and their fellow students – but in the main, they were a good bunch and I had no problems. I envied them really. I would have loved to have had the sort of education that would have enabled me to go to university, but it was not to be, so I got on with being a humble but happy trainee shoe shop manager. Happy, that is, until one day my boss called me into his tiny office. "Close the door and sit down, Richard," I did as I was asked. "I have some bad news for you I'm afraid." I looked at him, puzzled.

"Bad news?" I repeated.

"I'm afraid so," he hesitated, "there is no easy way for me to say this, so I'll come straight to the point." He looked grave. "I have to let you go – dismiss you."

I felt tears well up in my eyes, my stomach turned over. "B-b-b-but why?" I stammered, "W-w-w-what have I d-d-d-done?"

"Head Office wrote to your last employer and I'm afraid they have given you a very bad reference."

"B-b-b-but I told you about th-th-th-that, th-th-the leaky ceiling, and the b-b-bad heating, and I told y-y-y-you about th-th-the manager." I was falling over my words like I did at school, they all wanted to come out at once. I was so scared. "What will I do?"

"I'm sorry, Richard, I don't want to do this. I have pleaded with Head Office on your behalf, I have told them that I hold you in high regard – but Head Office – well, it's no good. I'm sorry."

He was very kind and paid me what money I had due, plus a small bonus that I'm sure came from his own pocket. "Now listen lad, when you apply for your next position, give my name for any reference you may need. Don't mention Head Office," he sighed a long sad sigh. "They don't care you know – they sit at their big desks and control the lives of hundreds of people – thousands possibly. I don't know," he shook his head, "I think they despise us, you know – resent us even. I wouldn't mind betting that there are some people at Head Office who wished they could do away with all the shops and just sell the shoes by the truckload straight from the factory. They're not shoe people you see – they don't appreciate the satisfaction you get when you fit a shoe on a customer and know that you have made that customer happy – grateful even – all they care about is a balance sheet." He looked at me and smiled weakly. "Hark at me – rambling on – I'm supposed to be a company man. I was too, when a manager really did manage his shop. But now, you see, lad – all we are – are puppets – they pull the string and we jump – yes, that's it, we don't manage, we just jump!" He held out his hand and I took it. His handshake was firm and sincere. "Take care lad, I wish you well. Best if you slip out now, no sense everybody knowing your business –not just now anyway."

I collected my things and he walked with me to the door. "I did tell you the truth, you know."

He nodded "I know you did. Don't worry, lad," he opened the door, "you'll find something soon, I'm sure." Then his mouth tightened and he said through clenched teeth "Bugger bloody Dolcis," and with a final pat of his hand on my arm he turned and disappeared back into the shop. I went to the nearest pub. I felt humiliated and angry and was close to tears. The pub was busy and as I pushed my way to the bar I wished I had hit that greasy little bastard in Plymouth. One thing was for sure: soon, someday, somebody would, and I just hoped it was sooner rather than later. I got to the bar and ordered a large gin and tonic, the first of several. By the end of lunchtime, I was three sheets to the wind, but I managed to find my way home and fell into a heap on the Put-U-Up. I woke up several hours later, it was dark and my mouth felt like the inside of a birdcage. I turned on the light and looked at my watch – it was nine o'clock. For a moment I wondered what the hell I was doing, then I remembered and felt full of despair. My heart started to race. "What," I thought, "am I going to do?" This had been the last thing I had expected, I had spent money on the flat – a few things for the kitchen, new towels and bits and pieces – and I had spent money on myself – a new dressing gown and shoes. I hadn't for one moment dreamt I would be sacked, and now here I was with just over a week's wages plus a couple of pounds I had left of my savings. I would have to do something very quickly or else I would be in big trouble.

There were quite a few jobs vacant that I applied for, but they all asked the same question: "How long were you at your last job and why did you leave?" When I told them "Only a few weeks," they all said they would let me know. I now owed two weeks' rent. I went to the Labour Exchange but because I had been dismissed for – as they put it – "misconduct," I was unable to get any dole money for six weeks! They sent me to the Unemployment Assistance Board, who in turn treated me with the utmost contempt – not only me, I suspect, but anybody else in those days unfortunate enough to be in need. By their standards, today's Social Services are like Lady Bountiful and the Good Samaritan rolled into one.

My landlady was by now getting uptight about her rent and my inability to pay it. I tried explaining, but all I heard in answer to my pleas of "Please be patient" was "I have bills to pay you know – this is a respectable house – all my gentlemen have jobs!" and so on. My days were spent looking for work and my nights worrying why I couldn't find any. Then one day, when I was on my rounds, I passed an Army Recruiting Office. I stopped, walked back, looked in the window, walked away again – and came back a second time.

"No, I can't, it would be madness – but then again," I thought, "I would have a roof over my head and food – but I couldn't – not the bloody Army – all that square-bashing, the training – me! no, not me." I had never liked physical exercise, I would much sooner read a book or do some gardening. Certainly, jumping over vaulting horses or climbing up ropes and wall bars were not me. So how could I join the Army? I walked away again. Then the thought occurred to me that there must be some jobs in the Army where being a Mr Universe was not a requirement, and it couldn't do any harm asking. "And anyway," I said to myself "desperate needs call for desperate measures." So I went back to the Office, and in I went.

The Office, as you would expect, was covered with posters extolling the virtues of the modern Army and its way of life. "A secure job", "See the world" and "A worthwhile career", all showing pictures of happy soldiers sitting on beaches or riding on tanks. I stared at them wondering if I could be like one of them, tanned and relaxed and looking so very happy. My thoughts were interrupted. "Yes, young man, and what can we do for you?" A man in military uniform came into the office from a back room. He was about forty and on a closer look, I saw he was a sergeant. He introduced himself and shook my hand, and asked me to sit down. He sat behind a desk covered in leaflets all in neat rows, and all proclaiming the same things as the wall posters. I told him my name and said I was interested in joining the Army.

"Oh yes," he was very pleasant, "and why would that be then?"

Without thinking of what I was saying, I told him I wanted a career in something worthwhile. "Christ!" I thought, "I'm quoting the bloody posters!" I went on telling him I hadn't found what I was looking for and that I thought the Army might be the answer.

"Well now lad, what branch of the Army were you thinking about, the Tank Corps or the Paras maybe? Which have you got in mind, eh?"

"Not the fucking Parachute Regiment that's for sure!" Jumping out of aeroplanes was not my idea of a good time, but I kept my thoughts to myself. He, meanwhile, was running through a list of different Regiments. I sat there and listened as he told me something about each one and what was expected of the men in them. My mind was now filled with horror pictures of me trying to complete assault courses, or lying under some huge Army truck or tank covered in oil as I tried to repair it. I shuddered to myself. I hated anything mechanical and I couldn't stand being dirty., so I had almost decided that Army life was not for me when suddenly the sergeant was asking me what skills I wanted to achieve. Again, before I could stop myself I said, "I want to be a chef!" He then asked me why I hadn't trained in civvy street and I told him some cock and bull story about my parents being too poor to send me to catering college, and that I had to leave school at fifteen to help the family budget. He then told me about Army pay and told me the longer I signed on for, the more money I would get each week, so right there and then I signed on for twelve years (the maximum) in Her Britannic Majesty's Royal Army Catering Corps. Two days later I found myself clutching a travel warrant and boarding a train on my way to Aldershot to begin my training, and this time there was no going back. "What have I done? Twelve years! Twelve fucking years!"

8 – MY SON THE SOLDIER

As the train neared Aldershot, my stomach tightened into nervous knots, and to calm myself I looked around and tried to spot any other new recruits. In one corner of my compartment was a huge black guy about my age reading a boxing magazine. "Well, he won't be spending the next few years boiling eggs! Probably a Para," I told myself. As for the callow youth with acne opposite me, well, who knows? A librarian, maybe. There was one other in the carriage, a man about thirty, but I thought him too old to be joining the Army. When the train pulled in at Aldershot we were met by some Army personnel and bundled into lorries. This time though, there were no pleasantries from the sergeant in charge or the two corporals helping him. They just barked out our names and pointed to the truck allocated to us, then one or all of them yelled, "Well don't just stand there! You scruffy little man – move it! You're in the Army now! God help us!"

I climbed into the truck and was amazed to see that among my fellow passengers were the big black guy, the callow youth and the thirty-something man. Soon we were all introducing ourselves to each other. The older guy was from Liverpool – he told us he was married, but missed Army life after his National Service, and had lost his job so had decided to re-enlist. "Just call me Scouse," he grinned a huge toothy grin. The young guy – Eddie Gower – was from the Midlands; the black guy was from south London, his parents were West Indian.

"Everyone calls me Kingy," he said quite softly, "my name's Leroy King, but just Kingy will do fine, what's your handle then?"

He looked at me with warm friendly eyes.

"My mates call me Chuck!" I lied. Why did I say that? I don't know – maybe a new start, a new name, I have no idea. It was out before I could stop it, and to me it sounded silly, but there in that lorry, as it made its way to Tourney Barracks, nobody questioned it or laughed. So, from then on, while I was in the Army I was called Chuck.

Once we reached the Barracks, we were lined up on the parade ground to meet our platoon sergeant. He turned out to be a dour Scotsman, about thirty-five with something of the look of Sean Connery about him. We also met our corporal, another Scot by the name of Wilson. After all this, we were marched off to collect our uniforms and then shown our barrack room. But at the time this was all done, our platoon only had about nine men in it. We would have to wait a few days for some more recruits to arrive before we could begin training, so we were allowed to relax. I took a bed next to Scouse, Kingy and Eddie were opposite. In the brick-built two-storey block, we were on the ground floor, and apart from us, the block was empty.

I was determined to make a go of the Army and soon made friends with the others in our billet. After a few days some more fellers arrived, and soon our side of the billet was full, but we still had to wait until the other side of the barrack block was full before we were up to strength. So still we couldn't train, but we were allowed into town and we would get drunk and mess about. The other fellers, of course, had wives or girlfriends, even Eddie, so I had to invent one. I called her Rita after one of my sister's friends. Being all men together the talk was nearly always of sex and sexual exploits, and I made mine as good and many times better than my mates. I would also chat up girls when we were in town, knowing full well I would never have to see them again, soon I was quite the Jack the Lad. Among the rest of the men, I was seen as a bit of a Romeo who could pull the birds wherever and whenever I wanted. That's not strictly true, some girls simply didn't fancy me, but in the main I had very little problem attracting members of the opposite sex. Even years later, when I would be standing at a bar in some club or other in full drag, women would come up to me and say things like "Are you really queer?" – and me in full make-up! I would tell them that I was indeed homosexual and invariably they would say "I could turn you straight." When I told them that I had no wish to be straight, some of them would storm away from me, calling me every name they could lay their tongues to – angry, I guess, that their womanly charms had no effect on me.

Right now, however, I was in the Army and as far as my mates were concerned I was a lady-killer. My cover was established and I would tell as many dirty stories as the next man, fall about laughing at shirtlifter gags, and even tell some myself – now I was one of the boys!

It was to take several weeks before or platoon was brought up to its quota, and even when it was we still couldn't train. The new intake brought in to make our number up arrived one day, we saw them all lining up on the parade ground and we were quite surprised to see that they were all black guys. Kingy, who was until now the only black bloke in our barracks, took a lot of good-natured abuse with remarks like "I see Kingy sent for the rest of his family!" or "What's up, Kingy, getting lonely?" He in turn would grin and say, "Getting worried, boys?" We watched as the new recruits were given the welcome lecture, then saw them marched away to collect their uniforms. The next morning, we were woken by the sergeant and Corporal Wilson banging on the metal bed frames and ordering us out of bed.

"Come on you lot out! now! get your 'orrible little bodies washed, have your breakfast, then get fell in on the parade ground. You got half an hour, so – move! Our easy lifestyle had come to an end. We all moaned as we rushed about like headless chickens – we had to wash, dress, make our beds, have our breakfast, all in thirty minutes.

"We'll never make it," we all said.

"If we don't," said Scouse, "we'll be for the high jump, so let's do it," and we did, by the skin of our teeth. As we lined up we all saw that the new guys hadn't appeared. Sergeant Muir was getting agitated and he sent a corporal over to find the missing men. Finally they appeared, dishevelled and bootless, and ambled across the parade ground while the poor corporal was blue in the face as he tried to get the men to hurry. We, of course, all collapsed into laughter at the sight of this, that is until Sergeant Muir yelled "Shut up!" then demanded to know from the corporal why the men had no boots on.

The corporal sprang to attention and said, "They can't walk in them, sergeant – they're too hard." The rest of us looked at each other, then down at the ground or up in the air, anywhere in fact so we couldn't see each other – all of us were on the verge of hysterical laughter.

Sergeant Muir on the other hand nearly burst a blood vessel as he yelled "Too hard! Too hard! Who said they were too hard?"

"The men, Sergeant," snapped back the corporal, still at attention.

"You lot," Sergeant Muir said addressing the rest of us, "dismissed. Get back to your billet and clean it from top to bottom, and," he added with some menace, "it had better be clean when I inspect it or I shall want to know the reason why." We then ran at the double back to the barrack room, and as soon as we were safely inside we fell onto our beds and almost cried with laughter.

And it was true – the men could not walk in their army boots. They had all been recruited in the West Indies and none of them had ever worn heavy army boots before. In their country, with its brilliant climate, there was no need to encase your feet in thick stiff leather – most of the time they would be barefoot. This meant that their feet had spread, so when they squeezed them into boots it was no wonder they couldn't walk! I forget how long it did take for these poor sods to get used to their boots but it was some weeks!

Soon we were in training proper, not only on the Square but in the vast kitchens, and the very first day in those kitchens I learnt that Army life was far removed from civilian life. We were being asked by a cook instructor how long it took to cook an egg. "Simple," I thought to myself, "three minutes," so I said so.

"Not in the Army!" the instructor bellowed. "It takes four minutes."

"But," I protested, "it'll be hard-boiled."

"Are you telling me I can't cook an egg, soldier?" His tone was not friendly, to say the least. "Well?" he persisted.

"All I'm trying to say is—" he cut me short.

"Don't you come in here and start telling me how to cook – you cocky little shit! You shut your mouth and listen. Do I make myself clear?"

"Y-y-y—" Christ! I was starting to stammer. "I must not stammer, please God don't let me stammer, please!" I think God came to my rescue because the instructor yelled again.

"If I want you to speak, soldier, I'll ask you, right?"

"Right," I replied.

"Right who!"

"Sergeant."

"And that goes for the rest of you – got it?"

They all said they had, and suddenly I was beginning to question what I had done by joining the Army, but I soon put it out of my mind. He was only one man and I wasn't going to let him spoil it for me.

My sex life at this point was nil and although I found it frustrating, and at times almost impossible to deal with, I nevertheless kept myself to myself. I really wanted to be like my mates, and the only way I could see of achieving that was by giving the Army my complete attention. Now I told myself I had to be 'normal' and as a part of that normalisation I decided to write home and tell my parents that I was now in the Army and doing a 'man's job'. As I put the finished letter in the post box I wondered what sort of reaction it would receive at home. I desperately wanted my family – I had all my new friends, but still I wanted something more personal. A lover was out of the question, but to feel the warmth of my family again would help me to get through. I waited for over a week before the reply came, I was so scared to open it my hands wouldn't keep still. I was sure my mates would see my nervousness, so I waited until I could open it in secret. That meant carrying the letter around for several more hours until I was off duty. Every few minutes, I found myself touching my pocket and feeling the pale blue envelope to make sure it was still there. Then, at last, I got the chance to open it. I took it from my pocket and sat staring at my mother's familiar handwriting for a long time, before finally ripping the envelope open and reading my fate. To my joy, my mother said how pleased both she and my Dad were to hear from me and that they were so pleased I was pursuing a career. She went on to tell me bits of family gossip and ended by saying that she hoped I would come and see them when I got some leave. I was over the moon – not a word was said about my being queer or any of the past few years. It meant I could start again with my family. I almost skipped back to my billet and I couldn't wait for some leave.

I hadn't realised when I joined up that Army cooks were expected to train every bit as hard as any other soldier, and that included days spent on assault courses, swinging on ropes over muddy pools, scrambling up nets and over brick walls, all the time wearing full kit. At school, as I have said, I shied away from such pursuits, but here I couldn't and as I had the respect of my mates in the Romeo stakes, I was determined that I shouldn't give the game away by appearing as a wimp in the physical trials. Although I was never the best, I made sure I came a close second. I'II never know how I found the strength or the courage to face some of those obstacles, but I did, and my reputation stayed intact.

Soon we were given leave. and although we were forbidden to wear our dress uniforms for anything other than ceremonials, quite a few of us put them on in order to impress our families and loved ones. As we sat on the train heading for London we were all full of excitement. All of us, I think, without exception had felt a failure in civvy street. Either we were not well enough educated or lacked self-assurance and self-esteem – or like me, were just running away from the truth or the past. But now, on that train, dressed in our best we were at last – in our own eyes at least –somebody. We belonged – we were soldiers, even though we hadn't finished our course.

When the train arrived at Waterloo I said goodbye to my mates and made my way to the Underground, intending to go to Liverpool Street Station and from there get a train home. As it was only mid-day I decided to have a look at the West End first. I hadn't told my parents about my leave, as I wanted to surprise them, so I thought few hours on my own looking at the sights would do me good. Anyway, I felt so good in uniform, and I felt sure people were looking at me with admiring glances – I didn't want it to end.

I went to Trafalgar Square and mixed in with the tourists feeding the pigeons, smiling broadly as they held out handfuls of bread to find themselves suddenly smothered by the birds as they swarmed over them to reach the food, sitting on heads and arms, anywhere in fact that gave them a vantage point, and crapping on their unsuspecting benefactors at the same time. It was spring. I walked around – my feet hardly seemed to touch the ground, I felt so good, so positive – my thoughts went back to Terry and Fred, and the love we had shared, and just how precious that love had been. I hoped they would both be as proud of me now as I was of myself.

I walked up Charing Cross Road and along Shaftesbury Avenue, then into Piccadilly Circus. By this time, I was in need of a drink so

I went into a bar, The White Bear, almost opposite the Café Royal. The bar was in the basement and as I walked down the short staircase and into the dimly lit bar, all heads turned to look at me. At first, I took no notice and ordered myself a drink. As I turned around from the bar with my drink in my hand I saw for the first time that all the customers were men – mainly middle-aged but with a few young guys among them. My heart started to race as it dawned on me that I was in a queer pub. I could see men smiling at me, all sorts of men, tall short, fat, thin, young and old. I looked down in embarrassment "Oh shit!" I said to myself, "it's the fucking uniform! That's what the attraction is – not me! The fucking uniform!" I turned to face the bar again. I could feel dozens of eyes boring into my back. I was just about to finish my drink and leave when a voice next to me said, "You're either a stranger to this cathouse or you're very brave to come here in uniform."

I turned towards the cultured voice to see the smiling face of a young West Indian. "My name's Emile." He put his hand out and I took it. He squeezed my hand gently.

"Ricky," I said as I shook his hand.

"You still haven't told me yet whether you are brave or a stranger?" he was still smiling, he had an almost girlish face. He was slim, about five feet six and dressed in very expensive and stylish clothes.

"A stranger," I replied, then I realised I had said it without even the hint of a stammer, which was unusual for me in a situation like this.

"Oh, I see," he laughed, "and is it a bit of a culture shock to see all these queens drooling at the mouth over you?"

"A bit, "I admitted, "but it's the uniform really – not me."

"Don't be so modest," he squeezed my arm, "you're very good looking."

At this point, I could feel myself colouring up and getting an erection at the same time. "Can I get you a drink?" I asked him, trying to take my mind off the ever-hardening lump in my trousers. He said yes, and suggested we go to a table in the corner. I had to stall him for a few moments until I could walk without showing the rest of the customers just how excited I was!

We drank and talked until closing time, he told me he was a student studying art and that he lived by himself in a flat in Notting

Hill. As we left the bar he said, "Why don't you come back for some coffee," he paused, "or whatever else you might like?" then he giggled. I could feel my trousers filling up once more, and before I could stop myself I said, "OK, let's go."

The flat turned out to be a couple of rooms on the second floor of a run-down Victorian house. As we climbed the stairs, the smells of the other tenants' cooking filled the air. Doors banged constantly and the sound of raised voices could be heard. We reached Emile's rooms and went into the living room which, although small, was spotlessly clean and neat. The walls were covered in pictures, mainly of husky men but also a couple of Marilyn Monroe. As I looked at these, Emile disappeared into the bedroom, then he called out, "Come here, soldier man." I went into the room and saw him lying on the bed, naked except for a pair of skimpy red underpants. He had an erection and the top of his cock burst through the thin waistband of the pants. His body seemed to glisten, it was black and inviting. He moaned as he lay there, moving his slender body into more and more erotic positions. I could feel my own dick aching as it tried to push open the buttons on my dress trousers. Suddenly I was consumed with lust and passion for the writhing body on the bed. I undressed, throwing my uniform on the floor – nothing else mattered. I threw myself on the bed and on top of him. Almost as soon as our bodies touched, I climaxed. I smothered his face in kisses as I let all the past months of frustration out. I kept telling him I was sorry for coming so quickly, he told me not to worry as he kissed me and rubbed his body over mine. It only took me a short while before I was once more rampant and ready to take him – he, in turn, was ready for me, forcing his slim body down harder and harder onto my cock. We stayed in bed almost solidly for twelve hours, enjoying each other at every chance. In the morning I got up, washed and dressed, and made myself some tea. Emile was still asleep when I left, about eight o'clock, but I left him a note and told him to keep going into the White Bear, and that I would see him there again on my next leave.

As I walked to Notting Hill tube station I began to question my actions from the previous night. What the hell was I doing, was I mad? I was supposed to be making a new life for myself, one where I would gain peoples' respect, one where I could be like any average guy. I mean, supposing somebody had seen me go into that bar and then come out with Emile? I was in full dress uniform for Christ's sake! My mind raged on and on, thinking what my parents would say, the hurt I would cause them all over again. Then I remembered the note I had left for Emile asking him to meet me again! Supposing he rang the Regiment! I was getting more and more paranoid. I bought a ticket at the station. As I stood on the platform I imagined the people around me looking at me with admiration – then I wondered what they would think of me if they knew where I had spent the night. I shivered with disgust and self-loathing. What had been for me a night of passion and emotion now became sordid and dirty. I hated myself and I hated Emile. "He made me do it!" I told myself, "He seduced me! Yes, that was it, it was Emile's fault not mine – I was drunk and he took advantage of the fact, that's how it happened."

I told myself all these things, trying desperately to find some way of justifying the previous night's events and at the same time absolving myself of any blame. The train came and I got on. By the time I had reached Liverpool Street Station I was feeling better about myself, and by the time I reached Enfield and was only a stone's throw from my parents' house, I had convinced myself that it was the booze and Emile and had nothing to do with me. I was simply in the wrong place at the wrong time. I ignored the nagging of my conscience, pushing it back into my mind, completely oblivious to the damage it was doing.

The sun shone as I walked through the neat little council estate. I held my back straight and imagined all my Mum's neighbours looking at me from behind net curtains telling their kids that the man in the smart uniform was Mrs Greene's soldier son. I walked up the short concrete path to my mother's house and knocked on the door, feeling very nervous and at the same time excited. I waited what seemed an age for the door to open, suddenly it did and there, with a look of shock and surprise on her face, was my Mum, still wearing her old green cardigan, her once jet-black hair now greying at the temples.

"Goodness, why didn't you let me know you were coming?"

I didn't even get a chance to say, "I wanted to surprise you."

"Well, you better come in," she said as she opened the door wider and walked into the kitchen. I went in and closed the door behind me and followed her into the kitchen. Nothing seemed to have changed. There was still one piece of wallpaper missing – my father had redecorated the room some years ago and had run out of paper. He had, of course, promised to finish it but that was as far as it got. I smiled to myself at the thought of it.

"Tea?" my mother asked without looking round as she filled the kettle from the tap over the sink and put it on the stove "How long are you staying?" she asked, busying herself with cups and saucers.

"Oh, just a couple of days. I have to be back at camp on Monday" I said in reply, trying to sound relaxed but failing dismally.

"Right. Well, in that case, you had better take your things upstairs –tea will take a few moments." She was still opening and closing cupboards and doors as she spoke. I picked up my things and went up to my room. As I entered the room I was swept back in time. Nothing had changed, the wallpaper was the same as were the rest of the furnishings. I closed the door and felt the familiarity and comfort of the room surround me. Downstairs, the atmosphere was strained and brittle, but here in my room I felt at ease and safe. I unpacked and went to the bathroom to freshen up after my journey. When I returned to the kitchen my mother seemed more relaxed. I gave her a cigarette and she told me the family news. She was worried about my sister's marriage – she told me my brother-in-law was a good for nothing, and that now I was home I should advise my sister and try to end the marriage. I said I would do what I could, but at the same time I vowed to myself that I would not interfere. My mother was happy to think that I was on her side. I tried to change the subject by asking how my father was. "I see Dad's still not finished this room then," nodding my head towards the bare strip on the wall.

Her voice turned cold again. "You know your father, full of promises he never keeps."

"How is he?" I asked.

"The same as ever, up and down like Tower Bridge. But if you mean is he still gambling, then yes." She said this with a tired, weary voice.

"Are you still—"

She pre-empted my question. "Talking? Yes, we're talking, I don't know for how long." She looked at her watch. "He should be in soon – he's only gone out for a haircut, or so he says."

I had some more tea and we chatted about everything and nothing. Then I heard a key in the front door. "That'll be your father now," she said getting up to fill the kettle once again. As he entered the kitchen my mother said to him, "Look who's here!" My father looked as though he was about to smile but he changed his mind. "Thrown you out already, have they?" he said, putting a bag of shopping on the table. "They hadn't got a small loaf so I got a large one." He was talking to my mother.

"Just as well now," was the reply as she unpacked the shopping. "Tea?" He nodded.

"I – er, I'm – on leave, Dad" It sounded like an apology.

"On bloody leave! You've only been in for five minutes."

I wanted to say what would he know about it, he had never been in the services, during the Second World War he had been a bus driver, so was exempt as he was doing a job of national importance. I explained to him about the hold-up in my training. Gradually, both of them softened. My father gave me a pack of Senior Service cigarettes, which was his way of saying Welcome Home. Not the most emotional of welcomes, I will admit, especially as I had been away for so long, but it was as much as I had hoped for so I was happy. Of course, I would have loved them to put their arms around me and hold me kiss me even, but it was not their way and I accepted it.

The next day things got even brighter with my mother showing me off to the neighbours. I had wanted to wear jeans and a t-shirt but she insisted I wore my uniform. In fact, I had to wear it for the rest of my leave, even when we went to the market at Edmonton where my brother-in-law's family had a fruit and veg stall. My Dad said I should wear it to please my mother and she told me to wear it to please him! So I guessed they were both proud really. Sergeant Muir would have blown a fuse had he ever found out, but I didn't care about him, I was just so pleased to be a part of my family again.

My leave was over all too quickly, and as I waved goodbye and walked away I was sure I saw my mother wipe a tear from her eye. I turned my head quickly away lest she should see the tears streaming down my face.

Once back at camp, we all each eagerly reported our exploits whilst on leave, and as usual, the tales were of sexual conquests and prowess. Not to be left out, when it came to my turn I told them all about the dark-skinned beauty I had met in a West End nightclub, then I proceeded to describe my night with Emile almost down to a tee. I just happened not to mention that instead of a great pair of tits he had a dick and a beautiful little arse! I wouldn't have believed it then that later in my life I was to meet people with all of these on the same body! My mates lapped up my account, demanding to know all the ins and outs. It was the start of the Swinging Sixties and for an ordinary white guy to pull a black girl was really way out, so once again I was Jack the Lad as far as the rest of my squad were concerned.

The problem now was that I could not stop thinking about Emile. l tried to stop myself by asking myself what would happen if anybody found out and of course I realised the risk I was running, but I couldn't help myself. The more I tried to push it to the back of my mind the more it came to the fore. It wasn't that I was I love with him – I knew that was not the case – but I had enjoyed our time together, especially the sex. Well, if I were to be honest it was only the sex. Emile was a good-looking boy but we had little in common apart from sex, he was from a different background to me, far better educated, he had talked about music and art, even philosophy. Although I liked classical music and art to some extent, he left me standing. I had not got a clue what he was talking about half the time, but in bed – well, in bed we both understood each other., and it was this that was driving me nuts. I still wanted to see him again, and some weeks later I was given the chance.

We had been given a forty-eight-hour pass, I made up my mind as to what I should do. Turning down my mates' invitations to spend our leave getting pissed in town, I told them I had to go home. Instead, I caught the first train to London and this time I was not in uniform. When the train arrived, I made my way straight to the White Bear. It was about two o'clock when I arrived and it was a Saturday. I made my way down the stairs and into the crowded bar, this time I attracted a few admiring glances but for the most part I was ignored, confirming my suspicion that the last time I had been there it was the uniform and not me that was the main attraction. I bought a drink and looked around. Emile was not there. I stood in the middle of the room so that I could see both the entrances, I waited until closing time but there was still no sign of Emile. I had been chatted up by a few people, two of whom under different circumstances I would have liked to have known better, but I wanted Emile.

Closing time found me out on the street feeling not only a little foolish but a bit sorry for myself, so not knowing quite what to do next I walked up Piccadilly towards Hyde Park Corner. I passed the Ritz and soon found myself in Victoria. Memories of my childhood came flooding back as I stood in front of the Victoria Palace. This was the home of the Crazy Gang, a group of seven very funny old comics who kept the country laughing through the forties, fifties and into the sixties. My Mum and Dad had loved the Gang and had taken me to see several of their shows, including "Knight of Madness" and "Ring Out the Bells". Little did I realise that thirty years later I would be a member of another troupe called The New Crazy Gang.

After my walk I was tired out, and it was still only tea-time, so I looked around until I found a cinema. The Bio-Graph looked a bit run-down and tatty, but I didn't care, I just wanted to sit down and rest, so I bought a ticket and in I went. The place was packed, but I found a seat on the end of a row and was about to settle down and enjoy the film when I had to stand up again and let somebody in to sit in the seat on my left. This done, I sat down again to watch the film, but people all over the cinema were getting up and changing seats. It never seemed to stop, and I was getting irritated by it – after all, I had paid to see a film, not to watch people moving from one row to another the whole time. I was just about to let my views be known when the young guy who had moved next to me asked me if I had a light. I dug my hands into my trouser pockets, took out my lighter and ignited it. The young man cupped both his hands around mine, brought his head close to mine and took a long drag on his cigarette as he did so he squeezed my hand gently but firmly before letting go and saying softly "Thanks." A tingle went through my body as I looked at the guy and said, "You're welcome." He was about eighteen, slim with blonde hair, he reminded me of Kevin. I put the lighter away and went back to trying to watch the film. I was pleased to see that, for the moment at least, calm had restored itself, and apart from a few people calling to friends or complaining about somebody or something, all was relatively quiet, so I settled back into my seat. I had only just done so when I felt the guy next to me pressing his leg into mine, gently at first, like his hands were around my hand, then gradually firmer and firmer and at the same time rubbing up and down. I could, I suppose, have moved my leg, but somehow I didn't want to. For a while, I didn't even think the guy knew it was my leg – I thought that maybe he thought he was rubbing against the seat – but whatever, I was finding it pleasurable. I glanced over at my neighbour out of the corner of my eye, he was looking straight ahead at the screen. The pressure and rubbing on my leg continued, and that convinced me he thought my leg was the seat that is until I glanced down at his leg – then I nearly passed out! His left leg was pushing into mine and his left hand was resting on his knee, but with his right hand he was gently masturbating his erect cock, which was by now completely exposed. Still he kept his eyes straight ahead onto the screen. I could now feel my own dick protesting at being kept in darkness and trying to push its way out of my flies! I didn't know what to do – I was shocked. I felt my body go rigid. I could hardly take my eye off the young guy and his cock, but I was scared, I suppose. "He must be some sort of nutcase," I told myself, "we are in the middle of a cinema for crying out loud!" Then suddenly it was taken out of my hands (if you will pardon the pun). The guy's left hand suddenly reached for my right hand. I didn't resist as he pulled my hand across his lap and onto his hard dick. I gripped it and felt it warm and hard as it throbbed in my hand. Then he was fumbling at my flies in a fury now to get to my now rigid cock. I helped him to achieve his goal and I heard him sigh as he clenched his hand around it and slowly move it up and down. I was, of course, doing the same thing to him. Then suddenly without a word he was down on me, his mouth warm and wet where his hand once was. Now I did start to panic – suppose we were seen? I looked around and nobody appeared to be taking the slightest notice. By this time his mouth was working overtime on me, I could feel myself being brought to a climax. I, of course, still had hold of him and I felt him stiffen and then the warm feel of his semen on my hand. At the same time, I released my own into his now-still mouth. He stayed on me for a couple of seconds then, pulling himself up and adjusting his dress he said, "Thank you very much," and was gone! I watched him as he walked around the auditorium then saw him make his way along a row of seats and sit next to somebody else. Very quickly I straightened my own clothes. I couldn't believe what had just happened. As I sat there looking at the screen without knowing what was taking place, somebody else came and sat beside me. As he sat down I looked at him. He was a small podgy man of about sixty with thin grey hair, and he was carrying a raincoat. As he sat down he looked at me and gave me a sweaty grin – I fled! I was, of course, later to learn that the Bio-Graph was a gay cinema and pick-up spot. I was to go back there quite a few times in later years, now though it has been pulled down and the space used as a car park. There were other cinemas with the same reputation, the Cartoon Cinema in Piccadilly – now a Hot Dog shop! – and the cinemas on Waterloo and Victoria stations, now also gone.

After leaving the Bio-Graph I found a café and had something to eat. I started to reflect on what had just happened. Well, at least it proved one thing to me – there were more people like me about than I had ever believed. But I asked myself, were they really like me? Were they also trying to live a lie, putting on the face of so-called normality for family and workmates, or did they live their lives without giving a damn about what other people thought? And if they did, where did they work? How did they make a living? How did they cope?

It was getting late so I made my way back to the White Bear. As I walked in I saw Emile talking to some fellers. I bought myself a drink and stood where he would see me. After a few minutes, he looked at me, did a double-take, smiled and came over.

"My, you look so different, thank you for the note – it was sweet" and then he kissed me on the cheek, I felt myself blush. "Christ, everyone's looking!" I said to myself. As though he had read my mind, he laughed and said, "Don't be so shy, they are all queens in here." I looked at the rest of the crowd. I was sure they couldn't all be queens but I knew what he meant. I bought him a drink and we sat down. "How long will you be in town?"

"Only twenty-four hours," was my reply.

"Oh well, in that case, it looks as though I have a guest for the night – always supposing you want to be my guest, of course?" he asked hesitantly.

"Why else would I be here?" I said, grinning like I had just won the pools.

At closing time Emile suggested we went on to a club. I readily agreed, never having been to a real nightclub before, let alone one in the West End of London. Sometime later after a short walk, we found ourselves entering a large shabby-looking terraced house. We went down a musty, dingy corridor, then down some stairs and into the basement. Emile knocked on a black-painted door: a spy hole slid back, Emile said "Hi", and the door opened. We entered a richly decorated room, packed with men of all ages. Heads turned as we entered, some merely to stare then turn away with a look of disdain on their faces, others beamed and welcomed Emile.

"Darling! bona to see you," said one greying man of about fifty, dressed elegantly, throwing his arms around Emile's neck and kissing him on both cheeks. Then he looked at me and, completely ignoring me, said, "Rough trade eh – you naughty boy! Pass it on to mother when you've finished!" I didn't have a clue what he was talking about, I just stood there smiling like a complete prat. Emile laughed and said something that I didn't hear, and he and the grey-haired man and a few of his friends all fell about laughing. With that, Emile took my arm and pushed me towards the bar.

Once at the bar and out of earshot of the man, I said to Emile "Who the bloody hell was that?"

"Just some stupid bitch with too much money, take no notice – she fancies you though, but then she fancies anything in trousers."

"Well, thank you very much!" I said indignantly.

"I didn't mean it like that," he replied, laughing, and squeezed my arm. Then he ordered drinks, and while he did this I looked around the room. Most of the men here looked as though they were not down to their last shilling. Some of the younger ones, although dressed well, were wearing cheaper, less well-cut clothes, like me. Suddenly, I caught the eye of my admirer – he was looking at me from across the room. He waved like the Queen Mother waved when she was driving around a racecourse in an open coach. then, smiling, he raised his glass to me. I turned quickly away, "Silly old bastard," I said to myself. Emile got the drinks and we made our way to another room. It was decorated like the last one but was much darker. Somebody was playing records and men were dancing with each other, holding each other tightly, and some were kissing. I looked on in amazement: the surprise must have shown on my face, because Emile was telling me there were lots of clubs like this in London. I thought back to when Fred and I slunk around, never daring to show any affection for each other in public, and now here I was watching and joining in as men relaxed with someone of their own sex, not caring who saw them as they hugged and kissed without any fear at all. I felt sad. Fred and I had lived under a great strain. Maybe if we had found a place like this with other people who understood our love, then maybe, just maybe, the choice of going back to Hungary would have been harder, and maybe, just maybe, he would have stayed with me.

We left the club in the early hours, both a little the worse for drink, but by the time we reached Emile's flat we were both ready for bed and not to sleep. We made glorious love, then the booze and tiredness got the better hand of us both, and we fell asleep. When I awoke next morning, it was late. Emile was not next to me but I could hear him in the small kitchen. My head felt like lead and my mouth like the proverbial bottom of a birdcage. Emile's head appeared around the door. "Oh, so my soldier boy's awake at last," he smiled – he was always smiling – "breakfast in ten minutes," then he was gone. The thought of breakfast made me almost want to throw up, but I got out of bed, went into the bathroom and got under the shower.

Breakfast was surprisingly good –fresh fruit, lightly boiled eggs and lots of toast and tea. We chatted as we ate about the previous night at the club, he said his friends had liked me and he asked me when he would be seeing me again. I, in turn, asked him for his phone number and promised I would call him as soon as I could. He asked about my mates in the Army and whether they knew about me or not. I told him about after my last leave when we had first met, and the story I told my mates about spending my leave with a beautiful black girl I had met in a nightclub. Emile thought this very funny. "You made out I was a girl!"

"Well, what else could I do?" I exclaimed, "I could hardly say I had been shagging a bloke, could I?"

"No, no, of course you couldn't," he said still laughing, then he left the table and went into the bedroom. He came out a few seconds later carrying a photograph. "Here, show this to your mates." He thrust the picture into my hand. I looked at it and saw a beautiful black girl with long hair lying seductively on a chaise longue. She was wearing a pale blue swimsuit and matching high-heeled shoes.

"She's lovely," I said, "is it your sister?"

He laughed again. "No, it's not my sister, keep it and you can tell your friends it's your girlfriend," he paused, "that is, unless you are ashamed of me." I looked at him and then at the photo.

"You! You mean this girl is you? I don't believe it." With that he disappeared again, only to return carrying a long black wig, a pale blue swimsuit and the matching shoes.

"Well, here she is "he grinned, "now do you believe me? I did it for a party last year."

"But you look stunning! Nobody would ever think it was a bloke."

"Well it is, and when you are telling your soldier friends about your nights of passion and you show them the photo, they will see her, but you will see me!" We both laughed and I asked him to write on the picture. He wrote, "To my darling Chuck, you taught me so much, all my love, Millie."

On the journey back to camp later that same day my head was full of all the things I had seen and done in such a short space of time – the pub, the cinema and then the club, and to cap it all this. I sat looking at the photograph that Emile had given me. "Incredible," I thought, "absolutely incredible." But that short leave had left me far more than a few vivid memories. It left me wondering just what I had done – the same burning question kept coming back to me. Had I known about Emile or about the Bio-Graph or the pub or the clubs, would I have joined the Army? More to the point, should I have joined the Army? lt was the one place where I would not find the love I craved. It had got me back my family, but at what price? And could I keep up the pretence, not just to Mum and Dad but to my mates? Even if I could, did I really want to go on living this double life? As I looked back over the past few years and thought about my secret life, and the fear and misery I felt in case I was caught, I wondered, would it always be like this? My mind turned to some of the people I had met whilst on leave. "Did they live in fear and dread?" I asked myself. It had not seemed that way as they kissed and danced the night away. I had no way of knowing that, over fifty years later in the so-called enlightened twenty-first century, hundreds, possibly thousands of gay men and women, young and old, would still live in fear of rejection from their families, friends and the people at their workplace. Even though there are now gay newspapers and advice centres, even TV shows for and about gay people, and the added fact that discrimination is being discouraged, still people find it difficult to come to terms with. lt was especially so for me and hundreds like me in the late fifties and early sixties. Queers were something we read about in our Sunday papers, and for some reason were thought by ordinary working-class people to come from the higher classes of society. Utter rubbish, of course –people of all social classes had the same problem to deal with – but to the average man in the street a poof would be one of the nobs, or at the very least an actor. It would be unimaginable to think of a factory worker or builder or postman or dustman to be queer – or, indeed, a soldier in the lower ranks.

I wondered just how many men and women like me were forced to live behind a facade. I put the photo away. "I have to be strong," I told myself, "I don't want to lose Mum and Dad again. I need them." I needed somebody, that was for sure.

When I walked into my billet, some of my mates were already there. Some hadn't gone home but stayed in camp, others, like me, had come back so as to save the rush to get to camp by roll call the following morning. As usual, they gave me the third degree. "Did yer get yer end away, yer dirty bugger?" they all laughed and asked the same question in a variety of ways. I flopped on my bed and listened while they told me of their exploits then it was my turn and I told them about 'Millie', the reaction was as I expected. "I bet she's some old scrubber you met in the Dilly," said one. I said nothing, but I got up from my bed and took my jacket off. As I folded it I slipped the photo from the inside pocket and dropped it as if by accident. Almost before it had hit the floor, a dozen or so hands had pounced on it. "Steady!" I yelled, "don't tear the bloody thing, it's all I've got." Scouse got it first. He looked at it long and hard then gave a long low whistle.

"Jesus Christ Chuck, that's some Judy yer got there, I've got to hand it to yer."

"Show me!" somebody else snatched it out of his hand and before long they were all drooling over 'Millie'. "You lucky bastard you – what you got I ain't – look at those legs – never mind the fucking legs look at the rest of her." I just lay back on my bed grinning. "If only they knew that between those legs was a fair-sized cock!" I laughed out loud.

"Smug bastard," said Kingy as he gave me the photo back.

I had never let myself think about any of the other guys in a sexual way and it was quite difficult at times – some of them were very good looking – but I knew that if I did I would be finished. That lasted until I met Woody. We were out on manoeuvres, having to lie in rain-soaked ditches covering ourselves in bracken, and then springing out on the 'enemy' as they passed. After a few hours of this we were sent to a field kitchen and there, serving the food with some others from his platoon, was Woody. He looked

Afro-Caribbean, aged about twenty with golden skin, slim with a mop of black hair or at least as much as the Army would allow. He was about five feet six and for me, it was love at first sight. I made sure he served me that day, and to make sure he noticed me, I dropped my tray. He smiled the most magnificent smile, told me not to worry and gave me a fresh meal. After that, I went out of my way to seek him out. Soon we were quite friendly. I never did or said anything to arouse his suspicion, he would talk about his girlfriend and I would show him 'Millie's' photo. I knew deep down I could never have him, but I couldn't stop seeing him at every chance I got. We even went out a few times drinking, I would pray that he might get a little drunk and let his guard slip and tell me he was queer. It was crazy, I know, but I was besotted with him. Soon my own mates, who I was neglecting, started to ask questions, in a flippant way but I could feel the underlying tone.

"What's with you and Woody? Not turning queer on us are you, Chuck?"

"Oh, he likes a bit of black does our Chuck, he's making out it's Millie!"

Of course, nobody really believed I was queer, and I laughed off their jibes and even made counter-claims as to their sexual preferences, but it did make me much more cautious. As much as I was attracted to Woody, I cut down drastically on the number of times I saw him and spent much more time with the blokes in my own billet. I did this gradually of course, but it tore me apart. I would watch Woody from a distance and it took all my self-control not to run up to him and tell him my feelings. The whole thing was absurd – it was like a drug – I was almost out of control but I couldn't stop. He, of course, knew nothing of the crush I had on him and I knew that was how it had to be, but my mind was in turmoil. I couldn't concentrate, my work began to suffer badly, I was continually getting bollockings for not paying attention, and eventually I was put on a charge. As a punishment I was made to scrub the paint-splattered floor of a newly decorated barrack room – but not with a scrubbing brush and water, that was far too sensible a way for the Army – no, I had to use a single-edge razor blade!

My mates could see things were going badly for me and tried to help. They would make sure my bed space passed inspection and even saw that my kit was in order. They were genuinely worried about me, but I wouldn't let them get close to me, and gradually I started to freeze them out. I became a loner. I needed my own space, I had to think things out. Much of my free time was spent walking round and round the camp hoping to get a glimpse of Woody. On those aimless walks I used to pass the Army chapel and one evening I went in. It was only a small wooden hut really, once inside it reminded me of the Sunday School I used to go to as a child, with the same musty smell of old books and dust. The room was sparsely furnished with an assortment of chairs and a few tables, some piled high with hymn books and Bibles. There were a couple of wooden cupboards and an old upright piano, complete with a battered piano stool. The walls of the hut, as you would expect, were covered in religious pictures and texts. In pride of place, of course, was a picture of the Queen in Garter robes. I walked around the room, not knowing why I was there. Then I sat at the piano and sorted through the pile of sheet music stacked on top. When I found something I knew, I played it, badly. I must have stayed there for about an hour just playing hymns. I found myself going back there whenever I could. I never saw the Chaplain, nor anybody else for that matter.

By now I was getting worse. I knew I had to get some help, some advice – but from who – who could I trust? Then one day I left a note for the Chaplain. It didn't give anything away, it simply asked him to meet me there the next evening. I didn't even give my name or number. The next day I was on edge the whole time, I snapped at anybody who spoke to me. Scouse tried talking to me but I told him to fuck off. I could see in his face that I had hurt him, he was only trying to help. I wanted to tell him I was sorry and explain what was wrong but I couldn't. Once we had been dismissed from duty that day I ran back to the billet and changed into civvies, then I raced round to the chapel. I crashed through the door and stood in the doorway trying to get my breath. I looked around – the room was empty. "Where the hell is he?" I was talking out loud to myself. I slammed the flat of my hand onto the piano keys – the noise echoed through the empty room. I went to the desk to look for my note. It wasn't there – but suppose the Chaplain didn't have it, suppose somebody else picked it up, what should I do, go or stay? The question was answered for me when the door opened and the Chaplain entered the room. He was a small, thin, odd-looking man in full uniform, his long thin face and large head topped with his peaked cap. He was about fifty. He smiled weakly as he came in. "Good evening, are you the soldier who left me the rather strange note?"

I nodded "Yes sir."

"Well, sit down soldier and tell me what all this is about," he spoke in a soft kindly voice. I felt a bit more relaxed. I sat down and looked at him, not quite knowing where to start.

"Well, come on man, spit it out. I haven't got all day you know."

Now I was physically shaking. My stammer came back with a vengeance, then before I knew what I was doing I was pouring my heart out to him. Oh, the relief – the relief. I told him I was homosexual. For the first time, I was admitting officially that I was queer. Then I told him I was in love with another soldier. I didn't name him, I told him the man didn't know, but what should I do? Would praying help? All this took quite some time as I stuttered and stammered trying to find the right words. He said nothing, he just let me talk and talk.

Eventually he said: "Is there much more of this that I have to listen to, or have you now bared your soul?" His tone had changed from the kindly man. I told him I had finished – in fact I could have gone on for hours, I wanted to go on, but his tone told me to stop. He asked for my rank and number, I told him and he said "Well, Private, if this is some cock-and-bull story to get you out of the Army, you've picked the wrong man. On the other hand, if what you say is true, then I suggest you start behaving like a man and stop all this whining. Have a cold shower twice a day and pull yourself together. Now get out!"

Dazed at what I heard I stood up and left. I couldn't believe what had happened. I came to this man – this Chaplain, this man of God – for help and all he says is "have a cold shower!" What the fuck would a cold shower do? Cleanse my mind? Wash away all thoughts of Woody and Fred and Terry and Alf and Emile? Would it make me normal, whatever that means? Would it fuck! By this time I was near to tears, I felt let down and humiliated and even more lost. I went to the NAAFI and got very very drunk. Some of my mates were in there and it was them who carried me back to the barrack room and put me to bed. I woke after a few hours, my eyes craved sleep but my mind wouldn't allow it. For a moment everything seemed OK, then I remembered the Chaplain and our meeting. I felt quite calm as I got out of bed and made my way to the bed of a guy desperate to get out of the Army, but who couldn't afford to buy himself out. I woke him gently, so as not to disturb the others. I whispered to him for a few moments. He looked at me, surprised, then he pulled back his bedclothes and I got into bed with him. We were found by the guards as they woke us next morning and put under close arrest. He was not homosexual and nothing happened between us that night or any other night, he didn't even know I was gay, all I told was that it was a sure-fire way of getting a discharge from the Army.

We were brought up before the Regimental Sergeant Major, a stocky man with a parlance for shouting at everybody – well, those below his own rank, that is. If this behaviour was supposed to scare the shit out of you, then he most certainly achieved his aim. We were marched in at the double by two burly military policemen. After we were brought to attention the RSM barked at us both, demanding to know what the bloody hell was going on. I told him that the other guy had been drunk and that I had got into bed with him because I fancied him. I watch the rage boil up in the RSM's face. He turned bright red, I thought he would burst a blood vessel. He came from behind his desk, stood in front of me and yelled abuse at me, spraying me with his saliva as he did so. I don't remember his words, just the force at which they came out. He barked at the guards and I was marched out at the double to the guardhouse. Once there I was pushed, punched and kicked into a cell. All that day officers and NCOs came in to look at me. It was like being in a zoo, except nobody was saying "Ooh, look at that nice homosexual." Some said nothing, just looked at me with contempt and loathing, others were far more vocal. "They should hang the bastard – Dirty fucking pervert – Cut the bastard's cock off!" and much much more. It seems ironic now that years later I would be booked dozens, if not hundreds, of times to appear before Army and other service audiences, sometimes in drag, sometimes as a stand-up comic. I always let them know that I was homosexual and ninety-nine times out of a hundred I got a terrific response! Ain't life strange?

Later I was told I was to be charged with homosexuality and for indecent assault, and as was my right I was allocated an officer who would act on my behalf as defence counsel. He was a tight-lipped first lieutenant not much older than I was, and he made it absolutely clear he would sooner have defended Hitler than defend me. Hours came and went and the barrage of abuse never ceased. At mealtimes my food was almost thrown at me, much of it falling on the floor which I had to clean. I didn't eat anyway, I could just imagine what was done to my food before it got to me! so refused to touch it. This infuriated my guards and their anger at my not eating confirmed my suspicions. They, of course, got their revenge but making me run on the spot at the double and do innumerable press-ups, until I realised that the Army was going to get its pound of flesh, so why should I care what the guards said? From then on I refused to take any more orders. On about the third day my 'counsel' informed me that the other man concerned was not pressing charges against me for indecent assault, so the Army was dropping that charge. I could tell by his tone that he was seething. "So your boyfriend has come to your rescue!"

"He is not my boyfriend – I have already said nothing happened that night." I realised he was trying to needle me so I said it quite casually.

Later that day I received a visit from a young second lieutenant. I recognised him and I assumed that he too had come to see the queer, but he asked to be let into the cell, then he sent the guard away. He introduced himself and said "I really am most terribly sorry. Your treatment here is appalling, but there is very little I can do, I'm afraid."

I looked at him. "If you're trying to catch me out you are wasting your time, Sir. I have only told the truth."

He shook his head. "I'm not trying anything of the sort – I want to help – if I can that is. You do realise they could send you to Colchester?" I nodded and went cold at the thought of it. Colchester was a tough military prison and the thought of going there scared the shit out of me. He offered me a cigarette, my first since I had been arrested. I accepted it gratefully and took long satisfying draws on it. "Are you certain you are homosexual and this isn't some game you're playing to get out of the Army?" I assured him I was gay and told him the truth about joining up – I needed the job – I was desperate – and I thought I could keep it under control, change even, but now I knew that was not possible. He looked at me and said, "I'll speak to the Officer acting for you," then he smiled, "chin up," and handed me the packet of cigarettes saying, "You will have to ask the guards for a light."

"They won't give me one."

"Oh yes, they will," he said firmly, "I'll have a word. Goodbye and good luck." Then he shook my hand and called the guard and was gone. I never saw him again, just as I never saw the Chaplain.

Two days later I was told I was to be dishonourably discharged. My things were brought from my billet, and I had to sign for my effects. One of the guards found Emile's photo. He looked at it and whistled. "Who's this then queer boy, your alibi? Some tart you conned into signing it? Or did one of your nancy-boy friends sign it for you?"

"She's a friend, that's all, just a friend," I told him.

"Oh, is she now? Well, queer boy, she's too good for you so I'm going to put her with my collection. You got a problem with that?" I said no and he kissed the picture and put it in his pocket. His mates laughed, so did I inside, thinking of this big ape pulling his pud over a photo of a man in drag! "Priceless," I thought. After a trip to the paymaster's office, where I was given a travel warrant and a few pounds in wages, I was ordered off the camp. By this time I was feeling very weak – I hadn't eaten in days and my head ached like it had never ached before. I knew I had to walk right through the camp, and it was quite a walk to the bus stop. I was determined that I would not slink out with my tail between my legs. I wondered what had happened to the other guy I was charged with, I thought maybe we would leave together, but I didn't see him again. I don't even know if he was thrown out or not, I hoped for his sake he had been. So I picked up my case and did as I had been trained. I put my shoulders back, held my head up and started walking. On the way out, I passed some guys I had known as mates. Some stood and stared, some turned their backs as if I had never existed. Then I saw Kingy, he gave me a sly wink, and that gave me the strength I needed to walk away from it all.

9 – MAYBE THIS TIME

By the time I had reached Aldershot station my headache was excruciating and I realised I must be having a migraine (they were to plague me on and off for the rest of my life). Now I had some idea how Dad must have suffered, he had migraine attacks quite often and would sit hunched up in his armchair shivering with cold, his forehead covered with a cloth soaked in vinegar. This was his mother's 'cure' for a headache, it never seemed to work for him. He was a stubborn man and refused to take any aspirin and lie in a darkened room as was recommended. "Vinegar-rag was good enough for my old man, so it's good enough for me," he would say if he were asked to go to bed or take a tablet. This would irritate my mother. She swore his migraines were an excuse for doing nothing, but if he felt only half as bad as I did on that station then she was completely wrong. I went into the buffet and bought a cup of tea and a piece of cake. I asked the lady behind the counter if she sold aspirin she said she was sorry but no. I must have looked ill by then because she asked me what was wrong. I told her and she picked up her handbag from under the counter and rummaged among its contents. Then with an exclamation of triumph, she pulled out a small bottle. "Ah! I knew I had some somewhere," she opened the bottle and shook out two tablets, changed her mind and made it three." Now you take these and go and lie down in the waiting room, and put something over your eyes to keep the light out." I thanked her and was about to say I didn't think the station staff would let me sleep in the waiting room when she interrupted me. "Don't worry about the staff, I'll have a chat with the station

master." I thanked her again and went to the waiting room.
I ate the cake and took all three tablets washing them down with the tea, then I lay down on one of the long seats, put my jacket over my eyes as the woman had said and tried to sleep. When I woke about four hours later, I felt a lot better. The flashing lights before my eyes had stopped and I no longer felt sick, and the pain in my head, although still hanging around, had all but disappeared. I put my coat on and went back into the buffet. The same lady was serving. When I asked for a cup of tea she looked and smiled. "Feel better now dear? I popped in a couple of times just to keep an eye on you – you know." I thanked her once again as she handed me the tea.
"How much?" I asked, indicating the tea.
"You have that one with me dear – oh and don't go off without this will you?" and she dragged my case from behind the counter. "You left it here," she smiled again. "Why can't more people be like her," I wondered, "I bet she wouldn't turn her back on you if had leprosy!" I drank my tea and said goodbye to the kindly middle-aged lady behind the counter. She was serving a customer but stopped to wave and call out, "Cheerio dear, good luck." I went to the booking office and bought a single ticket to Liverpool Street and was only just in time – the London train was already in the station. I got on with only seconds to spare. As I settled into a corner seat I thought "Now what?" then I thought of Emile. "Emile, that's it! I'll give him a ring when I get to London, and stay with him until I can sort myself out."
By the time the train had reached London my migraine had all but gone and I was feeling a little more optimistic about the future. I was also feeling weak from hunger, so as soon as I was through the ticket barrier I made straight for a cafeteria and there I ordered my favourite meal of double eggs and chips, bread and butter and a cup of tea. That meal tasted like a banquet and now I was ready to face the world. It felt very strange, I had only been in the Army for seven months but I had already got quite used to the regimentation, and now here I was again on my own and with no one to tell me what to do. I found some phone booths and rang Emile's number. It rang for quite some time before a gruff voice said, "Yeah, 'oo is it?" I thought at first I had the wrong number, so I asked the person at the other end of the line what number he was speaking from. He told me and it was Emile's number.

"Er-could I speak to Emile please?" I was almost apologetic.
"'Oo's calling?" the voice demanded to know.
"Ricky," I replied, still a little timidly, "just tell him it's Ricky." The voice then called out so loudly I had to hold the phone away from my ear.
"It's for you – some geezer called Ricky – come on yer lazy queen, get aht of bed!" then to me, "'e won't be long mate." Soon Emile's voice was asking "Who is this, please?"
"It's me, Ricky," I said impatiently.
"Oh right, Ricky, hi, how are you? How is life in the Army? Sorry, I didn't realise it was you," he giggled, "I had quite a night last night – what's the time?"
I looked up at the station clock and said with an icy edge to my voice, "Oh, it's only three – in the afternoon!"
He laughed. "My, my, really – oh well, who cares – so how are you?"
"In a word, free."
"Free? Free from what?" he sounded puzzled.
"Free from the Army of course. I resigned," I lied.
"Resigned! What, left – forever! But why?"
"Well, so I can see more of you for one thing."
"Oh, I see," he said, "of course I'm very flattered – so you mean it, you're really not a soldier boy anymore?"
"Yes, I really mean it – great, isn't it?" I was full of eager expectations now. "I wonder if I could stay with you – just for a while – until I get sorted." There was a long silence on the other end of the phone. "Emile, are you there? Emile!"
"Yes, I'm still here," the joy seemed to have left his voice. I supposed it was a bit of a shock to him – he is properly worried about me, I thought.
"Well, what do you think – shall I come straight over?"
"No – no, you can't, I have me – er, my brother staying here – it's just not – well, it's not convenient – please give me a ring when you get settled – bye." And the phone went dead. I looked at the receiver with total disbelief. I put it back slowly on to its cradle as I tried to grasp what I had just been told, which was to piss off! This was the last thing I had expected – my plans were once again falling apart. It wasn't that I really minded being dumped like that, it was simply that I hadn't put the possibility into the equation. The question was, with so little money left, what was I to do. After a

little thought, I took the bull by the horns and phoned my parents. It was my mother who answered.
"Hello Mum, it's me, Ricky, look, I've got some bad news. I have been thrown out of the Army on medical grounds."
Her tone was sharp. "What medical grounds?" I had to think quickly.
"Well, it seems that they have discovered the fact that I had osteomyelitis when I was younger, I never told them you see."
Now she sounded concerned. "Well, why didn't you tell them?" The lies got worse.
"Well, if I had I wouldn't have got in the first place and I just wanted a chance to prove myself." I said all of this so glibly that I almost believed it myself. I hated lying to my Mum like this, but had I told her the truth the telephone would have been slammed down in my ear.
"Where are you now?"
"Looking for digs in London."
"Why London?"
"I don't know really, I feel at a bit of a loss to know what to do." At last a chance to speak the truth.
"Well, you had better come home," this she said with some exasperation.
"What about Dad?" I asked.
"Don't worry, I'll explain to your father." I said thanks and rang off. I felt ashamed of myself. I had told the Army my full medical history and I had passed the medical A1. As I got on the train for home I thought that maybe this time things will be different.
The welcome I received from both my parents was one of understanding "At least you tried, son," my Dad told me proudly. Even my sister was understanding. My mother thought it was a disgrace that the Army threw me out for something that happened years ago and had not recurred since. I lapped up the new-found warmth shown to me by the family. Both my parents seemed to be trying to make up for the years we had lost. Finding a job was to prove a bit difficult. I didn't really know what I wanted to do – well, I did but if I had told Mum and Dad that I wanted to dress in drag and do an act, they would have been far from being amused – so it was agreed that I take any job until I had made up my mind.
That decision led to my working as a porter for a fruit and vegetable import company. It was my job to unload the lorries

bringing the goods in, and then reload them onto the lorries taking them out, very fulfilling work! Mostly it was boxes of oranges or sacks of onions. There was no such thing as a fork-lift truck, so I had to do it all by hand. I found it hard at first, but I was fit after my short time in the Army so I soon got used to it. I made friends with one of the drivers, Ronnie was about my age and hoped to be a guitarist. we would talk for hours about our dreams of showbiz – I told him I wanted to be a comic. He was fair-haired and quite good looking, but not my sort – he was tall and awkward – but we got on well. He also had a car, an old green Austin, quite a big car, in fact. The problem was it cost so much to run he hardly used it, so I suggested I pay half the running cost. He readily agreed and in our free time we would visit pubs that had entertainment and imagine ourselves on stage.

My mother, in the meantime, was concerned that I was getting into a rut and should be doing something worthwhile with my life. She still blamed the Army for ruining my career and wished more than once that she could have spoken to the people concerned and given them a piece of her mind. I told her to let it drop. A few days later I came home from work and could feel the frost in the atmosphere – nobody spoke to me apart from a curt yes and no. This went on for two days and no matter how hard I tried, I couldn't get any clue as to what was wrong, but on the morning of the third day, just after the post had arrived, the balloon went up. My mother read a letter then passed it to my father. When he had read it, he screwed it up and threw it at me. My Mum said, "You lying dirty pervert! I was worried about you so I phoned your Commanding Officer, and he told us the truth about your leaving the Army. It had nothing to do with any medical, did it? Well did it?" I hung my head.

"Answer your mother," my father snapped. I said nothing.

"You were dishonourably discharged, you were found in bed with another soldier, you filthy dirty creature." It was my mother speaking. I could feel my whole world crumble. Tears welled up in my eyes. Both my mother and father were now yelling at me, but I heard nothing just words – loud heated words, then I felt my mother's hand as it connected with my face. "Pack your bags and get out and this time don't bother to come back! Do you hear me?" I wanted to tell her what really happened, I wanted them to listen while I tried to explain the way I felt and the misery I was going through, but I knew that whatever I said would make not a scrap of difference. After all, I didn't understand it so why should they? But I didn't want to leave, I really didn't, I was scared and I told them so. "But you're not too scared to carry on with your disgusting habits, are you? Now go! Go on, get out!" and with those words ringing in my ears I went to my room and packed.

As I pushed the doorbell on Ronnie's front door, I wondered if I was doing the right thing, but I thought, "What the hell –whatever I do seems to be wrong, so once more won't make any difference at all." His mother opened the door. She was careworn, about forty, her once-red hair, now nearly all grey, was pulled back from her face and tied with a ribbon in a bunch behind her head. She didn't look at all surprised to see me. I saw her eyes move down and look at my case. "My washing," I said as though I had to explain. She simply said "Oh," then called over her shoulder.

"Ron! Ronnie, it's that mate of yours – he will be out in a bit," she said, then disappeared inside. Ronnie appeared looking tired, his hair a mess, and tucking his shirt into the waistband of his trousers."

"What brings you 'ere this time of night?" I looked at my watch – I had forgotten all about time.

"It's only ten – I thought you might fancy a drink."

"Oh, and you always go for a drink with your suitcase do you? What's up? Get chucked out?" He reached inside the door, took a jacket from an unseen hook and yelled back inside the house "Just going down the road." With one arm in his coat, he reached out with the other and slammed the door closed. The pub was only at the bottom of the street. I bought the drinks and we found a seat and I told him what had happened – well, that is I told him what I wanted him to believe had happened.

"They wanted me to get a better job – you know, one with prospects – whatever they are. When I said I wanted to be a comic they didn't think it was funny. There was a row and I walked out," I lied – yet again – well, I could hardly tell him the truth. "Oh, my Mum and Dad found out I was a queer – I got caught in bed with another soldier while I was in the Army, so they threw me out." It wasn't something that happened in ordinary life.

"Bit fucking hard ain't they? My old man and old lady know what I want to be and they couldn't give a toss."

"Well," I thought, "maybe that's the trouble, maybe my Mum and

Dad DO care and are worried about what will become of me." Then I thought about that and realised it was rubbish. You don't care about somebody and then throw them out without at least trying to help.
"So what are you going to do?" Ronnie was asking me.
"To tell the truth, I haven't got a clue – well that's not really true. I wouldn't mind going back to Cornwall. I worked a couple of clubs there some time ago, did pretty well as a matter of fact – one thing's for sure, I'm not staying around here for much longer."
He passed me a cigarette. "Why don't you wait until the end of the month, it's only a few days away, then we'll get our bonus and I'll come with you."
"You! Why? What for?"
"Well, there's fuck all doing here is there? So I might as well try a fresh place, and who knows there may be a guitarist job for me in one of them clubs you worked!"
"Shit," I thought," I hope he likes me in a frock!"
His mother let me sleep on the couch for the next week or so, and at the end of the month, with money in our pockets, we set off to find fame and fortune. As we drove towards the West Country, I had the most terrible feeling of foreboding. I tried to put it out of my mind by laughing and joking with Ronnie. He was chatting away the whole time about pulling 'birds' and finding work as a musician. I was beginning to regret painting such a rosy picture of my time in Cornwall. I did it in the first place because I loved the place and did genuinely love living there but – and it was a big but – I didn't tell him about living there in the winter once the visitors had left, with hotels and clubs closing and dances limited to maybe one night a week. "He must be a couple of pence short of a shilling anyway," I thought, "to think he would find work with a band in Cornwall when he had only lived a short distance from London." London was the place to be, and where remarkable changes in music style and dress were taking place. "In fact," I thought, "why am I not going to London?" I knew the answer to that – I lacked the self-confidence for one thing. It always seemed to me that London was too vast, had too much to offer .so why would anybody look at me twice? Whereas in the more provincial towns I seemed to adapt better, I felt more at ease. Maybe it has something to do with either being a small fish in a large pond or a large fish in a small pond, I don't really know.

We made quite slow progress by today's standards. The car, a 1938 Austin, was a bit temperamental, so we would have to stop to let it cool down or simply to give Ronnie a rest from driving. At that time I didn't drive, and even if I had, the thought of getting behind the wheel of a large pre-war car with a mind of its own – judging by the times Ronnie swore at it as he crashed through the gears – would not have filled me with joy. We passed through Bath and soon decided to camp on the outskirts of a village, we pitched the tent that Ronnie had brought with him on the edge of a small wood. The campsite was not visible from the road, the only access being via a narrow track with just enough room to turn the car around. We ate a makeshift meal. The evening was closing in, the only sounds we could hear – apart from a very occasional car – were of birds singing and the rustle of leaves as a slight breeze caught the trees. It was warm and balmy that September evening in 1964.

The silence was broken by Ronnie. "Oh, fuck this for a game of soldiers!" he moaned, "let's go and find a boozer or something. All this silence is getting on my nerves."

"Philistine!" I thought as I came out of a daydream. "What pub and where?" I asked, not really wanting to go.

"Any fucking pub, any-fucking-where, just as long as we don't have to sit 'ere all fucking night!" He was on his feet now and making for the car.

"Why don't we walk? It's not far."

"Walk! Are you sure? It could be miles."

"Well it could be, but it's not. We passed a pub about half a mile back and if we get pissed – and we might – I for one do not want to be driving back! OK?"

"Yeah, all right then," he said grudgingly, "we'll walk – but it had better only be 'arf a mile!"

The pub was small and friendly. We attracted a few looks from the locals and nods of "evening". After a few drinks we played darts, then Ronnie got talking to a couple of local girls and kept trying to get me to go over and meet them. "What the fuck's up with you?" he demanded to know, "they're all right – better than nothing."

I agreed they were all right, as he had put it, but I told him I felt sick. "Look, I'm going back to the tent. I'll see you later, I don't want to spoil your chances." with that I left the pub. Once outside, I breathed in the fresh night air and made my way back to the campsite. I was now regretting ever having come away with Ronnie. It was a mistake, "and when we get to Cornwall and he finds out the truth about me, what then?" I opened up the tent and lay down. I fell asleep. I woke up sometime later – something had disturbed me. I lay there in the dark listening, then I heard it – somebody was out there. I slowly opened the flysheet and looked outside. It was dark, but the moon shone just enough for me to see a few yards. I looked about me, the trees rustled their leaves. "I must have imagined it," I thought, "but where the hell is Ronnie?" I looked at my watch, the luminous dial telling me it was nearly one o'clock, then I heard the noise again. It was coming from the direction of the car. "Shit," I thought, "don't tell me somebody's trying to nick it!" I felt around in the tent until I touched the peg hammer. Grabbing it, I crawled slowly out of the tent and crept nearer the car, wishing that Ronnie would come back. As I got nearer the car I could hear voices. "Fuck!" I thought, "there's more than one!" I lay still in the dark, trying to think what the best thing to do was. I wanted to run and get the bloody hell out of there, but I couldn't just let these bastards take the car, so I crept nearer still. I could now touch the wheel I was so close. I listened – then I heard something that made my blood run cold at first then boil. It was a girl's voice first.

"Supposing your mate wakes up?"

"So what if he does?" It was Ronnie.

"Well he won't want to join in, will he? You know," she asked nervously.

Ronnie laughed, "You must be joking darling – him! He's as queer as a nine-bob note!"

I froze. "He knows, the bastard knows!" I wanted to get up and scream at him, "You bastard! You bastard!" but I didn't. I lay still on the damp grass. The girl spoke again.

"What! Don't tell me you're one as well! I'II scream, I will!" Now she was agitated.

"Shut up for Christ's sake," Ronnie hissed at her, "or you will wake 'im up. 'Ere, grab this – there, now do yer still think I'm queer?" He laughed again. "Come on babe, relax."

"Well, why are you with him then – if you're not like that?" she asked.

"Cos I need 'im – 'e's got a few bob and 'e knows people that can 'elp me get a job playing in a band. I think 'e fancies me, see, so I'm just using the queer bastard – now forget him – it's just you and me now."

I was boiling with rage and once again with humiliation. I crept quietly away from the car and back to the tent. I lay there trying to think what to do, my mind in a whirl by this latest turn of events. "Fancy him!" I said to myself, "the vain bastard. I have never fancied him," and nor had I. Time went by and I heard the car door slam. "Ssh! don't wake him now!" said Ronnie, "come on, I'll get you 'ome." I heard them make their way down the track, suddenly all was quiet. I left the tent and ran to the car. he had left it unlocked with his jacket on the back seat. I searched his pockets and found the car keys. I undid the boot and took my case out, then I went back to the tent, gathered my things and put them in the case. I went back to the car and looked through his coat again. This time I found his wallet. So far on this trip, I had bought all the petrol and food, so I took ten pounds from the wallet and put the wallet back inside his coat. This done, I let down the tent and threw the keys into the grass, then I made my way back to the main road.

I kept to the shadows as I walked, ducking into hedges when I heard a vehicle approaching, just in case Ronnie had found the keys and came looking for me – not out of concern for me, but for the ten pounds I had taken from his wallet. I began to feel guilty about it, but that feeling didn't last long as the conversation I overheard between the girl and Ronnie came rushing back into my mind. "Sod him!" I thought, "maybe this will teach him a lesson." It had certainly taught me one. The moon was high and the night very still, apart from a slight breeze that gently brushed the leaves on the trees, all I could hear was the sound of my own footsteps as I lugged my case along the tarmac road. Soon my humiliation and anger turned into despair as my case became heavier with each step I took. I looked for a place to sleep and soon found it in the shape of a Dutch barn picked out in the moonlight on the other side of a field. I threw my case over a small hedge and clambered after it. Once in the barn I made a bed of hay and lay down, thankful for the rest but sure I wouldn't sleep – but I did.

Each new day brings fresh hope, or so they say, but I certainly didn't feel that when I woke up next morning. I felt miserable and extremely lonely as I recalled the events of the previous night. A black cloud of despair hung over me as I made my way back to the

road and just to make me feel a little worse it started to rain. It was then I realised I had left my top coat in Ronnie's car. I had walked a few miles before I managed to get a lift. By this time I was soaked. I apologised to the driver, a guy about thirty.
"Don't worry about it," he sounded so bloody cheerful! "It's only the firm's car." He went on to tell me he was a rep for some company or other. When he asked what I was doing, walking through the rain at that time in the morning, I told him some cock and bull story about my car breaking down and having to get to London. The rep dropped me at Temple Meads station in Bristol, waved me a friendly goodbye and shouted, "Good luck." I had a feeling I was going to need it. After a wash and brush-up in the station lavatories, I went into the buffet and had some breakfast. I was being to feel a little better, I had some clean clothes on and the breakfast had restored my energy, now all I had to decide was what to do and where to go. When I looked at my options, I shuddered. I couldn't go home, that was for sure. I had walked out of my job so they wouldn't be too thrilled to see me again. I didn't want to stay in Bristol even though I liked the city, and Cornwall was out, I didn't understand for the life of me why I had suggested to Ronnie that we go there. I loved the place and the people, but it was in the past and the memories were still too painful. What I needed was somewhere new, somewhere that I could begin afresh. I picked up my case and walked across the station concourse and stood before the destination board.

10 – MY OWN PRIVATE NIGHTMARE

Why did I choose it? I'll never know, but as I got off the train in Leeds I felt good, and glad that I had. Strange, but I had always thought of the north of England as being full of coal mines, cotton mills and row after row of small grimy terraced houses, so it was quite a culture shock for me when I walked into Leeds city centre, with its huge town hall and shops full of expensive and up-to-date goods. It was also arrogant of me to think it would be any different, but in those days a southerner's conception of what the north was like was coloured by what we saw on TV and read in our school books. Think of the North, and we in the South thought of Gracie Fields and George Formby and films like Saturday Night and Sunday Morning. North of Watford might as well have been a foreign country.

I walked around for a long time getting used to the feel of the place and the Yorkshire accent. "Was this my chance," I wondered, "to escape my past?" I didn't know then that you could never really escape from your past, no matter how hard you try or how many lies you tell. You may convince others, but you never really deep down convince yourself. You can only disguise your past with a thin veneer, but soon even that will crack.

A job and somewhere to live were my first priority. I was directed to Chapeltown, a fairly run-down area but with an arty atmosphere. Many of the people living in the bedsits and flats were hippies and sixties 'flower people'. I found a bed and breakfast that would do until I could afford a flat. Full of eager anticipation I went to the Labour Exchange to sign on. I couldn't claim any money as I had left my previous job of my own free will, but they sent me for several interviews, none of which turned out to be successful. The days turned into weeks and it was now October, and still I didn't have a job. Things were looking black and my money was disappearing at an alarming rate. My optimism turned to desperation and I took a part-time job as a potman in the Peel Hotel on the Headrow, one of the main streets in the centre of Leeds. The job paid very little, just a couple of pounds a night, but the manager said I could expect quite good tips. I thought if I could do this until I was eligible for unemployment money I would be all right. My first night in the job, I was scared to death. The place was packed and people kept calling me from all sides. I did my best as I tried to clean the tables and take orders, but I found the accent hard to follow with all the noise around me. I had to keep asking people to repeat their orders, which didn't please most of them. As a result, my tips were almost nothing. After a few days I got used to it, but I rarely made more than ten bob a night extra. Some of the customers treated me as a sort of skivvy, which to a degree I suppose I was, and because I was doing a menial job a lot treated me with contempt, snapping their fingers at me, whistling for me to serve them and so on. But I stood for it and tried very hard not to let my feelings show – after all I needed this job, they didn't need me.

Soon it was just impossible for me to go on paying for my digs, so I left and started sleeping rough anywhere I could – derelict buildings, shop doorways – anywhere dry. By day I would wash and shave in public lavatories. The lack of proper sleep was now taking its toll and my self-respect was non-existent. I began believing that I was a low-life, destined for nothing but the gutter. The nights were the worst. After leaving work, I would walk around the station making out I was a passenger until all the drunks were off the streets. Then, when I thought it safe, I would find a place to sleep, but sleep was not easy. Every slight sound woke me. I was scared stiff of being beaten up and robbed of what few possessions I had left. My days were spent in cheap cafés, drinking endless cups of tea in an attempt to keep warm. One night at work I mixed up an order for one table. The man who had ordered the drinks was a loud-mouthed pig of a man, about forty probably, a rep or an office manager. He clicked his fingers and beckoned me over to the table. "I don't know if you're deaf or just plain stupid," he sneered at me while his friends laughed. He pointed to the tray of drinks. "Now run along back to the bar and take this lot with you, and when you come back make sure you have the right order – is that clear?" I nodded. He continued, "Well, don't just stand there, you stupid cockney bastard – get the drinks!" I picked up the tray of drinks and threw the lot into his lap. The whole room heard the commotion and turned to look at the man and me. I snapped – I called the man and his friends all stupid bastards, and threatened to put the table over their heads. Then I asked those watching what the fuck they were staring at. I barged through the crowd and into the staff room and grabbed my case. Just as I was leaving the manager asked what the hell I thought I was doing.

"Just showing those bastards the same respect they showed me," was my reply.

"If you think I'm paying you for tonight you're wrong!" he yelled.

"Shove it up your arse!" I yelled back and walked out into the night. "Not very clever," I told myself, then I found the two-pound float I was given each night still in my pocket. I made my way to the nearest pub and by the time the last bell went, I was well and truly pissed. I was also in turmoil and a state of high anxiety. I felt cold as I left the pub, and this time I didn't go to the station, I just walked and walked. I wanted to get out of Leeds. What a few weeks ago had seemed my chance for a fresh start had now turned sour, as had everything else in my life. I was now completely alone, with no home, no job and worst of all no hope. I felt completely abandoned.

I don't know how I got onto the road, but I did. It was a long country road with hedges either side. I remember wanting to speak to my mother, and I remember opening my case. I was sitting on a wall or some stones and the razor blade, I remember the razor blade, then somebody shaking me, but I wanted to sleep, it was cold and I just wanted to sleep, then nothing. Someone was calling me. "Richard! Richard!"

I looked and everything was white, all around me was white – then the white separated, and there were people, and the people were in white. One of them was talking to me.

"So, you're back with us – good." He went on talking but I was so tired.

The next time I woke, a young man, about twenty-five with

long fair hair, was looking down at me. He was smiling. "Hi, welcome to St James."

"St James?" I thought I was dead for a moment until the young man spoke again. "How are you feeling, Richard?"

I looked at him. He was slim and wearing a dressing-gown. "They don't wear those in heaven, I'm sure!" I thought. "It's Ricky," I corrected him, "I'm Ricky, not Richard."

He apologised. "Sorry," he was still grinning, "I'll get a nurse."

"Why?" I asked.

"They said when you wake up we had to tell them." He called a nurse. When the nurse arrived, it was a man. He told me I was in St James's Hospital in Leeds and that a doctor would see me soon. In fact, a short time later I saw two doctors. One told me I had been found on a roadside with both my wrists slashed. I looked down and saw both my wrists swathed in bandages.

"You are a very lucky young man," the doctor smiled benignly as he spoke, "it was a cold night – your blood congealed."

I felt like saying "You stupid bastard, that's not good luck – good luck would have meant I would be dead by now, and not looking at you grinning at me," but in the event I said nothing – what was the point? The doctors were still talking, whether to themselves or me I didn't know or care. I just wanted to get out of there and quick. I pulled at the bedclothes and tried to sit up, but a hand pushed me gently but firmly back onto the pillows.

"Sorry, you can't do that."

"But I want to go – I'm not staying here."

"I'm sorry but you must – you attempted to take your own life and that is an offence in law. It also means that we have to keep you here until you're well enough to leave."

I protested. "You can't do that! You can't keep me here if I don't want to stay."

"Oh, but we can – you are being held under section." He went on and on, but by now my head was spinning. What was happening to me? Why were they doing this?

I lay there for two, maybe three days, waking only when I was forced to, either for food – which I left – or for pills, which were pushed into my mouth. I didn't speak to anybody, they spoke to me but I never replied. It was all so unreal – like a bad dream, but unlike a dream, it was there even when I was awake.

When I was able to sit up, propped against my pillows, the

long-haired guy came back and sat next to me. "How are you doing?" he asked, his face quite solemn. I felt my eyes fill with tears, I couldn't stop them – they spilt down over my cheeks, hot and burning. I felt so ashamed. I turned my head away from the young man. He took my hand very gently. "Hey, don't let them get to you –or is it my ugly mug that's upset you?" I turned to look at him, my eyes now so full of tears I could hardly see him. I wiped them on the bandage of my free wrist. He was smiling now. "That's good – so it's not me!" he laughed softly.

"I feel so lost." was all I could say.

"I know, Ricky – see, I got your name right this time – we are all lost, that's why we are here – lost souls together – and that lot." He waved his hand in the direction of the nurses. "They are trying to find the answers – but I doubt if they will. Only God knows all the answers, and he ain't ready to tell." He squeezed my hand gently. "What about a guided tour of the 'Hotel'?" I looked at him, unsure. Somehow, I had begun to feel safe in my bed.

"Come on – just for a while." He lifted my arm up and pulled the bedclothes back, then he took my legs and swung them over the edge of the bed. "Stay there," he ordered, as if I were about to make a run for it, but I felt so weak and worn out that I did as I was told. He rushed off and came back a few moments later with a dressing gown one, of those thick, woolly checked ones that seem to be the norm in hospitals everywhere. I stood up and was surprised to find myself swaying like a drunk. I grabbed hold of him. "It's OK, you're all right – it's the pills," he steadied me, "all right now?"

I nodded and for the first time in days felt myself smile. "Thought I was pissed."

"When you're feeling better, we'll get pissed together. Now, are you ready for that tour?"

I told him yes. The ward was on the ground floor and we were in the psychiatric ward, the sound of it made me shudder. Mike, my new-found friend, must have sensed my concern. He took my arm. "You are not insane and nor am I – well, I might be!" he laughed, "you have been through a rough time, that's all." Thus reassured, we continued the tour. He introduced me to some other patients. One was a middle-aged man, short, slight with a mop of steel-grey frizzy hair. He was wearing his own clothes, a grey suit and tie. He didn't look ill at all. "Barry, this is Ricky, our latest recruit." I held out my hand.

Barry took it, and said, “Got a ciggie I could borrow?” I said sorry, I hadn’t and he shuffled off.

“What’s up with him?” I asked.

“Well, believe it or not, he’s a comedian, or so he says. He’s just depressed, that’s all, like a lot of us.”

“And you – why are you here? You don’t sound depressed.”

He took some time to answer. “My wife's idea. I have all these things in my head and they won't come out – well not properly anyway – I want to say so much, but it all gets jumbled up.” I was to find out about this later when I would see him walk up and down the ward for hours on end, reciting poetry he had written and getting mad at himself because he thought was lousy. Most of the time he was all right, but the look in his eyes when he was having a bad day was quite scary – yet I was never frightened of him. He took me to see other people, all men, old and young, some in bed, some like Barry in their own clothes. One, a young black guy, I still remember vividly. He lay on his bed staring at the ceiling. Every now and then he would rub his skin really hard and say over and over, “I can’t get it off – I can’t get it off.” I asked Mike what was wrong with him. He told me the boy had been taunted at school, and later in his first job called a black bastard and worse. Now he thought he was white and that someone had painted his skin. He was ill for a long time, but I did see him leave and he was better. I only hope he managed to cope with life when he left.

I spent lots of time with the doctors as they tried to find out what my problem was, but I was unable to tell them the truth. I felt ashamed, I could not say “I am homosexual”, I simply couldn’t. I was scared of the reaction firstly. After all, the only other person I had confided in, apart from lovers, was a vicar or at least a Chaplain – a man of God, a supposed Christian – and what had he done? Nothing – even while I was locked up in the guardhouse up he never came near me – so what hope did I have of a doctor understanding? I told them about my family and that we were estranged. They suggested I write to them and tell them where I was and what had happened. I was very dubious but was assured it would be the right thing to do and it would help to build bridges.

I had to wait a week for the reply and when the nurse handed me the letter, I recognised my mother's handwriting. Mike saw the look on my face and came over to join me. "Everything OK?" I showed him the unopened letter.

"From my Mum."

He nodded. "That's good." I sat on the edge of my bed turning the envelope over and over in my hands. "You have to tear the top to open it," said Mike. I handed him the letter.

"You do it – please." He gave it back to me.

"We are mates, but this is one you have to do for yourself."

I knew he was right, so I ripped open the envelope, took out the familiar blue notepaper and read what my mother had to say. I never did finish reading it. I got to the part where she had written, "And as far as I am concerned I have only one son. You have not existed and do not exist." I dropped the letter and it fell on the floor. I climbed back into my bed fully clothed, pulled the bedclothes tightly over my head and wept.

The hospital had forwarded my sick certificates to the Ministry of Health and I was now getting a small amount of money each week for which I was very grateful. It gave me a measure of independence, I could now buy cigarettes and a newspaper if I wanted one. Not much of an independence, you may think, but from having absolutely nothing to having cash in your pocket, however small the amount, was to be rich. It gave you the power of choice – to spend or not. I was reading a newspaper – my newspaper – one morning when a woman, aged about thirty-five and wearing a dark green uniform and heavy framed glasses, almost bounced up to my bed. "Hello," she gushed, her plump face radiant. She held her hand out. "I'm Margaret," she beamed, "Margaret Washbrook, occupational therapy department. Charge Nurse says you might like to come down to the unit and meet the rest of our jolly gang." That's just how she spoke, all Joyce Grenfellish, but not quite as awkward as Joyce. She really is the one person whose name I have never forgotten from that period of my life that I wouldn't have wished on anybody. The faces of the rest of the staff – doctors, charge nurses and nurses – are forever engraved on my mind, but their names I discarded a long time ago. Some I never even knew.

"He said that did he?" I said in reply.

"I'm sure you'll have a jolly time – there is so much to do. There is—" and she went on to tell a whole list of things that I could do. When she got to basket weaving, I nearly choked.

"I'll think about it." I shook her hand and she bustled off.

Mike, who was standing close and had seen her come in, said, "What's the matter – don't you fancy a spot of basket weaving?"

"She's a bit – well, pushy."

"She's all right is our Margaret, and she's right – now you're allowed down to occupational therapy, we can go and have a cuppa in the tea bar."

He was right about Margaret. Once I got to know her, and that didn't take long, she turned out to be one of the kindest, nicest people I have ever met. She never pried or made judgements, she just coaxed people back to being alive again. Some people were in a far worse state than others, some had almost reached the point of no return, yet I never saw her give up or lose her patience with anybody.

To get to the occupational therapy department we had to go down past the women's ward and down a long corridor. What I saw on the way distressed me. There were men and women, young and old, walking up and down the corridor as though in a trance. They looked like zombies, their faces gaunt, eyes staring into nowhere. Occasionally one would ask for a cigarette, but in the main they said nothing, just walked up and down. Mike saw the look on my face.

"That's one thing you must not let them do."

"What? "I said, not understanding what he was trying to say.

"Electric shock treatment – that's what all these have every week."

"What the fucking hell for?"

"It's their cure."

"Cure from what? They look like the living dead!"

"If you had been strapped down and had electricity pumped through your brain you would look like that – come on," he took my arm, "let's go – you'll get used to it."

But I never did.

We went into the residents' day room, a pleasant place filled with tables and chairs, and a tea bar in one corner selling not only teas but a variety of things including sweets and cigarettes. There were quite a few people about. We sat at a table where two smartly dressed women sat sipping tea and smoking cigarettes. Both women were in their late thirties or early forties.

"Hiya girls, meet Ricky," Mike then introduced me to Ann and

May.

We all shook hands, then Ann quipped, "Well, your friend isn't looking very happy – nothing to do with us I hope?" She spoke in a broad Scots brogue. The three of them laughed, I felt myself blush. "Bitch," I thought. Mike then explained my lack of carefree abandon by telling them about my encounter with the people in the corridor. "Oh, I'm sorry, I didn't realise." It was Ann – she squeezed my hand.

"You'll get used to it in time," this time it was May talking, "if it's possible to get used to it, that is."

I started to stammer, but this time nobody mocked me for it – they just sat there, waiting for me to say what I had to in my own time. "I will never get used to it – it's barbaric."

"Aye, we know – just you make sure it doesn't happen to you."

"How could I stop it?" I was puzzled by her remark.

It was Mike who answered for her. "Play them at their own game" was his advice and the two women nodded in agreement. "When you see the doctors, kid them on that the junk they are giving you is doing the trick – try to look happy."

"It's true, love," May said, lighting another cigarette and blowing a cloud of smoke into the air. "That's why the two of us always try to dress to the nines – we feel like hell some days, but we force ourselves to make the effort – that way the staff think we are improving."

"But that can't be right," I was calmer now, "that can't be the way to cure people, surely?"

"What's right got to do with anything? It's not right that we are in here in the first place! And as for a cure – cure of what? Can you cure other people's insensitivity towards you? If somebody keeps beating you or abusing you in other ways, why should you be cured? Surely the person who needs the cure is the perpetrator?" I couldn't argue with that – after all, the only real reason I was there was because I was born differently from most other men. I hadn't chosen to be homosexual, it had just happened.

Ann carried the argument further. "Most of us in here are only here because of other people's lack of understanding or downright indifference – or in some cases because we won't comply and follow like sheep. We all react in different ways – some people are strong-willed and can fight back, others crumble. I used to be strong-minded, but my husband was stronger, much more determined. He wanted me out of his life. I thought that I could change his mind – after all, I loved him and had done for twenty-two years. We had worked together, building our lives with the children, making a lovely home, through good and bad times. I never once thought of leaving him – why should I? He was my life. Then one day he said, 'It's over,' and I very stupidly said, 'What's over, darling?' and without even lowering his newspaper he said, 'This empty shell of a marriage of ours. I want a divorce!' I won't bore you with the details but I had no intention of just letting him go. I thought maybe he was at some crisis point in his life, so I decided to fight for him. He was worth it, I told myself – but all I got for my efforts were taunts and jibes. He told people, my friends, our friends, that I was losing my mind. He played terrible tricks on me and in the end, I fell to pieces. I thought I was mad, and I know she won't mind me saying so, but May's husband did a similar thing to her only he was even more evil." May nodded and wiped a tear from her eye.

"Then." Mike said, "when you finally end up in one of these places because you can't take any more, not only are you in some way tainted, but the quacks start to try and look into your mind – to dissect your brain almost – in order to see why you couldn't take any more, when any bloody fool knows that everybody is different. Some people can take a lot more stress than others who are much more sensitive, and all they really need is a chance to come to terms with themselves and their problems."

"And not to be turned into a cabbage!" I added.

All that may sound a little simplistic, but from that day to this I have never understood psychiatrists or the need for them. They are, in my book, a bit like modern-day social workers. I'm not saying for one moment that they are not decent dedicated people who believe in what they are doing – they probably are – but they haven't a clue how anybody feels really feels when their lives collapse before their eyes, when they have nothing left to live for or to aim for. Before you can help you have to understand, really understand – you have to have been there and bought the T-shirt, not just to some academic establishment reading everything from textbooks. You have to be able to feel the hurt – feel the distress – relive the experiences. That's why I think that Alcoholics Anonymous works, because the people giving the helping hand have been through the pain. They understand – which is all most people want.

Mike was now able to go home for short visits. I missed him and spent more and more time with May and Ann. Margaret, in the meantime, had got me involved with the patients' social life. Soon I was running a weekly Beetle Drive and even a dance. I was, however, getting more and more concerned about my treatment and what they were treating me for. I still had meetings with the psychiatrist, I was no nearer a release date and I still had to take a daily dose of pills. When I asked about release, the answer was always the same: "It's early days yet." Early days! It was now Christmas and I had been in hospital for two months! And as I had not told them I was queer – what the fuck were they treating me for?

I was allowed out for Christmas Day. I felt very nervous about going out in public so Mike had me collected by car. The day itself was great. Mike, his wife and little girl and their friends and family made me feel really special. We played silly games, drank a great deal and smoked a little 'wacky baccy.' Seeing them all so happy did, in a strange way, make me feel even more alone. I knew Mike was my friend, of course, but somehow it was not enough. Going back to the hospital was, I was surprised to find, a relief, like finding a safe haven. This, in turn, made me anxious. Was I really getting so used to this place that I would soon not want to leave? The thought frightened me and the fear of electric shock treatment still hovered over me. I told Mike of these fears. "Don't let them give you that treatment – promise me."

I promised but said, "How can I stop them?"

He thought for a moment, then said, "You will just have to get out."

"But," I protested, "I'm under a section – they will call the police if I just try to walk out, and then where will I end up?" The outlook seemed black.

"Well," he sighed, "suppose you will just have to take your pills and keep your nose clean." He was right, I thought, but it meant I was trapped!

A young guy about eighteen, also called Mike, had been a patient for about three weeks and was in a side ward on his own, but he did come and mix with the rest of us and one day I found myself telling him my fears.

"What are you going to do – get thrown out?" His words hit me like a sledgehammer.

"Christ!" I thought "Dare I do it again?" The thought stayed. "It worked once, but would it work a second time?"

"You all right Ricky?" he sounded concerned, "you've gone as white as a ghost."

I told him I was fine. The thought of going through all that again scared the shit out of me, but at the same time, the idea did excite me – not the thought of getting into bed with young Mike – the thought of getting out.

When I did think about the two of us sharing a bed, it occurred to me that since my stay in hospital I had not had any sexual urges, and I began to wonder why. Maybe the doctors did know what was wrong with me, without my saying a word – and maybe all those pills I have been taking were starting to work – but how did the doctors know? Then I thought about it some more, and looking back I couldn't think of anybody, male or female making a pass at me, nor had I seen anybody flirting with anybody else. Then it dawned on me what had they all got in common – the pills! "Of course, the pills! I bet one of them at least is to control sexual appetite!" The more I thought about it, the more it made sense. All those men and women, all or most upset, some even traumatised, most at the very least depressed, all thrown together into one small community, able to socialise, they must give us something – nature being nature something had to happen – and nothing had. So if I was right – and I had to suppose I was – would my plan still work or would they know it was a try-on?

I told Mike–not young Mike but my friend – I told him how I had got out of the Army. I didn't tell him why though. When I had told him the story, he said "Wow man, do you mean that? You pulled that off? Oh, that is brilliant! What a gas!" He made it sound like some schoolboy prank. I dared not tell him the real story, the heartache it caused, the anguish I went through. He was still laughing and slapping his side. "Oh, it's just great, what a stunt." Now I was laughing with him – but from nerves.

"The thing is, Mike, I want to try it again – here. I want to see if they will throw me out of here too." He looked at me his eyes alive with mischief.

"Here? You crazy bastard," he said, and thought about it. "It might work."

"Might? Might's not good enough – suppose it doesn't work,

what happens to me then? Will they throw away the key?"

"No – I can't see how it can fail. They wouldn't want a queer in here, would they? The trouble is, they know I'm married—" I cut him short.

"Not you! I wasn't thinking of you! Young Mike – in the side ward." He feigned a hurt look.

"Oh I see, you've gone off me now, have you?" For a split second I thought he meant it, then I realised he was joking – but he didn't know how wrong he was – in a different place and situation I would have been very happy to have had a relationship with him. He was thoughtful, good looking and he made me feel happy – but I knew it was never to be.

"You're much too old – I like 'em young." We both laughed.

"Have you asked him?"

"Christ no, I've only just thought of it and I wanted to talk it over with you."

"Go get it – if he will play ball!" another laugh, "oops, sorry about the pun."

"Come and see him with me "I pleaded, he agreed.

The look on young Mike's face when we told him the plan was a picture. He came from a tough working-class Yorkshire family. "You're fucking mad the pair of you, it's no wonder you're in 'ere."

"So are you." I pointed out.

"Only cos I can't keep me fingers off other folks' stuff. I'm in for reports, tha knows," he grinned a cheeky boyish grin.

"No," I said, "I didn't know."

"Why don't you do it if it's so bloody easy?" he pointed to Mike.

"They know I'm married."

"I see." There was a pause. "Well, if I do it – and I'm not saying I will, mind – what's in it for me?"

I looked at Mike, he looked at me and we both looked at our young friend. "Nothing "It was Mike who spoke first "Ricky has been shut up in here under a section for months now, and still they won't let him out."

"And I am worried that they might start to give me shock treatment. There's nothing else to tell you."

"But suppose they think I'm queer! My old man would kill me."

"I know the feeling," I thought. "They won't. I'll tell them you were asleep and didn't know I was there until you woke up, and

Mike here will vouch for you as well."

Mike nodded. "No problem."

"All right yer bastards, but if owt goes wrong it's down to you two – right?"

We both said "Right."

Then we made plans for the following night.

The next day dragged on and on, I was getting very tense. Mike said we should keep away from the residents' lounge because I was so on edge. "You might just give something away – try reading a book – what about The Wooden Horse? Good book!"

"Bastard!" But, as all days do, it finally passed. After lights out I lay in my bed, wishing I hadn't started the whole thing. Then I thought of the many more months I could be here, and how I could end up, so I reckoned I had little choice. At about two o'clock, when the night charge nurse had finished his rounds and was back in his office, I crept out of bed and made my way to the side ward. Mike was still awake and waved goodbye to me. Just as I was passing Barry's bed a hand grabbed my shoulder. My heart jumped so much I thought it would stop beating. I stood there frozen to the spot and a voice asked, "Have you got a ciggie?" I could hear Mike sniggering. I rushed back to my locker and got a cigarette, and pushed it into Barry's waiting hand. "There – now piss off!" When I finally reached the side ward young Mike was fast asleep, so I gently eased back the covers and got in beside him. He grunted and groaned but didn't wake up.

"He is either a bloody good actor or he really is asleep," I told myself. I was far too scared to sleep – or so I thought, because the next thing I can remember is being hauled out of the bed and thrown on the floor. For a moment I thought it was a bad dream. I lay there, the sudden light in my eyes blinding me.

"You dirty sodding queer! Get up!" I recognised the voice of the charge nurse. He grabbed me by the hair, almost tearing it out as he pulled me from the floor. "Get up, you disgusting creature – quick, grab the shit!" He was talking to somebody else. I felt hands strong hands grip my arms, then they pushed me to the door. Other nurses were now in the corridor, more hands grabbed me then I heard a door being open and somebody shouting, "Quick, give me a hand!" I started to panic, kicking wildly and blindly, screaming for help. Someone got my head in an armlock, I could feel my arms being pulled tight across my chest, then I was violently pushed as a voice said, "That's got the bastard." I fell towards the floor, keeping my eyes tightly shut – believing, like the ostrich, that if I couldn't see what was happening it would go away. I hit the floor with a thud and apart from the initial shock of the sudden end to my fall I was unhurt. "Right, get those down!" a voice ordered, and I felt hands pulling at my pyjama bottoms ripping them away from my body until my lower half was naked. People were still pulling at me, trying to turn me around. I was still screaming at the top of my voice, begging them to stop, trying to tell them it was all a try-on – nobody listened. "This will keep the dirty sod quiet," and I felt the sudden sharp momentary pain as a hypodermic needle pierced the flesh on my thigh – then nothing.

I have no idea how long I lay there – it might have been minutes, hours or even days – I had no way of telling. When I did awake my head hurt, throbbing at the temples. The pain seemed to be shooting all over my body and it felt as if somebody was still holding my arms. I wouldn't open my eyes, I called out for them to let me go – there was nothing – just silence. Slowly I released the tight grip I had put on my eyes. I was on my back and the light from directly above me shone into my eyes, causing me to shut them again almost immediately. Slowly they got used to the harsh light. I tried to sit up but my arms would not move, then I saw why. I had not hurt myself in the fall to the floor – I was in a padded cell wearing a straitjacket. For a moment, I just stared at the padded walls, not being able to take in what was happening to me. Then I tried to call out, but my mouth was so dry no sound would come. I ran my tongue over my lips, they felt dry and swollen. I tried calling again without success, then I fell back and the tears rolled hot and burning down my cheeks. I must have cried myself to sleep because the next thing I remember was somebody shaking me and calling, "Come on, wake up – you're not going to sleep your way out of this." It was a charge nurse. I asked for a drink. "It's not a drink you need – it's a bloody good hiding." I tried to tell him it was all a mistake, but as I could hardly speak, the words were almost inaudible. In any case, he was not listening to me. He was talking about young Mike and the harm I had caused him. I tried again to explain but it was of no use. He did release me from the straitjacket on condition I behaved myself. I assured him I would – then he left.

Having my arms free again felt wonderful but I needed a drink desperately. It was what seemed like hours before I was given one, and only then if I took yet more pills. It took me some time to realise that I was naked from the waist down and that people passing outside in the corridor were able to look in at me through a small observation window in the door, so I moved to the wall to one side of the door, out of sight of prying eyes. I was to stay in that cell for two more days. Finally, on the third day, I was thrown some clean pyjamas and taken to a small side ward nearby. It was empty except for a bed and a side locker. I hadn't been in bed very long when a doctor came in. He asked me why I had committed such an act, and I told him it was just a plan to get out. I went on to tell him about my getting out of the Army in a similar way. He then asked me if I thought I was homosexual. I said yes, I knew that I was. When he then asked why I had not told him or some other member of staff all this before, I told him the truth.

"I was scared for one –and secondly – I was ashamed."

"Why were you scared?" he wanted to know.

"Because of the way I've been treated by people in the past when they found out about me."

"Why ashamed then?" he continued.

"I don't know. I have tried to be normal but it didn't feel right, so then I felt ashamed because I couldn't be like most other men, and I had to sneak around leading a sort of double life and telling lies to people so they wouldn't find out."

He went on "Would you like to be normal?"

"I feel I am when I'm with people like me – it's only when I'm with ordinary people that I feel different. I don't know what normal means."

"It means," he said sharply, "that you have the normal sexual relation with women that God intended, and you do not commit perverted acts such as buggery with members of your own sex." With that, he asked one last question. "Do you drink alcohol?"

I told him I did – when he left, saying he would see me again later.

A few hours later he returned and, to my amazement, he pushed a trolley laden with all sorts of things, including a quantity of spirits – gin, rum, whiskey – into the room. He was smiling. He chatted while he set some equipment up on my locker, including a tape recorder. Then he asked what was my favourite drink. I said I didn't mind – I liked gin but not neat, I didn't really like rum, so I supposed whiskey – and to my astonishment, he poured me a large glassful. "Now drink it all down," he smiled.

"But I'll get pissed."

"That's not important. You have been through a rough patch, you have earned a drink." So I drank it. Then he gave me an injection in my arm. It seemed to take effect almost immediately and I started to feel sick. Then he switched on the tape recorder and a voice started to tell me how disgusting I was, and how revolting it was to be homosexual, and didn't I realise how loathsome I and my kind were in the eyes of decent people. By this time I was being violently sick. I had had nothing to eat for days, so after clearing my stomach of what there was, I was left just to retch as the tape continued telling me how vile homosexuality was. After a while, the doctor left. I carried on throwing up for about two hours. Just as I as I lay back on my bed, exhausted, the doctor came back and the whole process started again. This went on for four days and nights, every two hours without food and, apart from the whiskey, only a little water. I would roll around the room screaming to be let out, banging on the door, but nobody came. The stench of my own filth was unbelievable. One day, the second I think, I saw Mike's face at the small window in the door. When he saw the state I was in, he started banging and pushing on the door. I managed to get over to it and tried pulling at the handle. I was screaming at him, begging him to get me out. By now he too was yelling and screaming, tears streaming down both our faces, then some staff came and pulled him, still screaming, away. I collapsed onto the floor.

On the morning of the fifth day when the doctor came in, I begged him to stop.

"No more, please, no more, I'm cured now, I swear – I'm not queer anymore, I promise I am cured." I was taken from the room and given a bath and some clean clothes, then to the ward where I slept for hours.

When I finally woke up, I wondered where I was, and breathed a sigh of relief when I recognised the ward. Then I had vivid flashbacks of my 'treatment'. I shivered at the thought, then I also remembered that I was now cured. The trouble was, I didn't feel any different, but was I supposed to? Should I have had a sudden urge to make love to a woman? Or would that come about in a different way? Then I thought about having sex with a woman and it filled me with horror – even the thought of it made me cringe – it appalled me. "But if I don't do it they will never let me out," I thought, "somehow I have to prove that I am straight – but how, and who with?" I started to panic again. "Suppose I can't do it? What excuse can I make?" Paranoia set in once more. I had to find Mike, I needed to talk to somebody I could trust. When I had got dressed I asked one of the blokes in the ward if he knew where Mike was. This particular man was no great talker and didn't mix in very much so I was not really surprised when he turned his head and refused to speak to me. "He's having a bad day – poor sod," or so I thought. But then I spoke to one or two more on the ward and they all gave me the cold shoulder. Then, of course, I realised that they all knew about my being in bed with young Mike. "But I'm cured now!" I said to one bloke as he turned away from me. "Bollocks!" was all he said as he walked away. I started to shake. "They don't believe me, I have been through all that and they still don't believe me." I went out into the corridor and was about to go into young Mike's side ward when a nurse barred my way.

"Oh no you don't," he said through clenched teeth, "he wants you to stay away from him – is that clear?" I looked into his eyes and saw the loathing.

"Tell him – tell him I'm sorry," then I walked on down the corridor. I could feel the tears well up in my eyes. "I must keep in control," I kept saying to myself, "I must not give way – I have to be strong," but the tears still came.

"Got a ciggie?" Barry was tugging at my sleeve – well at least he was still talking to me, I gave him a cigarette.

"Seen Mike, Barry?"

"Not since he went. no," he said examining the cigarette before putting it into the corner of his mouth. "Light?" he asked.

"What do you mean – not since he went – went where?" I asked him as I gave him my box of matches, he struck a match and carefully put the flame to the end of the cigarette, sucking on it at the same time and taking great gulps of tobacco smoke into his lungs. He coughed and spluttered a bit.

"These are good," he coughed again and I gave him two more from my packet. "Ta," he said as he put them carefully into his pocket.

"Barry," I was getting agitated now, "what do you mean? Where did Mike go?"

He looked at me, surprised. "Why, home of course – he was sent home a couple of days ago – you know, discharged!" Then he was gone, blowing cigarette smoke into the air. I was stunned. I walked into the OT room. Margaret Washbrook looked up from what she was doing when she heard the door open and seeing me she hurried over.

"Come over here and sit down, you look awful." She put her hands gently around my shoulders and led me to a quiet corner, out of earshot of the others in the room. "I heard about it, of course – it was pretty bad, I imagine."

I looked at her, my composure now gone completely, and through great sobs, I said, "Mike's gone – he just left."

"Now listen to me Ricky – he has gone, yes, but he didn't want to go like that," I looked at her, "he saw you in that side ward. He went berserk almost when he saw the state you were in and the nursing staff had to subdue him for his own sake. Then when he had recovered it was felt he was well enough to go home – and," she added, "he told me to tell you he will see you soon – feel better now?" I said yes, and apologised for being a pain in the arse. "Come on," she said brightly, "let's get a nice cup of tea."

We went to the lounge and sat at a table drinking our tea. A little while later May and Ann joined us. After some small talk, Margaret excused herself and went back to work.

"She's very matey today," Ann said sarcastically.

"I've always found her to be very nice," I could feel myself being defensive towards her.

"I know – I know. I was only saying – it wasn't meant badly."

May interrupted. "How are you anyway? We heard you were having treatment."

I almost snapped back "I'm fine – just fine." Then, realising I was being a pain, I said, "I'm sorry, I'm just a bit on edge – Mike's gone, did you know?"

"Yes." It was Ann speaking. "He went a couple of days ago, he was upset about you – but he said he would be back – and you know Mike."

"We go tomorrow," May said almost casually. "It will be your turn soon."

"Both of you!" I exclaimed.

"Yes, thank God, the nightmare will soon be over," Ann said, offering me a cigarette.

"Yours may be," I thought, "but mine's still with me." I took the cigarette and lit it. "So you're both going eh? I'll be on my own."

"Not for long," May was saying. "anyway, you can always come for a visit."

"That's sure to please your husband – having me to visit!"

"I have applied for a divorce, so I don't really care what he thinks."

The next few days were unpleasant, to say the least. I found myself being snubbed by fellow patients and staff alike. The one thing that gave me a lift was passing young Mike in the corridor one day. He was walking towards me accompanied by a doctor. As they saw me, the doctor spoke to Mike, who then hung his head so that our eyes did not meet – but as he passed me, he quickly squeezed my hand without the doctor seeing. I felt ten feet tall. I almost skipped into the occupational therapy room. As I sat at a table I could still feel the warmth of his hand as he touched me. I was to remember that for a long while. Later that same day my heart was lifted even higher – Mike came to visit me. I was in the lounge when he came in. We flung our arms around each other's necks and hugged and laughed together. We both started talking at once. As I looked at him, I knew I was in love at that moment, I didn't care. He was telling me how much he had missed me and what he had felt like the day he saw me through the window in that side ward. I also knew by the look in his eyes that this was more than just two mates talking, but he never put it into words and neither did I. He stayed for over an hour and promised to see me again. That night as I lay in bed I could only think of him but then quite suddenly I was gripped with a fear – a fear that unless I gave up all of my past, and the way I felt about my own sex, I would be damned forever. He had a wife and child anyway, so if he could do it so could I – there was no future for me unless I changed. My family wouldn't have me, neither would most of society. I was the odd one out, so it was me who would have to change. Why, even the doctors had told me this. This hospital would one day be featured in its own television series, called "Jimmy's". People would sit and watch with awe at the miracles performed there by all the medical staff – except me. I always turned it off, not able to bear watching people in the hospital that was to me my own private nightmare. So there I lay, all those years ago, my mind mauled by doctors, knowing I was still gay but having to live a lie and telling people I was not. But then I thought I had to do more than just say these things – I had to do something tangible, something that people could relate to. My chance came a couple of days later. I had a phone call from May, her husband was away for a few days and would I like to visit? I asked for permission for a day's leave and it was granted.

When I got on the bus outside the hospital I was very nervous, firstly because I had not been out on my own for months and I thought people would know and point at me, and secondly, I didn't know what to expect from my visit. I found the house in a well-to-do area in Leeds. May opened the door looking her usual smart self and we had a pleasant day, talking about people we had met and life in general. When I said I should be going, she asked me why the rush. "Why not stay the night you're not scared of me are you?" I laughed and said of course not, and in the end I stayed. As we prepared for bed I was shaking inside. I watched her undress, hoping it would arouse me but it didn't. I wanted to get dressed and run, but I am ashamed to say I lacked the courage. We got into bed. she put the light out and I felt her hands on my body. I felt my body tense up, my heart pounding. "What's wrong – don't you like me?"

I should have told the truth there and then – I should have yelled so the world could have heard me, "I'm queer, I have not been cured and I don't want to be cured," but I didn't. I said "Your husband might come home "

"Silly," she said, "he is probably in bed with some little tart right now." Then she went down on me. I could do nothing but lie there, then it was my turn.

"Kiss me all over" she whispered so I did, first her small flat breasts, then further down. I closed my eyes and just went everywhere I thought I should go. She was moaning softly. Then she put a sheath on me and put my cock inside her. With my head one side of hers, so that she could not see my face, I performed the act of sex – but I was thinking about Mike. The next morning, she brought me breakfast in bed and said: "Was it all right for you last night?"

"Yes," I lied, "great, and for you?"

"Wonderful. If only we could always be like this."

"We can," I said without hesitation, "marry me."

They say the road to hell is paved with good intentions. That one little question was to prove it right in my case. So, after all the beatings, the rejection of me by my family, all the tears, the dreams, but most of all the lies, when I did tell the truth to the Church (the Army Chaplain) his answer "cold showers", was this what God wanted? Did he want me to be an outcast? One thing that was certain now, I had told those doctors that I was straight, and now I had asked May to marry me because I couldn't go through that torture again. All their pills and chats, their psychotherapy – not to mention their whisky! – had done not one thing to change me. I was still queer, and now I had to tell even bigger lies! St. James's – 'Jimmy's' – hospital in Leeds has a lot to answer for.

So dear reader, this ends the first part of my story. In part two I will tell you more about my relationship with May and the work I did as a stand-up comedian, including my time at Thames Television with Michael Barrymore and the hit show Strike It Lucky, and much more!

ABOUT THE AUTHOR

Lee Tracey writer/comedian, was born in London hackney one of twins, born to their mother Ivy a cook and father Ted a tram driver. His life at school blighted by a stammer, he tells us he learnt very little at school, due mainly to his affliction. So he has relied on the university of life for his education. Lee left school at 15, and had a variety of mundane jobs. His love of Jazz led him to start singing with local bands, in doing this he was eventually able to overcome his stammer.

Always an avid reader, he would lose himself in the works of Charles Dickens and P.G. Wood House. A great lover of comedy, at the age of 19 he was entertaining his friends with comedy routines and soon found himself working in the stand up. Later he was to form his own production company, "The Pure Corn Co", with other talented artists Chubby Oates, Tommy Osbourne, David Limelight, Lee Anne Robinson and Rex Jameson (Mrs Shufflewick). Working in theatres like the the Theatre Royal Stratford East and The Wimbledon Theatre and many more. Lee wrote the scripts and directed as well as appearing. The company stayed together for 15 hilarious years. He also wrote many pantomimes and spent 12 years as the writer for Michael Barrymore's show "Strike it Lucky". He toured the country and abroad with his stand up and later went into drag but still in stand up mode. Working with artists such as Frank Carson, Mike Read, Bobby Davro, Joan Turner and many more.

Now after a life time on stage, he is going back to his first love of books and writing!